FROM APRIL'S BITTER GLOOM . . .

"I didn't come to New York to become a star. I brought my star with me."　　　　　　　　　**—Reggie Jackson**

"I got my habits. I'm not going to change my habits. If they don't want my habits, then trade me."　　**—Mickey Rivers**

"If they paid me, I'd be out on the field, running forty laps. But he (Steinbrenner) doesn't want to, so it's war."
　　　　　　　　　　　　　　　　　—Dock Ellis

" 'Problems are the price you pay for progress' . . . We're in a time of re-evaluation in baseball."　　　**—Gabe Paul**

"If anybody says I've been on Billy Martin's butt, he's a liar."　　　　　　　　**—George Steinbrenner**

"This has been the worst spring training in my whole history in baseball."　　　　　　　　　**—Billy Martin**

. . . TO SEPTEMBER GLORY

"BILLY MARTIN! I LOVE THE MAN. I LOVE BILLY MARTIN . . . THERE'S NOBODY ELSE I'D RATHER PLAY FOR."　　　　　　　　**—Reggie Jackson**

"WE'LL WIN AGAIN NEXT YEAR."　　　**—Billy Martin**

. . . And all the innings, the outs, the out-maneuverings and outrages are here inside Ed Linn's . . .

INSIDE THE YANKEES:
THE CHAMPIONSHIP YEAR

INSIDE THE YANKEES: THE CHAMPIONSHIP YEAR

Ed Linn

BALLANTINE BOOKS • NEW YORK

To Hildy
My own designated hitter,
pinch runner, and coach

CONTENTS

I

THE BEST TEAM
MONEY COULD BUY

*"I didn't come to New York to be a star. I brought my
star with me."*
                    —the Wit & Wisdom of Reggie Jackson

On November 29, 1976, a day that will live in the
annals of show business, high finance and all other forms
of organized chaos, the New York Yankees held a
press conference at the Versailles Terrace Room of
the Americana Hotel to announce the signing of Reggie
Jackson. Reggie, who is a practitioner of high visibility,
was wearing a vested gray flannel suit with gold buttons, fitted to him with exquisite care by the folk at
Geoffrey Beene, whose clothes he was being paid to
promote. A dark blue tie, flecked with hand-painted
leaves of gold, nestled against his tapered sky-blue shirt.
On one wrist he wore a gold bracelet upon which the
name *Reggie* shone forth in a dazzlement of diamonds;
on the other he wore a glittering gold watch and an
even more glittering World Series ring.

Although the pool of light in which he floated was
for the TV cameras, there was a sense that wherever
Reggie Jackson moved, a spotlight moved with him.
Darold Knowles, a teammate at Oakland, had pinned
him to the screen forever with the immortal line, "There

isn't enough mustard in the whole world to cover this hot dog." Reggie did not come to the TV lights as a stranger. He is a verbalizer, is Reggie Jackson, which, in these days when the communicator is king, makes him a performer for all seasons.

Although his deal with the Yankees called for something like $2.93 million over five years, he wanted the press to understand that both Montreal and San Diego had offered him considerably more. "I considered the sociology and all of that," he explained. "I wanted the place that was best for me."

Most of all, he had been bagged for the Yankees by the enlightened attitude of George Steinbrenner, the Yankees' principal owner. "The reason why I am a Yankee is because George Steinbrenner outhustled everybody. George Steinbrenner dealt with me as a man and a person. . . . Steinbrenner is like me, he's a little crazy and he's a hustler. And there were certain things he expressed to me, and certain ideologies and philosophies that we reached an accord on."

Sociology, ideologies and philosophies. Reggie Jackson talks like that. Even when he isn't talking like that, Reggie is some phrase maker.

"If I was playing in New York," he once told a group of New York writers, "they'd name a candy bar after me."

Asked about that now, he made it emphatic that he didn't have to come to New York for the commercial tie-ins. He already had so many of *those* that even with the $3 million contract he would be making more money from his outside activities than from baseball.

"I didn't come to New York to become a star," he said. (Ready for this?) "I brought my star with me."

But wouldn't he have been lost, he was asked, if he had signed with Montreal or San Diego?

"Fort Knox is in Kentucky," said Reggie Jackson. "But Fort Knox isn't lost. Everybody knows where Fort Knox is." That was Reggie, all right. Even his analogies were sparkling with gold that morning.

When you come right down to it, what's so bad sociologically, culturally, spiritually or intellectually about Montreal? The Expos had offered him a small fortune, far more than he was getting from the Yankees.

2

Gary Walker, his best friend and agent, had urged Montreal upon him because he really believed that Reggie would be happier there than any place else.

Reggie wanted New York. It always had galled him that he had been forced to play in Oakland instead of New York only because the Mets, who had had first crack at him in the college draft, had passed him by. He had a right. The only item in the Mets' scouting report that had meant anything to them was that he liked to go out with white women.

During the previous season, in fact, Reggie had sent a message of sorts to Steinbrenner. The Yankees had just bought his old teammate Vida Blue (they thought), for $1.5 million, and had also completed a trade for another former Oakland pitching star, Ken Holtzman. By one of those rare coincidences, the Baltimore Orioles, who had just finished a series with the White Sox, were leaving the Executive House in Chicago just as the Yankees were coming in. "Tell the man to save some money," Reggie told a couple of Yankee officials. "I'll be there next year."

And do you know what the funny part of it is? The funny part of it is that the Yankees hadn't wanted him at all. George Steinbrenner had gone after him only because the Yankees had no other choice. Literally, no other choice. Steinbrenner had done it because his ego, which is every bit as wondrous to behold as Reggie's, had been bruised, and he had done it against the advice and pleadings of his brain trust.

The 1977 season didn't start with the signing of Jackson. It started three weeks earlier, at the Plaza Hotel, with the first Free Agent Re-Entry Draft. To give Steinbrenner his due, he had recognized from the beginning that the free agent revolution was not the end of our way of life, but—given his circumstances and his geography—a once-in-a-lifetime opportunity, a gift from the gods. As a businessman accustomed to thinking in terms of the marketplace, he had understood instantly that while the tremendous increase in the cost of doing business was going to be too rich for the blood of many clubs, the New York Yankees—just by being the New York Yankees—had the ability to recover almost any amount of money he had to put up. And more than that, if he was able to use that natural advantage to build the Yankees into a winner, the increase in revenues would far outrun the increase in expenses.

What that means in simple English is that Steinbrenner was prepared, from the beginning, to spend whatever had to be spent. When Catfish Hunter came on the market in 1975, in what seemed to be a one-shot fluke (Oakland owner Charlie Finley had abrogated his contract by refusing to give him some money that was due him), Steinbrenner was able to give the Yankees respectability by outbidding everybody else. In 1976, he paid the asking price on both Andy Messersmith, who had been declared a free agent in the landmark case on the reserve clause, and Vida Blue, the most expensive item in Charlie Finley's June 15 clearance sale. Never mind that both the Messersmith and the Blue deals were invalidated by Commissioner Bowie Kuhn. The thing to remember is that Steinbrenner was willing to pay whatever had to be paid for them.

The day after the Yankees were wiped out by Cincinnati in the 1976 World Series, the brain trust met in Steinbrenner's office to decide which two players would best fill their needs.

As pennant winners, they were able to be very selective. George Steinbrenner's first words were, "We are not going to win a championship with Fred Stanley at shortstop." The same words he had uttered after Stanley's throwing error, with two out in the ninth inning, had cost them Game Two. (Steinbrenner is always getting rid of players immediately after they make an error or strike out. That's the difference between an enthusiastic amateur like George and a professional baseball man like Gabe Paul, the Yankee president. Shortstop was the weak position in 1976 because it was the only position on the team that wasn't manned by a player who had been on an All-Star team.)

Selectivity comes in two parts. What you need and who is available. The only real shortstop on the list was Bert Campaneris, another refugee from Charlie

Finley's paradise on the Pacific. Campaneris, however, was thirty-four years old and clearly on the downgrade, hardly a man to be given a long-term contract.

In the mind of Gabe Paul, the best available shortstop was Bobby Grich, who had been playing second base for Baltimore. Grich had been a great shortstop in the minor leagues (the Minor League Player of the Year before he came up), and had been moved to second base only because Baltimore already had the best defensive shortstop in baseball in Mark Belanger. Grich had been a magnificent second baseman for the Orioles, setting four all-time fielding records, and Gabe Paul was convinced that he would be an equally magnificent major-league shortstop. In addition to that, Grich would be filling another of the Yankees' needs: he'd be another good right-handed hitter to balance off the predominantly left-handed power.

The other choice was just as easy to make. The class pitcher on the list was clearly Don Gullett, who had defeated the Yankees in the opening game of the World Series. Gullett was only twenty-five, he was a left-hander (another commodity always in short supply), and although he never seemed to be able to get through a season without some kind of injury, he always seemed to end with a tremendous won-lost percentage. Gullett, in fact, had the best won-lost percentage in all of baseball, and that's what baseball is all about. Winning more games than you lose.

If Manager Billy Martin had been given a say, which he wasn't, his choice would have been Joe Rudi, a solid all-around outfielder who delighted baseball men by all the things he could do that didn't show up in the box score. Rudi had been called the most underrated player in baseball for so long that, far from being underrated any more, it was generally accepted that he was going to be the most sought-after of the free agents. Rudi would not only give the Yankees the other solid right-handed hitter they were looking for; he was also a great left-fielder with an excellent arm. He was also thirty-one years old, he lacked speed, and the Yankees were already loaded down with thirtyish outfielders.

One other thing: although conventional wisdom held that Cincinnati had exposed the woefully weak throwing arms in the Yankee outfield, it was Gabe Paul's belief, going back to his early days as a disciple of Branch Rickey, that you could compensate for a poor throwing arm by getting the ball away quickly and hitting the cut-off man. Something that both Mickey Rivers and Roy White, who owned those weak arms, did very well. (The other way to compensate was to have a strong arm on the bench for specific late-inning situations. Before the meeting at the Plaza Hotel, Paul had sent his discontented substitute center fielder, Elliott Maddox, to Baltimore in return for their discontented center fielder, Paul Blair, a quiet little trade that turned out to be another Gabe Paul steal.)

The outfielder who best fitted their needs, in Paul's opinion, was twenty-seven-year-old Don Baylor, and he couldn't throw at all. Baylor could hit with power, he had great speed, and he would fit in nicely either in left field or as their Designated Hitter.

Yeah, but what about Reggie Jackson? Where did he come in? Well, Steinbrenner did have a yen for Reggie Jackson because Jackson was the most glamorous of the lot probably. But if he did, he never mentioned it. Possibly because he was also aware that Reggie Jackson was exactly what they didn't need, another left-handed power hitter.

The way the Re-Entry Draft worked was this:

1. Each team was entitled to sign two players or, in the event that more than two of its own players had declared themselves free agents, as many players as it stood to lose. (The latter provision would become critical to the signing of Jackson.)

2. Each of the free agents would remain in the sweep-stakes until the right to negotiate with him had been claimed by twelve teams.

3. Each team could draft negotiating rights to as many free agents as it wished for as long as the players remained eligible.

As American League pennant winners, the Yankees drafted last in every round. They selected nine players, in the following order: Bobby Grich, Don Baylor, Don

Gullett, Gary Matthews, Wayne Garland, Reggie Jackson, Bert Campaneris, Dave Cash and Billy Smith.

Baylor had been named ahead of Gullett only because four clubs had already selected him by the end of the second round, while only two had named Gullett. Reggie Jackson had been picked low for the same reason. Matthews, a speedy twenty-six-year-old outfielder with right-handed power, had been picked by eight clubs by the end of the fourth round, and Jackson by only two. When the Yankees' turn came around again, Wayne Garland, twenty-six, the second-best starting pitcher on the list, had been named by ten clubs, and Jackson by only four.

"Grich, Gullett, Baylor and Jackson are the players we're most interested in," Steinbrenner said. Note the order. He wasn't interested in *signing* Jackson, he was interested in letting the world know that he wasn't backing away from the player who would be asking the most money.

They knew who they wanted: Grich and Gullett. They had so little doubt they were going to get them that they didn't even bother to open negotiations for Baylor, even though Baylor was represented by Jerry Kapstein, the same agent with whom they were dealing for Grich and Gullett. Kapstein was told that in return for the right to make the last bid, the Yankees would guarantee to top anything anybody else offered.

So where did it go wrong? Well, you have to remember that this was the first time anything like the Re-Entry Draft had ever happened. There were no guidelines. Kapstein, who had ten of the twenty-two drafted players, set up new offices in Providence, Rhode Island, and before you could say Roger Williams, Providence had become the center of the baseball universe.

The way things developed, the bidding for Gullett heated up first. St. Louis moved in with an offer that came very close to what Kapstein was asking. On Wednesday, November 17, Steinbrenner and Paul went to Providence to meet with Kapstein and Gullett, and closed the deal by the simple expedient of giving Gullett whatever he wanted.

Wednesday, November 17. Hold on to that date. A busy day for Kapstein at the end of what had been a very busy two weeks. Before the day was over, he had announced the signing of three of his other clients: Joe Rudi (California), Bert Campaneris (Texas) and Dave Cash (Montreal). A day earlier he had announced the signing of Baylor (also to California). On other fronts, Atlanta was just about to announce that they had signed Gary Matthews, and Cleveland that they were signing Wayne Garland. You see what was happening here? The negotiations for the most sought-after players were all coming to a head at the same time.

And something else was happening in Kapstein's office on Wednesday, November 17, something that left the Yankees worrying furiously about their chances of signing Bobby Grich, their prime target.

As he habitually did at the end of every season, Bobby Grich had been wending his way across the country from Baltimore to his home in Long Beach, California, leisurely visiting various national parks and American landmarks in a trip that usually took between two and three weeks. It was while he was clambering around the Aztec ruins in New Mexico, the last stop on his itinerary, that he learned that Don Baylor had signed with the Angels. Grich and Baylor are close friends. They had roomed together at Rochester in 1971 and again at Baltimore the following year. Immediately, Grich put in a call to Kapstein, with whom he had been in constant contact anyway. From the beginning, he had informed Kapstein that he wouldn't mind signing with California. For one thing, he lived in Long Beach, which was only a few miles from Anaheim. For another, he had been signed to his original baseball contract by Harry Dalton, the general manager of the Angels, when Dalton was farm director at Baltimore, and the two had remained very close friends. Grich's only real reservation was that he wanted to go with a winner, which the Yankees certainly were and the Angels certainly weren't. Nevertheless, the chance to rejoin Don Baylor certainly made the Angels more attractive to him.

The following morning, Grich was driving along the outskirts of Las Vegas on the final leg of the long journey home when he heard over the car radio that the Angels had called a press conference to announce that they had signed Joe Rudi. And now Grich was really excited. With Rudi and Baylor, California had suddenly become a team to reckon with. And—here's what had him so excited—California had lost three players to the draft: Lonnie Dade and Billy Smith, two infielders of limited major-league experience, plus Tim Nordbrook, the utility infielder they had bought from Baltimore at the end of the season in anticipation of replacing the other two. And that meant they had the right to sign a third player.

At the next gas station, Grich drove off the road to place another call to Jerry Kapstein.

Harry Dalton had remained in Providence to nail down the final details on Joe Rudi's contract, after which an announcement was to be made simultaneously from Providence and Anaheim Stadium by means of a telephone hookup. The first thing Kapstein said to him, after the deal had been closed, was "What about Grich?"

Dalton's answer was that Baylor and Rudi had been so expensive that they had eaten up the entire budget set for him by the Angels' owner, Gene Autry. "From a practical standpoint," Dalton said, "I'm just afraid that Bobby is expecting too much from the market for us to stay in." Grich, after all, had been the number one selection of three clubs, and the number two choice of two others. From an even more practical standpoint, said Dalton, California was pretty much out of the market.

When Kapstein repeated the gist of that conversation to Grich a few minutes later, Bobby couldn't believe it. That wasn't what he had expected to hear at all. He knew Mr. Autry had the finances, and he knew they were eligible to sign three players. "I don't understand why they'd drop out. If they want to build up their ball club, it would make sense to me that they would try to get three free agents. I'm still available. Then why would they drop out?"

Grich asked Kapstein to put Dalton on the phone. "Listen, Harry," he said. "I want very much to play for the California ball club." He wasn't sure how much the market was going to bring him, he said, but he wanted

Dalton to know that he would be willing to sign with California for considerably less than he might get elsewhere.

"Well, then, stand by," Harry told him. "I'll talk to Gene Autry and see if there's a chance we can come in with a serious bid for you."

Now comes the second coincidence. Dalton's call reached Red Patterson, the club president, just as Autry was coming into Anaheim Stadium for the press conference. The press conference was held in the staff room right across from Patterson's office. Patterson looked up, saw Autry about to enter and was able to catch him and put him on the phone. Consider the situation. Autry is all pumped up because he is going to announce that he has bagged Joe Rudi, the most sought-after player of them all. (For $2.09 million over five years, with $1 million of it in the form of a bonus.) Plus Baylor ($1.6 million over six years, with $500,000 in the form of a bonus). In a different setting, in the solitude of his own home, Autry might very well have said to himself, "We don't even need the guy that much. Enough is enough." But in his excited state, all he hears is that he can have Grich in addition to Rudi and Baylor and become an instant contender, which is what this whole thing is about. After a minimum of thought, Autry decides that if Grich is really serious about not getting them involved in another bidding war, he'll reach into his own pocket for the money. What the hell, Autry is so rich that he could tuck George Steinbrenner into the southeast corner of his corral, which shows how far a nasal baritone can take you if you also can't play a guitar very well. "Any ballplayer who wants to play for us that bad," he says, "let's go get him."

The ironic part of it was that California hadn't even selected Grich that high. They already had an excellent second baseman in Jerry Remy, they had two excellent young shortstops coming along in their minor-league chain, and, most important of all, they had heard through the grapevine that the Yankees were prepared to pay whatever it took to get him. They had, in fact, passed Grich by in the sixth round, even though ten clubs had already selected him, and instead had taken Reggie Jackson, who had then been picked by only four clubs. When Grich was still around in the seventh round, they had added him to their list, making California the twelfth and last club eligible to draft him. All the clubs were doing that kind of thing by then, adding the name players who hadn't been closed out yet to make their lists look as strong as possible.

With Grich on his way home and Dalton scheduled to fly back to California immediately after the press conference, Dalton and Kapstein agreed that the best way to handle it would be for Dalton and Grich to get on the phone with Kapstein from Anaheim the next day and work out the details.

The first thing Dalton did when he walked into his house, therefore, was to call Providence to confirm that Jerry had passed the word on to Bobby. "Things have changed," Jerry told him. Kapstein had talked to Grich, all right, and Grich was flying back to Providence. Which left Dalton with nothing much to do except grab some sleep before flying back to Providence himself in the morning.

What had happened was this: Kapstein had called the Yankees to pass on the information about Grich's preference for California, as he was clearly obligated to do, and Steinbrenner had presumably reminded him that the Yankees had been promised a chance to put in the last bid. Or, anyway, a chance to talk to Grich. The least he was entitled to under these new circumstances, Steinbrenner felt, was the opportunity to tell Grich what the Yankees and New York City had to offer.

Halfway between Las Vegas and Los Angeles, Grich had called Kapstein again and was informed that Autry had given Dalton the green light. "But before you make a final decision," Kapstein said, "I want you to talk to Steinbrenner and Gabe Paul." Grich not only owed it to them, Kapstein told him, he owed it to himself.

"I will," Grich said. "I'll talk to them, and I'll listen to them, and I'll see what they have to say before I make up my mind."

Following Kapstein's instructions, Bobby drove straight home, packed a bag and caught the first flight to Providence.

On Thursday morning, the Yankees held their press conference at the Americana Hotel to announce the signing of Don Gullett. As soon as it was over, Steinbrenner and Paul headed for the airport. But not before Steinbrenner had informed the press that the Yankees were now in competition with California for Bobby Grich, and had accused Harry Dalton of committing "an unethical ploy" in putting the Angels in position to sign a third player. According to Steinbrenner, California had deliberately brought the two unsigned minor-league infielders, Smith and Dade, up to their club late in the season, and then bought the also unsigned Nordbrook from Baltimore so that they could lose him too. Lest there be any doubt that the Yankees were still doing everything possible to get Grich, Steinbrenner went so far as to ask the Commissioner to conduct an investigation. (The Commissioner dutifully asked the Angels if they had done such a dastardly thing, and the Angels said, Goodness gracious, no.)

On Thursday evening, Steinbrenner and Paul met with Grich in Kapstein's office and tried to sell him on the advantages of playing in New York. George Steinbrenner spoke of his determination to build the Yankees into a world championship ball club, regardless of the cost. He told Grich how much he wanted Bobby to play shortstop for him. Not only because his presence in the line-up would guarantee a world championship but also because he was the kind of high-type young man who fit the Yankee mold. Gabe Paul, echoing George, spoke of his confidence in Bobby's ability to do the job for them at shortstop. "In my opinion, Bobby, you're just one heck of a ballplayer. I want nothing more than to have you play for us."

And they had him wavering. George was so encouraged at one point that he advised Bobby to get all the work he could at shortstop during the winter. While no actual figures were being thrown around, Grich was led to believe that he could pretty well write his own ticket.

For his part, Bobby reminded the Yankee front office that he was a California boy, that he had always dreamed of playing for the Angels, that he had family and friends in California, and that a move to New York would constitute a drastic change for him and his family. "My hopes are leaning strongly toward California,"

12

he told them. "But my mind isn't completely made up. I'll think very seriously about what you have said."

That wasn't good enough for Steinbrenner. George is a super-salesman and he was there to make a sale. Having failed to sell Grich on the positive advantages of playing in New York City, he turned his attention to the opposition. Because of the unfair methods Harry Dalton had used, he warned Grich, he didn't think California was entitled to sign a third player. If Bobby did sign with the Angels, he told him bluntly, the Yankees would ask the Commissioner to conduct a full-scale investigation into the legitimacy of the Angels' efforts to sign the three players, and the contract would quite probably be nullified.

Well, that was a mistake. Bobby Grich had a relationship with Harry Dalton, and Harry Dalton has an excellent reputation. In fact, Dalton's besetting weakness, in the eyes of most baseball men, is that he's such a nice guy that he allows people to take advantage of him.

The first thing Grich did upon meeting with Dalton on Friday morning was to ask him whether there was any substance in Steinbrenner's charges. "Not only isn't it true," Dalton told him, "it's the very opposite of the truth." Beyond that, he wanted Bobby to know that playing fast and loose with rules was not the California club's way of doing things, and it certainly wasn't Harry Dalton's way of doing things, either. An agreement was reached between them very quickly, and since Dalton had to be in Hawaii on Monday, they arranged to come back in on Saturday morning to wrap the whole thing up. By Saturday morning, however, Kapstein had decided that before the negotiations went any further, he wanted something in writing from the Commissioner clearing the Angels of Steinbrenner's charge.

On Monday, Kuhn sent a telegram clearing California of any misconduct, and Steinbrenner immediately withdrew his protest. By then, of course, Dalton was in Hawaii. The ultimate effect of the delay was to push the announcement of the signing over to Wednesday, which, by a coincidence that can only be deemed fortuitous, was the day before Thanksgiving.

For Steinbrenner, the delay had positive value. From

the moment he heard that Grich was going to sign with California, Steinbrenner went after Reggie Jackson. Why Reggie? Because he had always wanted a **Star Name** and if he couldn't have the player he wanted, he could at least have the *Star* he wanted? Well, that's probably true, but it wasn't the real reason. Because Reggie Jackson was the only player who had the stature, impact and general all-around charisma to make everybody forget that Grich was the man the Yankees were really after?

Well, no. It may be true but that wasn't the real reason, either.

For the real reason, you have only to look back at the list of players who were signed, or wrapped up, within that hectic forty-eight-hour period: Campaneris, Cash, Baylor, Matthews and Garland. Gullett, the Yankees had signed themselves. *When Bobby Grich turned George Steinbrenner down the following day, Reggie Jackson was the only player on the Yankee list who was left.* Unless, of course, you want to count Billy Smith.

Steinbrenner had to sign Reggie Jackson or suffer the humiliation of emerging from the Great Re-Entry Draft, after all his big talk, with only one player. And still Gabe Paul counseled against it. It wasn't a matter of overbalancing the line-up with left-handed power any more. Nor was it a question of weakening the team defensively. Those were arguments to be used when the choice was between Jackson and somebody else. Now that it had come down to Jackson or nobody, Gabe Paul was casting his vote for nobody. Under normal circumstances, old baseball hands like Gabe Paul don't give a damn about personality conflicts or internal disputes. If you have enough talent you will win, they will tell you. If you don't have enough talent, you will lose. Dissension in the ranks? That's newspaper talk as far as they're concerned. But Jackson was unique. They would be imposing a mercurial, wildly articulate, ego-driven player upon a pennant-winning team, and they would be paying him far more than they were paying any of the players who had won it for them.

There was no way Jackson could be brought into

this particular situation, Paul felt, without becoming a destructive force.

Steinbrenner's response was to order Paul to find out where Jackson could be reached.

The following evening, according to one version, Steinbrenner was on the phone with Reggie. "I want you more than anything in the world," Steinbrenner was supposed to have said. "What do you want more than anything in the world?"

"A Corniche Rolls-Royce," Reggie says. The top of the Rolls line. Goes for a scant $63,000. Among his myriad talents, Reggie is one hell of an automobile mechanic.

The Corniche was his. "All I'm asking in return," Steinbrenner says, "is the right to be the last person to talk to you before you make up your mind."

Beautiful. So beautiful as to perhaps be untrue. The car was given to him after the fact, Reggie says. Not before. And he wasn't given the car, he was given a sum of money which he chose to use to buy it. What George really said in that introductory phone call, according to Reggie, was that although everybody in his organization was after him to sign Grich he felt that if he was going to spend that kind of money he wanted Reggie. And that Thurman Munson, who had come to New York for the Gullett signing, agreed with him.

Immediately, word was leaked that it was the Yankees who had changed their mind about Grich. They were now, wrote Murray Chass of *The New York Times,* in hot pursuit of Reggie Jackson. "A source close to the free-agent scene said yesterday that the Yankees apparently had backed off in their quest for Grich because they weren't convinced they should pay close to $2 million to find out if he could make the switch back from second base to shortstop . . . the source said that Steinbrenner has favored signing Jackson from the time the Yankees drafted negotiation rights to him and has slowly brought Paul around to his way of thinking."

When Billy Martin heard about it, he complained: "Don't I have anything to say about it, as the manager?"

No, he didn't.

During the telephone conversation on Saturday,

Reggie had told George that he was going to be in New York on Monday for a fitting. He came to George's apartment in the Carlyle Hotel. George asked what it would take to sign him. He wasn't handling that kind of thing himself, Reggie told him. "I just wanted to meet with you and see what kind of money you're talking." The fact is that Reggie had already set a price, but he had always left his options open for those "sociological and philosophical considerations" that were so important to him. George then did something very smart. He didn't go high; he went low. Probably no more than $2 million. "We can't do business," Reggie laughed. They spent a couple of hours together in Steinbrenner's apartment, and George took him to lunch at "21." George is a charmer. They hit it off, as Reggie likes to say, "as people."

It took two more days to lock Jackson up. Reggie and his advisors had already sent word to those clubs who were still interested in seeing how rich they could make him that they would be taking on all comers at the Water Tower Hyatt Hotel in Chicago on Wednesday, November 24, which, remember, was the day before Thanksgiving.

Steinbrenner was in Culver, Indiana, visiting his son at the Culver Military Academy. He chartered a small plane to Chicago in the early morning hours, laid his proposition out to Reggie's lawyer and agent, flew back to Culver to spend the rest of the day with his son and was back in Chicago to meet with them again in the evening. Whether it was by prior commitment, gentleman's agreement, or just sheer persistence, George was indeed going to be the last person to talk to Reggie before he made up his mind. After the terms were discussed, Reggie's advisors left him and George alone to work out whatever remained to be worked out between themselves.

The next morning, which was Thanksgiving, they had breakfast together. But the deal had already been set, Reggie says, when George volunteered to add another sum of money to the contract—a hundred G's maybe? —as a kind of personal gift to Reggie to more or less commemorate the occasion.

It makes sense. Top of the Rolls-Royce line, hell! If

Reggie had known how desperately Steinbrenner needed him, he could have held out for a DC-10. That's what makes it so ironic. With all the turmoil and jealousy that was to arise over Reggie's $3 million deal, Steinbrenner got him cheap.

Four days later—a week to the day after Reggie had come to George's apartment at the Carlyle—he was standing under the crystal chandeliers of the Versailles Terrace Room, wearing his star in his lapel and his heart on his sleeve. The way Steinbrenner had gone after him, he told the assemblage of newspapermen, it was "like trying to hustle a girl at a bar." Reggie, who can wield an analogy with the best of them, didn't know how aptly he had wielded that one. He also didn't know —to hold to the analogy—that George had come to hustle him only after he had been spurned by the girl of his dreams.

"It will be exciting hitting a home run in Yankee Stadium as a Yankee," he beamed. "For me to get applause from the crowd or slaps on the back or have George Steinbrenner say to me that he felt he wanted me to play here and always wanted me here, that's something I never had. I never felt wanted like that."

It's very important to Reggie to feel wanted. It really is.

By the All-Star break, the symbolic dividing point of the season, the whole experience had turned into such a horror for him that he could only wail, in a cry torn from the heart, "I don't want to play in New York. I don't want to be here any more."

2

SPRING TRAINING DIARY

"I am the hunted on the team of the hunted."
—The Wit and Wisdom of Reggie Jackson

"It was the worst training camp I've ever been in."
—Billy Martin

March 1. Reggie Jackson swept into camp on opening day, carrying an Oakland A's equipment bag and a pocketful of lines. The New York press was waiting. The New York writers had known him through the years as good copy and a likeable guy. Speaking of good lines, he had told a Coast writer a few days earlier that he hadn't been comfortable with the ten Yankee teammates he had met in Hawaii, while he was announcing their *Superteams* competition against the Cincinnati Reds for ABC-TV. "When I walk outside, and it's 30 degrees, I'm not comfortable," he had explained. "I don't feel comfortable if I'm in the ocean and it's filled with clams. And I don't feel comfortable if I go in the bathtub and it's filled only with cold water."

The coldness had set in well before that. There were any number of reasons why Billy Martin didn't want him, beyond the obvious one that he had preferred Joe Rudi. Given Jackson's reputation and personality, there were going to be clashes. Martin, being no dummy, understood very well that if it ever came to a showdown it would not be the $3 million player who departed the scene, it would be the $70 thousand a year manager.

Billy had not been at the hotel when Jackson was unveiled. Nor had he made the routine telephone call, welcoming the new man aboard. There had been one brief accidental meeting over the winter. Unknown to each other, they were both in New York at the same time. Unknown to each other, they were both staying at the St. Moritz. Jackson had walked into the coffee shop while Billy Martin was there. Each waited for the other to make the first move. Neither of them would. Both felt slighted.

Unlike his manager, Thurman Munson had every reason to be happy about the arrival of Reggie Jackson. Unlike his manager, Munson had been there to lend his presence to the announcement. Why not? He had an agreement with Steinbrenner that nobody on the team would be getting paid more than him except Catfish Hunter (who had already been signed). Shortly after Reggie came aboard, Thurman's salary was raised from $165 thousand to $200 thousand for the three remaining years of his contract, and the contract was also extended for two years beyond that at something like $250 thousand and $280 thousand.

And then Thurman discovered that in addition to the salary, Jackson's contract called for $132 thousand a year in deferred payment. Munson held, with seemingly faultless logic, that the New York Yankees were paying Jackson $320 thousand on their books, and that's what they should be paying him too. Steinbrenner held that salary meant salary.

Eleven days after Munson signed the new contract, he dropped the word to a Canadian broadcaster that he would offer to buy out his contract or asked to be traded. Steinbrenner's response was to neglect to show up at a dinner that was being held for Munson in his hometown of Canton, Ohio, in honor of his being named the Most Valuable Player in the American League. Munson's anger was directed at Steinbrenner, not Jackson. But, somehow, Reggie always seemed to be in the line of fire.

When, in the course of the opening day interview, the reporters asked Reggie about the *Superteams* quote, he dismissed it with a shrug. He had only been answering the man's question, Reggie said. "That's the way I felt when the guy asked me."

Sure, Reggie. And with that presumably casual answer he was also setting the agenda for this Opening-Day interview.

Today, Reggie was holding court, the Plato of the Playing Fields. The Greeks had a word for it, all right: Ego. "You never met anyone like me, I'm not just a ballplayer, I'm a multi-faceted person, a myriad of personalities. There's a lot of stories you can write about me. I'm a businessman who happens to be an athlete."

What dost thou mean by that, O Reggie? Art thou thinking about the land holdings in Arizona thou and thy partners are reputed to have amassed, or the income from licensing and endorsing, or the ABC-TV contract? Instantly, he made it clear that the office he was talking about was on the ball field. "I've got my case here," he said, indicating the equipment bag. "My files, my tools."

Actually, Reggie has been using that line for years. Except that sometimes he is a surgeon, and his bat is his scalpel. The "myriad of personalities" is also a maze of contradictions. As much as he wants to impress upon his audience that he is more than an athlete, he has never lost his adolescent delight in being a ballplayer. He still had his collection of bubble-gum pictures intact when he was in Oakland, and he probably still does. He is in awe of any Hall-of-Fame player.

"I haven't come here to create controversy. I don't know me that way. That's not the me I read about. The only publicity I want is to be at the top of the home-run and RBI leaders every day. I don't want to be there just on Sunday." Only the leaders are printed every day, you see. Everybody's statistics are printed on Sunday.

His relations with Thurman Munson? "I don't know the man. Why do you want to write it? I don't want to deal with that. I don't want that foul play." Like all refugees from Oakland, he talks as if he is a survivor of the Battle of Charley Finley. "Even the coolness in

20

Hawaii didn't bother me. Hey, I come from Oakland, man. I hit cleanup on that club. I missed a month and a half of last season in Baltimore, and still hit 27 home runs. People were waiting to see me fail. I started behind, but I caught up. I'm used to being the hunted."

Either he liked the sound of that or he was easing himself into a prepared line. "Part of the reason they pay me is that I like living in this environment. They're looking for me here. I'm the hunted. I'm the hunted on the team of the hunted."

"I don't know what Reggie's talking about. Reggie's full of shit, anyway. He probably meant nobody gave a damn about him. We were over there, we're like a bunch of guys. You know, who gives a bleep who Reggie is? I guess he wanted someone to kiss his ass or something. I mean, we all spoke to him. 'What's happening?' and 'Howya doing?' 'Glad to have you on the team.' All that stuff. But what are we supposed to do, take him out to dinner? When he said that, I was surprised. But he got a right to say what he wants . . . Hey, it's all up to the individual. After you're turned twenty-one, you shouldn't give a damn who cares about you, as long as you do your job. If he was looking for someone to kiss him and carry on, no, they wouldn't do it. They don't do that anywhere."

—Yankee player's view

Around the clubhouse, the players eyed the scene without noticeable pleasure. The same scene was going to be repeated almost daily during the season, and when you talk about the New York press during the season, you're not talking about half a dozen guys from four papers. You're talking about thirty-five guys from three states.

Jackson's old teammate Catfish Hunter, viewing the scene from the other side of the clubhouse, said, "The thing about Reggie is that you know he's going to produce. And if he doesn't, he's going to talk enough to make people think he's going to produce."

The Cat had a piece of it. Reggie writes his own script. He is Autobiography in a roomful of biography.

For a man who has the soul of a poet, Reggie has overlooked the one perfect metaphor. Reggie is a living manuscript, and his bat is the pen with which he writes his continuing saga. In his first day in a Yankee uniform, he was setting forth the main theme and conflicts, orchestrating the characters and, indubitably, announcing the star.

Scratch Plato. This is the Orson Welles of the Playing Fields. Produced and directed by Reginald Martinez Jackson. Written by Reggie Jackson. Starring Reggie Jax.

"Part of what they pay me for is what I have to deal with emotionally, psychologically, and socially. When I was a free agent, I didn't go around to anybody and ask for a certain amount. Anybody wants to make money, play out your option. But as soon as I get here, people want to create controversy. Hey, I'm a good dude."

Reggie goes for high drama. *Sturm und Drang*. Lots of agony and torment. An abundance of emotional crises. Reggie suffers before Reggie triumphs. That bat of his is some dramatic instrument. The sonofabitch writes one hell of a script.

"I haven't come here to look for jealousy. I just want to take my tool [his bat] and do my job. But sell your newspapers. If there's a man that can handle it, here he is. I can deal with it like a big dog."

He had been holding court for a while before Billy Martin came over. "Hi, Big Guy," Billy said, sticking out his hand. That was the extent of it until Martin called Reggie into the manager's office a couple of days later, for a talk.

When he was ready to hit, he couldn't find a batting helmet that fit. He took a notebook from the *New York Times* reporter and wrote, "Jax shows up in camp, has no helmet, wants to know if he's been forgotten already." He's pretty media-wise. Jax is a nice little name to fit a headline. It has character, color and subliminal identification. Jax as in Ax.

Mickey Rivers came out onto the field, in civvies, an hour and a half after the workout had begun. In his locker, he had found a typewritten note from Billy Martin. "I really didn't read it," Rivers said, "but I think it says I'm going to be fined." Mickey had an excellent excuse: "I didn't feel like coming out early. I work slow."

Mickey was upset, he let it be known, because they were pressuring him again. They had told him they wanted him to take more pitches this season, and get more walks. Nothing illogical about that. Batting lead-off, Rivers had walked only twelve times in 612 times at bat, a figure which doesn't seem possible. They also wanted him to take lessons in drag bunting from the master bunter, Phil Rizzuto. Nothing illogical about that, either. Mickey gets down to first base faster than is humanly possible. A drag bunt, where he is running when he makes contact, and (holy smoke) he'd probably beat it out if it went back to the pitcher.

But there was a greater logic in Mickey's position. "I got my habits. I'm not going to change my habits. If they don't want my habits, then trade me. I ain't gonna work on my weaknesses because it don't do any good. I build my strengths. I'm not gonna do nothing extra to please anybody but myself."

On the face of it, that sounds ridiculous. It was quoted, with a smirk, as another sign of Mickey's incurable dumbness. Not a bit. The man is right. It was his strong points that had brought him to the big leagues, and it was his strong points that would keep him there.

On that essential point, he and Gabe Paul were in complete agreement. People do what they do, and people are what they are. Baseball is a game of reflex and habit. Gabe Paul is an old Branch Rickey man, and all old Rickey men are forever quoting the Master. One of Rickey's favorite adages was, "A full bat is an empty mind." Swinging at the pitches he swung at, and bunting his own way, Mickey had hit .312 and knocked in 67 runs. In the opinion of most of the Yankee players, he had been their most valuable player. He probably would have been voted MVP in the American League if he hadn't insisted upon sitting out the last month of the season with what seemed to be the world's slowest-healing shoulder injury. And even then he had finished third to Thurman Munson and Al Cowan in the voting.

"If they want to change my habits," he said, "let them get rid of me. I signed my contract because I thought it would be best at that time, but I didn't really like it. I'm sorry I signed it."

Mickey's problem is money. He was badly in debt when the Yankees got him, and he was badly in debt still. Mickey had signed a three-year contract calling for $100,000 in the first year, graduated up to $125,000 in the third. It doesn't seem like a lot of money these days, but it was more than George Steinbrenner wanted to pay him. But then, who knows how much money Steinbrenner had given him that was being forgiven? And, perhaps more to the point, how much more, George had reason to suspect, he would be giving Mickey in the future? Who else can you name who buys rhinestone socks?

When Mickey's debts pile up, he gets moody. He loses interest. He doesn't run out hits. "Personal problems," he says. Management decided somewhere along the line that the way to get Mickey's mind back on the game was to give him enough money to meet his more pressing problems.

Very dangerous. Aha, says Mickey. So that's how it's done. You play your tail off and nobody notices. You drag yourself around and they give you money.

"They would play games with Mickey. They would play on his gullibility. Mickey is the kind that resents authority. Being hounded. He'll rebel against it. They'll play good-guy bad-guy with him. Billy will win Mickey's friendship, as if that's how to get Mickey to play every day. Somebody's got to be a bad guy, and somebody's got to be a good guy, and he's going to rescue him and he'll want to play for me. I don't know if they think it's successful. I think they ought to give Mickey a little credit for seeing through that kind of crap."

—Yankee player's view

As far as George is concerned, Rivers is trouble, Rivers is a pain, but, most of all, he's just a "skinny little kid." Steinbrenner was an assistant football coach in the Big Ten. He likes big, strapping guys who can powder the ball over the fences.

Mickey Rivers doesn't even look like a ballplayer. He has the worst-looking throwing motion this side of a game of beach ball, a quick, short-armed jabbing motion. Instead of a follow-through, he has a follow-back, like a rifle's recoil, in which his collar bones shoot straight back like wings. He comes to the plate on the balls of his feet, as if it pains him beyond endurance to touch the ground. Old Man Rivers. As he waits for the pitch, he doubles over and pushes the bat forward as if he is about to conk a butterfly upon its head. And then he hits the ball and—wooooosh!

Out on the field, Munson comes up to Jackson, who has just come in toward the batting cage. "Hey, you have to run now. The way we do it here, you run before you hit." It is the grumpy Munson's way of making contact, of moving in to give the Living Presence a chance to show he's a hard worker. Jackson, who is, in fact, a hard worker, doesn't choose to interpret it that way. To Reggie, it's Cap'n Munson asserting his leadership. "Yeah," Reggie says. "But if I run now, I'll be too tired to hit later."

"Yeah, but if you don't run now, it'll make a bad impression on the other guys."

There it is. All Reggie has to say is, "I never thought of that, Thurman. Thanks."

But that isn't the game Reggie is playing. Reggie has come to be the leader, and in order to be the leader, he has to take Munson on. "I'll ask one of the coaches," he says. He lifts his voice to Dick Howser, standing in the grass behind short. "Should I run now, or hit?"

"The hell with running," says Howser, as Reggie knows damn well he will. "Get in there and hit."

Okay, the captain has tried, and Reggie has spit in his eye. Left him standing there with his thumb in his ear, hearing the silent laughter.

Okay, Reggie, baby, if that's the way you want it.

March 2. Mickey Rivers no longer wants to be traded. "We talked about things. We came to a conclusion and

I feel a lot better." Paul and Martin have assured him that they appreciate his habits.

Fred Stanley is "disappointed and annoyed." They have handed his job to a rookie, Mickey Klutts. A year earlier, Klutts had been sent to Syracuse to be transformed from a shortstop to a third baseman. But Klutts can give them the right-handed power they're looking for, and they are now transforming him back. Just in case. Immediately after the Yankees struck out on Grich, Gabe Paul had tried to make a deal with Texas for Toby Harrah. Texas had signed Bert Campaneris, with the intention of playing Harrah at third, where most baseball men thought he belonged. Paul thought Harrah was a perfectly acceptable shortstop, and there was no question at all about his bat. Overloaded as the Yankees were with left-handed hitters, Paul had offered them Graig Nettles. Not even-up, though. Paul wanted something extra thrown in, and it was in the negotiations for balancing off the something extra that the deal had finally fallen through.

It was no secret that the Yankees were now renewing their efforts to make a deal with the Chicago White Sox for their unsigned Bucky Dent. Stanley himself is one of six unsigned Yankees. The others are Roy White, Chris Chambliss, Dock Ellis, Oscar Gamble and the absent Sparky Lyle.

The Yankees send a telegram to Sparky Lyle, informing him that they are activating his contract. What that means is that if he doesn't come to terms, he will have to play out his option year at a 20 percent cut from last year's salary. Sparky hates spring training. He always comes late. This year he also hates the contract they have sent, the same $90,000 as the year before. Sparky led the league in saves last season with twenty-three, but eighteen of them had come before the All-Star break. Over the last six weeks of the season, he had not only lost his effectiveness, he had lost his job as left-handed relief pitcher to Grant Jackson. The fact is that they are not counting on Lyle this year. They have a tremendous prospect coming in, Ron Guidry. Super-scout Birdie Tebbetts' report says he has the strongest left arm in baseball. They are so sure that Guidry is going to be the best relief pitcher in baseball that they

26

had put Grant Jackson on the list of players eligible to be drafted by the two new expansion clubs, gambling that he was too old to be selected. They lost him.

Reggie Jackson isn't in camp. He had been given permission to tape a television commercial in Philadephia. Jackson had made a point of informing everybody that the taping had originally been scheduled for January and had been postponed, and: "It won't happen again."

Thurman Munson doesn't have Jax in camp to contend with, but he does have a pair of expensive brown alligator shoes that are filled with shaving cream. In just retribution, he sets on fire the underwear of the suspected culprit, Catfish Hunter.

March 3. Catfish Hunter is worried about his arm. His ineffectiveness in the last half of the 1976 season had been diagnosed as due to tendonitis in his shoulder. The diagnosis had been scrupulously kept from the press, presumably so the opposition wouldn't know he was having all that trouble. Billy Martin's policy on injuries, and on the nature of baseball competition, is perfectly summed up in one simple sentence: "The United States Army doesn't reveal its casualty figures to the enemy, does it?" Unhappily, what counted wasn't whether the enemy knew the Cat's arm was sore, it was what the sore arm was throwing up there. What the sore arm had been throwing, wasn't much.

Reggie is back in camp, and before the day is over he is worrying furiously, too. He has never had a sore arm in his life before, and all of a sudden his elbow hurts like hell when he throws. It even hurts when he hits. He tells nobody. Billy Martin views the opposing team as the enemy, but to Reggie, the whole wide world is the camp of the enemy.

March 4. The Yankees notify Sparky Lyle, via telegram, that they will take disciplinary action if he doesn't report to training camp by tomorrow. Lyle doesn't receive it, because he is on the road, driving down.

March 5. Reggie's elbow is getting worse. And that isn't all. With the turmoil surrounding the free agency drama, and his TV commentating, and his commercial enterprises, he had done almost nothing over the winter to stay in shape. Just an occasional pressing of the weights in his home gymnasium in Arizona. Normally, Reggie does a lot of running over the winter. Normally, he does a lot of gym work. He is almost thirty-one years old, and he is in the worst shape of his life. Far worse than he had thought possible. His interviews are undergoing an abrupt change of tone. If he can do everything he wants to do in two years, he suddenly tells Murray Chass, he will retire. "You have to prepare yourself mentally to play in New York," he says. If he led the league in everything, and was MVP, and the Yankees won the World Series, people would only say, "He should have done that. Look what they're paying him." If he didn't do it, and the Yankees didn't win, it was all going to be his fault. "Steinbrenner fouled up. Jackson's no good, he hurt the club, he created dissension."

Yes, he knows he's being carefully scrutinized. "But the pressure won't affect me . . . I think Reggie Jackson on your ball club is a part of a show of force. It's a show of power. I help to intimidate the opposition, just because I'm here. That's part of my role. In order to do that, I have to come early and stay late. These are all things that go into winning."

As to his critics: "I don't bother anybody. I don't say anything. I work hard. I do whatever they ask of me. I show up on time. When I was in Oakland, they won. When I left, they didn't win. They lost by two games last year. If I had been there, they wouldn't have lost."

He also has a word for those players who are so critical of all the money he's getting. "Well, play your option out, or shut the hell up. Take a chance on hurting your arm, breaking your leg. Play with no security except yourself . . . Take the scrutiny, lie under the microscope, and then you can get it. Do it. If not, shut up. Jim Palmer and all the rest of you. Don't talk, go do it." How many would be able to take the scrutiny? A lot of them would get it. Some of them wouldn't make it. "I know one that will."

March 6. Sparky Lyle arrives in camp. Unhappy with his contract, but not unhappy otherwise. Sparky enjoys life too much for that. He has the perfect temperament for a relief pitcher. "I have my one pitch," he says. A hard slider. "If it gets them, I'm better than them; if it doesn't, they're better than me." Sparky is not only in the habit of arriving late, he likes to make an entrance. His famous entrance was in 1975, the one year he did come on time. There was a reason: It was the year of the Catfish, and the camp was teeming with newspapermen and television crews. NBC was shooting a segment for Joe Garagiola's show, in which Catfish would come marching out of a Brink's truck, and walk to the pitcher's mound. Sparky's original plan was to hire a helicopter and have it land on the pitcher's mound. He discovered at the last minute that they couldn't do it without a license or something, and so he shifted plans.

Everybody was gathered around Catfish, writing furiously, when Sparky was driven onto the field in his car, emerged with his left arm and leg in casts, and went limping out to the pitching mound. It seems that Sparky has a doctor friend in Fort Lauderdale who had been willing to go along with the gag. The casts served another exemplary purpose. Sparky could hardly go out on the practice field encased in plaster.

Sparky didn't make a helicopter entrance this year, either. Not at these prices. Sparky settled for a big, white, plantation hat and a pair of rainbow sandals with two-inch platforms.

Reggie surprised everybody by going over to shake his hand. "I appreciate your being late and everything," he said, putting the arrival of Sparky Lyle in its proper perspective. "It takes the heat off me."

Lyle had informed Gabe Paul upon his arrival that he wanted to be signed or traded. He did not want to play out his option. Possibly because he was thirty-two, but also possibly because he had promised Bob Lemon, who had been the Yankee pitching coach last year, that he wasn't going to become one of those greedy guys. He wanted $500,000 for three years, with some of it in the form of deferred payments that would be guaranteed, "even if the club goes defunct. That's it in a nutshell."

He had also told Paul that he wasn't going out onto the field until he knew there was a chance they could get together. Shortly thereafter, Paul called Sparky back in, and offered him $125,000 a year for two years. Sparky turned it down, but agreed to work out the next day. But that was all he would do until he had a contract. He would pitch batting practice, but he would not pitch in a game. Makes sense. If he didn't go onto the field, they could fine him.

March 7. Reggie has more on his mind than the growing anxiety about his physical condition. After one week in camp, his relationship with his teammates is kaput. They are a cold, stand-offish group to begin with, slow to accept new players. Chris Chambliss and Dick Tidrow, quiet and unassuming men both, were frozen out for a full season after they arrived in a trade for four pitchers, all of whom had been popular members of the team. Oddly enough, Chambliss and Tidrow are among the coolest to Reggie. Reggie is stand-offish, too. One of the conflicts in his nature is that, as talkative and friendly as he can be with strangers, he is not very good in personal relationships. "I remain a stranger for a long time," is the way he puts it. And Reggie can be perverse. Possibly because he feels rejected by the team as a whole, he has rejected the companionship of the few players who have made overtures, who have even suggested having dinner or a couple of drinks with him. He has taken to talking about "those dumb ballplayers with their low I.Q.'s."

By the end of the first week, he has only one friend in the clubhouse, Jim Wynn. Jimmy Wynn is a right-handed power hitter Gabe Paul grabbed onto shortly after Reggie was signed. Jimmy Wynn is one of the old black stars Reggie admires, and he is a highly intelligent man. He is also, by nature, a peacemaker. Wynn has been trying to tell Jax that in order to be liked and accepted by the players, he is going to have to stop being Reggie Jackson, the millionaire sports commentator, and just be Reggie Jackson, the man.

When Reggie gets into one of his boastful moods about his physical prowess and great intellect, he knows what the reaction is going to be. He can't help himself. It wrecked his marriage, as he openly admits. An article about him in *Sports Illustrated* had been titled "Maris and the Babe, Move Over!" and had shown him naked from the waist up. There was a line in there about how intelligent and articulate he was, and Reggie went strutting around the house until he became unbearable. The breakup of his marriage is the great tragedy of his life. He will admit that the fault is his; he will admit he became impossible to live with. "But she should have been more understanding," he will add wistfully. "She should have recognized immaturity."

Recognizing all that, he repeats it. He has, in fact, developed a brand-new compulsion. Just as the first recognition in a national magazine had overwhelmed him, the $3 million has overwhelmed him. The new compulsion is counting his money, talking about it. On the way to the training field, he sits with the writers in the front of the bus more often than with the players, takes out his wallet, and counts his money. Every day. Never misses. All hundred-dollar bills. He would do the same thing while being interviewed. He would do it while talking to his teammates. It continues all through spring training; all through the year.

"It never stopped. He might be talking to you in the hotel bar or something, you've been living with the guy for six months. "You know, I make three million a year, and they're telling me to do this or do that." That figure always comes up in a conversation, how much money he makes. I don't know whether that's to immediately perk your ears up that whatever he is saying from then on is going to be gospel, or whatever I say must be the truth because I make three million, or whatever. He'd do it with ballplayers making a hundred and fifty thousand a year, and he'd do it with newspapermen making twenty thousand."
—a Yankee player's view

March 8. Robert Ward is taking it all in. Ward is a writer sent down by *Sport Magazine* to write an article about Reggie. He is a tall, slim young man. At the same time that he's writing about Reggie, he's writing a novel and a screenplay. He writes for *New Times* and *Crawdaddy.* He's the new kind of writer who goes out

31

with the players, and drinks with them, and tries to find out what makes them tick.

Reggie is holding forth on his "tremendous intellect" and his position as "a black man who . . ." while a couple of lockers away, Chris Chambliss, a black man who worked like hell to get where he is, lets a cold eye run over Reggie and moves off.

In the evening, they meet at the Banana Boat Bar, a Fort Lauderdale bar where the players hang out. Reggie is wearing his "SUPERSTAR!" T-shirt, just in case nobody knows. Billy Martin is there, playing backgammon with Mickey Mantle and Whitey Ford, the three nightriders of the old Yankees. They have been close friends from their earliest days with the Yankees, across a span of thirty years.

Jackson sends a drink across to them. Whitey Ford sends the waitress back with a message that he appreciates "the offer" of a drink but he would rather have his "SUPERSTAR!" T-shirt. Jackson takes the shirt off and goes across to present it to him personally. Ford, one-upping him again, takes off his gorgeous pink cashmere sweater and gives it to him in return.

Jackson seems overjoyed. Whitey Ford, a Hall-of-Famer, giving him his sweater! "I'll always keep this." But he has been put down. He is one against three. As they watch the three musketeers play a wild, cheating game of backgammon, he is ignored. He goes back to the bar, Ward joins him, and Reggie starts to talk again. He is in a wildly boastful mood, a pontificating mood. "Everything stems from me . . ." And then he's ripping Thurman Munson apart.

"Do you want me to print that?" Ward asks.

Reggie raps his knuckles on the bar. "I want you to print that," he says. "I want to see that in print."

He is a man trying to surmount his insecurities by accusing everybody else of being insecure. "I am the situation," he will say at the end of the season. He is a man making the situation. Writing his own steamy little scenario. Choreographing the coming events by setting up the inevitable reaction. He is a strange man, a fascinating man, a man who has something steaming inside him. An apostolic view of himself, perhaps, that he was destined to perform greater deeds, in larger arenas. Not just a great black athlete, but a great intellectual. Not just a ballplayer, but a leader. Not just Reggie Jackson, perhaps, but Jesse Jackson. Not just Jesse Jackson, perhaps, but Martin Luther King, Jr.

Ward has come to find out what makes Reggie tick, and Reggie has handed him a bomb that will be ticking away through the early weeks of the season.

March 9. Mickey Rivers declines an invitation to attend Phil Rizzuto's class on bunting. Mickey still doesn't want anybody fooling around with his habits.

March 10. Graig Nettles has a wart removed from his right hand, and will be unable to swing a bat for a few days.

March 11. The Yankees meet the Texas Rangers in the first exhibition game. Jim Wynn is given the right-handed DH spot over Lou Piniella, who had held it through most of the previous year. Reggie Jackson bats twice. Grounds out and strikes out.

Toby Harrah, the shortstop who got away, hits two home runs as the Yankees lose, 4-3.

March 12. Mickey Klutts breaks a bone in his left hand in a freak injury as he is tagging a Baltimore runner out at second. The Yankees try to hide it from the press, and from the White Sox, by reporting it as a sprain. This is a rather difficult deception to maintain, since the writers have heard Klutts screaming on the trainer's table and have seen Martin come out, saying grimly, "We've got trouble with Klutts."

March 14. Catfish Hunter, who is the main project for the coaching staff, goes three innings against Texas, allows five hits and two runs. He reports that his arm didn't hurt, but that he hadn't felt natural, either. Catfish never alibis, never complains, so who knows? "If I can't pitch," Cat says, "I'll wash George's boats for five years."

After seven outs, Reggie Jackson gets his first hit as a Yankee, a line-drive single, and follows it with a vicious line-drive double. "That's what separates me

33

from the rest of the guys," he gloats. "Nobody else can hit it that hard."

Gabe Paul, trying to keep the price down on Bucky Dent, trades a minor-league outfielder to San Francisco for Marty Perez. Perez hasn't signed his contract, tells the press he hasn't played shortstop for two years, hates playing third base, and doesn't want to be a utility player.

March 15. Dock Ellis announces that he doesn't think his agent is going to be able to keep him quiet much longer. Nobody on God's green earth has ever been able to keep Dock Ellis quiet. Dock isn't even certain the Yankees want to sign him. "If I don't, that's when I become oppressed. That's when I become very hostile . . . I will become the hanger, not the hangee." Ellis came to the Yankees with the reputation of being a troublemaker. He turned out to be exactly the opposite. Very bright and extremely popular. So popular that he had been elected player representative. Billy Martin loves him. He is Martin's representative in the clubhouse, a very valuable man under the circumstances. Dock drops the hint that if he isn't signed, "It would make me cautious of the other players on the team." Translation: "If I don't get what I want, you can forget about me keeping peace around here."

Ellis has a case. After he came to the Yankees, along with Willie Randolph, in what turned out to be Gabe Paul's greatest trade, Dock agreed to take the same $80,000 salary he had been getting in Pittsburgh with the understanding that he would want a good raise if he produced. And that wasn't all. During one of his pep talks, Steinbrenner had got carried away, and promised the players that they would be amply rewarded if they won the pennant. Dock's 17-8 record had been far beyond anybody's expectations. (Ellis was nine games over .500, and the Yankees won by ten games.) But Ellis and Lyle are thirty-two, Roy White is thirty-three, and the Yankee policy was not to give those magnificent long-term contracts to players who were going to be past their prime before the contract ran its course. That's the reality Paul is talking about.

It had reached the point, Dock said, where he had

cursed his own sister for the first time in his life. He had explained why he was holding out, and when he mentioned the paltry sum they were offering—$350,000 over three years—she had squealed, "Get the money, look at how much they're offering you."

"I told her she sounded just like them. Hell, they ain't ever gonna run dry."

On March 15, Ron Blomberg, who has been swinging the best bat in camp, hits a towering two-run home run against Minnesota. Blomberg is back after a shoulder operation. If he can take over the left-handed DH role, Oscar Gamble, who became expendable with the signing of Reggie, will become even more expendable. This is an item of some importance, since Gamble is the player being offered to the White Sox in the Bucky Dent talks.

March 16. The Yankees and the Red Sox meet in an exhibition game, and almost have another brawl when Ed Figueroa decks Carlton Fisk after home runs by Yastrzemski and Scott.

Bill Lee, the major casualty in last year's brawl, gives his version of the circumstances that put him out of action: "I was assaulted by George Steinbrenner's Nazis, his Brown Shirts. He brainwashes those kids over there and they're led by Billy Martin—Hermann Goering the Second. They've got a convicted felon running the club, what else do you expect?" (George Steinbrenner was the first businessman indicted by Leon Jaworski's Watergate Investigation Commission for illegal campaign contributions. He pleaded guilty.)

Ron Guidry comes in, with the score tied in the ninth inning, and gives up three hits, capped by a tremendous home run drive by Carl Yastrzemski. While Guidry is about it, he also pulls a muscle in his right thigh.

March 17. The Yankees sign Stanley to a three-year contract. Gabe Paul implies that the Dent deal has fallen through, and Stanley will be the regular shortstop.

Mickey Rivers, tired from rising early to make the 140-mile-long bus trip to Vero Beach, fails to run out a ground ball as leadoff man of the game, and is taken out. Rivers says Martin just wanted to give another center fielder a chance to play. Billy says three players and a coach jumped all over him. An unidentified player, who sounds like Lou Piniella, says, "Is it possible that the man can be punished and not even know it? I wish I had that going for me."

When a Los Angeles cameraman asks to take a picture, Reggie says, "Better get it now. I may not be wearing this uniform very long."

March 18. Reggie Jackson hits his first home run as a Yankee, a two-run drive against Texas.

Marty Perez plays third base, and announces that he wants to be traded.

White, Chambliss and Ellis are all beginning to show anger about their contracts. White, who had gone through the dog days with the club, is in his twelfth year with the Yankees. He hit .286 the previous year, and led the league in runs scored. For that, he has been offered a raise from $90,000 to $100,000, even though he has super-agent Jerry Kapstein working for him. White is thirty-three, and the Yankees are clearly planning to phase him out. In the old days, that would have been expected. These are the new days. You look at Reggie's $3 million, and a $10,000 raise becomes a bloody insult.

Gabe Paul tells White that in the new order of things, there are those who gain and those who get hurt.

March 19. Martin says he will probably bat Chambliss fourth and Jackson fifth. Steinbrenner doesn't like it. Jackson hates it.

Steinbrenner didn't like the idea of Chambliss batting fourth last year, when they *didn't* have Reggie. But Chambliss, according to Billy, makes contact, and with the Yankees' running game, they can't afford a cleanup man who strikes out as much as Reggie. Steinbrenner isn't crazy about Chambliss in any capacity. Chris is a Gabe Paul man all the way. Gabe signed him out of college for Cleveland, and made the deal that brought him to the Yankees. Chris has the ability to knock in runs without hitting too many home runs. In the field, he has developed from a poor fielder to a determined fielder, although he's still so weak on pop flies that Willie Randolph is under instructions to run him off on anything Willie can get to.

Everything Reggie is, Chris is not. He is so uncharismatic that he wasn't able to cash in at all on the ninth-inning home run that put the Yankees in the World Series, a failure that has left Chris so sour that he no longer wants to hear anything about the home run.

March 20. Mickey Rivers is taken out of the game against Philadelphia for failing to hustle on two consecutive fly balls. First, he lets a line drive skip past him, and jogs lazily after it. Then, he loafs back on the ball, puts his glove up with a clear lack of interest, and drops it. Martin says he'll talk to him to find out whether anything is bothering him. "He's one of the fastest guys in baseball, and he doesn't want to run."

Munson suffers a three-inch cut when the pitcher steps on his ankle on a play at first base.

Nettles, playing in his first exhibition game, fumbles the first ball hit to him.

Lou Piniella is angry about the coddling of Rivers. Elrod Hendricks believes it sets a bad example for the younger players. "What if Willie Randolph started doing this?" Fat chance. Willie does everything, hustles all the time, and never opens his mouth. Willie's left knee was operated on over the winter and he was glad to sign a four-year contract, starting at something like $70,000. Which makes him the most underpaid player in baseball. But he's young, he's willing to wait and he's happy to be playing ball.

March 21. Everything is fine and dandy with Rivers, after a meeting with Martin. Carlos May and Oscar Gamble, who are his friends and fellow good-humor men, had already talked to Mickey, suggesting that they ought to take him out in the alley and knock some sense into him. Billy Martin has made the same suggestion, but has added that he just wants Mickey to make him understand why he was loafing. "Because I know you don't play ball like that." Which must have come as a surprise to Mickey. Especially since Martin has also told him that there were players who couldn't understand why he hadn't punched Rivers on the nose last year.

"Me and Billy don't have any problems," Rivers says. "He's taken time to understand. I think Billy helps me a lot. He helps me when I get down, and I've been down for three months. But I'd rather not discuss it. I believe it will go away."

Everything is not fine and dandy with the holdouts. Steinbrenner has come to camp, possibly to find out what's going on with Mickey Rivers. Walking into the clubhouse, Steinbrenner found Dock Ellis at his locker, wearing his earring. Listen, Dock likes to wear an earring. Dock was the first player to appear on the field —well, lolling outside the dugout, anyway—with his hair in curlers, and that was back in 1971, when the Pirates were winning the pennant. George said something that could not, by any stretch of the imagination, be taken as a compliment, and Dock said, "Watch it, or I'll wear this *bleeping* earring on the field. The only reason I don't do it is because I don't want to rock your little boat." George told him he wouldn't rock it a second time, and Dock screamed, "Okay, *bleeper-bleeper,* get ready to trade me. I'll have four teams ready to hand you tomorrow. Let's get it on. Anything you want to talk about, you talk to me through the papers. I'm going to kill you through the papers. This is war!"

Ellis went out and told Martin that anything that happened wasn't to be taken as a reflection on him. Billy understood perfectly. Billy was extremely fond of Dock, wanted to keep him, and knew that he wasn't going to be able to.

"If they paid me," Dock told the press, "I'd be out on the field, running forty laps. But he doesn't want to, so it's war."

Graig Nettles does have a contract. He wants to renegotiate. Nettles is the home-run champion of the American League, and he is also the best defensive third basemen. He had held out through the first half of the previous season before signing a three-year contract at $100,000 for that season, and $140,000 for the next two. Unfortunately, he had done it all wrong. To begin with, he had signed in July, after a typically awful first half, and had then proceeded, as Nettles always does, to a great second half. To make it worse, the new player agreement with the owners held that a player who had signed his contract after August 9, was no longer bound by the reserve clause. Worse yet, he had insisted upon having the contract written so that he could take his deferred payments whenever he wanted to, instead of setting up the kind of irrevocable schedule of payments that would have given him a tax break.

All things considered, Nettles didn't really seem to be asking for so much. He wanted to protect himself by having the contract extended for the same $140,000 over two more years and, having discovered that the tax bite was going to be far beyond anything he had dreamed, he wanted to have it rewritten.

Nettles' agent was in town, and Steinbrenner wasn't interested in talking to him. "They don't want to take care of some of us who made the Yankees a good team, and an attractive package that made other guys want to play here. It seems the only way to make money with the Yankees is to play for another team."

He had more than that to say. "It seems the guys who make money are the flamboyant, controversial guys. On this club, at least. Maybe I should pull something controversial. I have a few shockers in store for people."

Sparky Lyle had been saying that if he didn't get the contract he wanted, he would leave camp. If Steinbrenner wouldn't talk to his agent, said Nettles, he just might join Sparky.

March 23. Steinbrenner is ripping mad because he has taken guests to watch his team of champions play the University of Florida in Gainesville, and it takes a six-run ninth inning, capped by Graig Nettle's three-run home run, to defeat them, 10-9. Steinbrenner, who is active in civic affairs, had donated the lights for the University Stadium. After the game, the Yankees discovered that a thief had broken into their locker room and stolen some gloves, sweatshirts and equipment bags. "I think George should have installed burglar alarms instead of lights," says Oscar Gamble.

George is so mad that he orders Ken Clay and Randy Neimann, the two rookie pitchers who were hit so hard by the collegians, back to the minors.

The Yankees announce that they have renewed Dock Ellis' contract, with the 20 percent pay cut. Ellis says he will not recognize the contract. War!

Gabe Paul is in Sarasota, discussing the deal for Bucky Dent, which has been in various forms of discussion, hot and cold, for four months now. Both Gabe Paul and Bill Veeck are old baseball men who know how to sit and wait. "We had a delightful lunch," says Gabe upon his return. "Bill is one of my favorite guys."

"It's always a delight to spend an afternoon swapping lies with Gabe," says Veeck, from Sarasota. "Gabe has been a good friend through lo, these many years, in good times and bad. Too bad he had to get tied up with a bum like Steinbrenner."

As far as Ellis and Lyle are concerned, Gabe says once again, "There's a new reserve system, and there's a lot of good and bad in it. We have taken the bad, and realistically understood we must live with it. The players have to do the same thing. They can't have their cake and eat it, too."

March 24. Steinbrenner brings guests and family to see his team play Minnesota in Tampa, where he has his home. It's the first of five games to be played in the Tampa area. Minnesota wallops Ken Holtzman for eight runs and ten hits in five innings, while three Minnesota rookies are holding the Yankees to six hits, all of them coming in the final three innings.

Elston Howard has refused to go out to the bull pen as bull pen catcher as long as the new pitching coach, Cloyd Boyer, runs the bull pen. Elston's proposition is that he should run the bull pen while Boyer remains on the bench and watches the pitcher on the mound, which is the way most clubs do it. But if Boyer is on the bench, what are they going to do with Yogi Berra? In previous years, Howard has been the first-base coach. This year, the Yankees have brought Bobby Cox, as well as Boyer, up from their minor-league system. Cox had won the Little World Series at Syracuse, and the

Yankees didn't want to lose him. A week earlier, Elston had offered to accept a front-office job, which had been offered to him at the time Billy Martin came. "You told me you didn't want it then" is Steinbrenner's answer. Obviously, they don't want to give it to him now. If Howard felt that he was a fifth wheel, who could blame him? If he feels they would be delighted if he quit, who could argue with him?

None of the coaches is Martin's, another point of dispute. Billy has been known to say that, between Elston Howard and Yogi Berra, he might as well do it himself because he's going to end up doing it, anyway.

Billy Martin sends word to the bull pen for Lyle to warm up. Lyle sends back word that he isn't going to pitch in any exhibition games until he has a contract. "If they don't make a deal I might not show up for opening day. I'm serious."

"Nobody can make a guy pitch," Gabe Paul says. "But I'm getting sick and tired of his bullshit. He's under contract and we expect him to pitch. The reserve system has changed and there are pluses and minuses for the players. He happens to be in one of the minus categories."

Says Lyle: "George Steinbrenner talks about loyalty. He told us to be loyal to him and he would be good to us. His loyalty went out the window. We helped him win. I'm not using any specific player as an example but as soon as a good player becomes available, there goes $2 million or $3 million to him. But the guys who won for him see very little of it."

March 25. "I don't want to make you nervous," Martin tells Catfish Hunter, as the Cat goes out to face the Phillies in Clearwater, "but remember what happened to Clay and Neimann." Hunter's first pitch is thereupon hit for a home run. There is a three-run home run later, and the Yankees lose, 5-3. It is the Cat's third attempt to pitch, but he insists his arm feels great, and his fast ball has been popping. "Before, I was throwing the ball too weak for them to hit it out," says the Cat. Hunter always jokes about his generosity in giving up home runs.

Jackson's elbow is hurt further in a jarring crash at

41

the plate in the first inning, but he hits a home run the next time up.

Ron Guidry, back in action, pitches the last two innings, and allows one run on a massive blow over Mickey Rivers' head by a weak-hitting infielder, Fred Andrews. He reduces his ERA from 11.25 to 9.00 for the spring.

A testimonial dinner is held for the team at a Tampa bank. Steinbrenner orders all the Yankee players to be there. Lyle and Ellis don't show up. Nettles has a bitter argument with Steinbrenner and stalks out. For the first time, Jackson apparently tells Steinbrenner how bad his arm really is. It not only hurts when he tries to throw, it hurts when he swings the bat.

March 26. The Yankees lose to the Mets, 6-0, in St. Petersburg. Reggie's arm is hurting so bad that he can't start, even though the game is being telecast back to New York. But he does come up as pinch hitter late in the game, and lines out a single.

After the game, George was unhappy. He was unhappy because he had just learned how bad Reggie's arm was. He was unhappy because Martin had sent in a team of substitutes over the last few innings. And he was unhappy because his team was losing so consistently. But there was another source of his unhappiness, going back to the beginning of spring training.

Billy Martin's marriage had broken up. He was living a bachelor life in Boca Raton with his buddy, Mickey Mantle, and driving to the practice field every morning, not necessarily on time or alone. Gabe Paul had told him at the beginning that the team couldn't stand that kind of thing. Paul had ordered him to move to Fort Lauderdale, and drive back and forth on the team bus. Billy went over Paul's head to Steinbrenner, and George, being a more understanding man, or being in a particularly indulgent mood, had told him it would be all right to stay where he was and live his own life.

That was a mistake. Billy runs a loose training camp these days, anyway, as a kind of bow to the modern ballplayer. If they want to take part in the exercises, they can; if they don't want to, they don't have to. With Billy coming in late, some of the players began to come in late, too. It was a terribly disorganized camp. Respect for the manager diminished daily.

With the Yankees quartered in Tampa for the five games in the area, Steinbrenner had been telling Billy that if things didn't get straightened out immediately, they weren't going to be ready to start the season. "Preparation" is the word Steinbrenner likes to use. George was an assistant football coach in the Big Ten, and he views preparation in football terms: statistical breakdowns, tendencies, films. Things which Martin, the old baseball man, finds ridiculous. But most of all, George wanted Billy on the practice field on time, and he wanted him to ride the team bus with the players. And there is no question that he had reason to believe he had Martin's promise to do so.

When George came to the clubhouse after the Mets game, he was already upset about the failure to start Reggie, and furious about the use of the second stringers in the latter part of the game. Parked in front of the clubhouse was the players' bus, already more than half full. Parked nearby was Billy Martin's car. It took only a few words with the bus driver to determine that Billy had driven to St. Petersburg, and was going to be driving back.

Into the clubhouse went George, storming. "I want to see you *now*," he screamed at Billy. "I want you to ride on the team bus."

"You don't tell me where to ride, you sonofabitch," Martin yelled back.

"Hey, watch yourself," Gabe Paul said. "Watch yourself."

"You lied to me!" Steinbrenner shouted.

"You're a lying sonofabitch," Martin shouted back.

The bus wasn't the only thing Billy had lied to him about, Steinbrenner screamed, apparently referring to the fact that Billy had not played the starters all the way.

"Don't tell me how to manage my ball team," Martin told him. "I'm the manager, and I'll manage how I want to manage. This is an *exhibition* game. This is not a game you leave your blood and guts on the field to win. This is a game where you prepare yourself to have a winning season." He had done things, he yelled, that he wouldn't be doing during the season. "But I wanted to try some things out. There are things I have to find out now."

Those were the kinds of things he should have already found out, Steinbrenner felt. "I ought to get rid of you," he said.

"Fire me right now if you want to," Billy shot back. "But leave me the hell alone."

In the morning, the three of them had breakfast together, and Billy Martin never yelled at George in public again.

March 27. After the breakfast meeting with Martin, George invited Munson up to talk about the progress of the team, and perhaps even about the state of his relationship with Jackson. Munson told him he had better sign Sparky Lyle fast, because the team wasn't going to win without him.

Lyle had fallen back to sleep watching television, when the phone rang. "Now, Sparky," said a voice, "we got to get this thing settled."

"Oh, George, it's you." Even half-awake, Sparky knew that nobody else wakes you up and expects you to know who it is. Lyle was willing to take $450,000 over three years. "I figure I got a three-year contract plus a needed wake-up call," Sparky said.

Roy White was also signed before the morning was over. White will be getting $125,000 a year for three years. That leaves Ellis, Chambliss and Gamble unsigned, and Nettles wanting to talk about it.

Sparky pitches one inning against the team that had humiliated them in the World Series. He gets three straight outs on three long, long fly balls.

The game goes into the tenth inning. It shouldn't have. Batting with men on first and third and one out, Reggie Jax had hit a ground ball off the end of the bat. There would have been no chance of a double play if the ball hadn't stung him right up through the elbow, and taken his breath away. It hurt so much that he had to stop running. In the tenth inning, with a Cincinnati runner on second base, a line drive came out to Reggie on one hop. The runner was sent in. Any kind of a throw and he's an easy out. To make it ridiculous, the

44

runner pulls a hamstring muscle rounding third and comes hopping and limping the rest of the way. But there is no throw. Reggie has taken the ball and run right off the field.

The sore elbow is no longer a secret. Reggie can't throw at all. Tendonitis, says the trainer. Reggie had been under orders not to throw, goes the official statement, because he was scheduled for a shot of cortisone in the morning. That's why they had him playing, I guess. Because they knew he couldn't throw.

March 28. The Yankees complete their five games in the Tampa area by losing, 6-5, to Detroit in Lakeland. Ron Guidry, sent in to protect a two-run lead in the eighth, is hammered for four hits and the tying runs. "The trouble with you," Steinbrenner has already told Paul, "is that you love Tebbetts so much that you take everything he says as gospel." Even Paul is beginning to wonder whether Guidry might not be one of those players who have everything except the ability to stand up under pressure.

March 29. Graig Nettles jumps camp without a word to anybody, and Gabe Paul announces that he will be fined $500 a day, "unless he can show proper cause." The quiet ones will do it to you every time. Nettles is the kind of guy who has very little to say but always seems to be walking by at precisely the right moment to deliver a witty line, a characteristic which has earned him the nickname "Puff." Here and gone, like a puff of smoke.

During his early days in the majors, his nickname was "Clank." As in iron glove. By dint of hard work, he has made himself into a perfectly marvelous third baseman during his three years with the Yankees, the best third baseman in baseball now that Brooks Robinson is fading. He has a sense of humor about that, too. On the inside strap of his glove, where the players traditionally write their names, Graig still writes "E-5," the scorer's code for "error by the third baseman." He has one of those picture swings that only a left-hander seems to have, the kind of swing that would seem to be slump-proof. On the contrary, he runs hot and cold. His history is that he is mostly cold during the first half of any season, and hot as a firecracker during the second half. No matter how cold he is at bat, it doesn't affect his fielding. He'll come onto the field after striking out with men on base, and you can almost see him spit, as if to say, "I couldn't get them up there, I'll get them out here." And, as often as not, he will. He plays hurt, almost never missing a game. He is thirty-four years old, though, and he missed his chance when he decided to sign the contract at midseason. Sal Bando, a year older than Nettles, played out his option, and signed a five-year contract for $1.4 million. Nettles has outhit him the past few years, and Bando can't hold Nettles' glove.

"We're in a time of re-evaluation in baseball," Paul says, yet again. "Now we're left with a residue. A lot of players benefited. Some didn't."

Steinbrenner is more than willing to make a test case out of it. "If Graig's not there on opening day, we'll go after damages to our ball club. A contract is a contract. A player has got to realize that." It's no different, as far as George is concerned, from a rock singer who fails to show up to give a performance he has contracted for.

March 30. "This has been the worst spring training in my whole history in baseball," says Billy Martin.

Up to now, he has been able to kid about his squabbling charges. Not infrequently, he would open his press conferences by saying, "Only two murders and one suicide today. We've eliminated the fighting and gone right to the killing." Or by ridiculing Steinbrenner's insistence upon winning these exhibition games. "We've got to win today, George says it's a real big one. *Ditdedah dedadit.*" The *ditdedahs* represented the sound of a computer churning out the statistical data that George was forever sending down to Billy and that Billy would, of course, dutifully ignore.

At more relaxed times, when he was alone in his office with a writer he trusted, Billy would shake his head and sigh, "When I get through managing, I'm going to open up a kindergarten."

But now he wanted to put himself squarely behind Nettles. "He just wants to talk to the man," he re-

46

minded everybody. "The man doesn't want to talk to him."

Billy Martin was, in fact, putting himself solidly behind all his dissidents. "Baseball better find a cure for how it's going to pay money, because it's getting to be a cancer. The free agent gets it all. One guy, they want to pay nothing because he's too old; another guy, they don't want to give him nothing because they don't like him." Nobody else had expressed the slightest sympathy for Nettles. Neither his teammates nor the writers. Okay, looking back, it was a bad contract. But it hadn't looked so bad to him when he signed it.

"He made a business deal," Steinbrenner says, "and he's going to be made to abide by his contract. He's going to understand the facts of life. Does it make any sense as a businessman to guarantee anybody a hundred and forty thousand at the age of thirty-six and thirty-seven?" Nettles is in a no-win situation, and Steinbrenner is putting it to him. "If Graig realizes he made a mistake leaving the team, and learns from it, I'm willing to sit down and help him, within the confines of his existing contract. But he has to stand up like a man and admit he made a mistake." If he didn't stand up and admit it, there would be no negotiations whatsoever.

By one of those ironies, the Yankees were in Winter Haven to play the Red Sox, a team which had blown its chances to repeat last year because three of their players—Fred Lynn, Rick Burleson and Carlton Fisk —had played most of the season unsigned. By the time the club surrendered, the Red Sox were fifteen games behind.

"We'll be eleven games ahead of you by May 1," the Boston *Globe*'s feisty Clif Keane tells Billy Martin.

"That's all right," Martin shoots back. "I'll catch you with another team."

The Yankees managed to win this one for him, 9-6. It was not a happy win. Ron Blomberg had run into a cinder-block cement wall in left field and had been carried from the field, and Ron Guidry had once again shown nothing. The Yankees announced that Blomberg had a bruised left knee. They were still saying that Klutts had a "jammed sprain," while in reality he had two broken bones and a dislocated finger. "I should have caught the ball," said Blomberg. "Is the wall still standing?"

Guidry pitched the ninth inning, and the guy who hit the two-run homer this time was Jim Rice.

Reggie Jax, back in the line-up as DH after the cortisone shot, had two smoking doubles.

March 31. Graig Nettles is back in camp, although there is nothing to negotiate except the articles of surrender. "I understand Graig feels badly, and feels he made a mistake," Steinbrenner gloats. "That's the only positive thing to come out of it, and it will make a better man of him. When I'm convinced of that, there'll be no fine.

"I was really itching for this battle," Steinbrenner says, "and I really licked their tails. These guys can't go through life walking through obligations."

He insisted that three of his fellow owners had called to congratulate him on the stand he had taken. "What was going to happen if I had backed down is that a lot of players get this idea in their head that a contract is a unilateral document: if he has a bad year, the club has to make good on it; if he has a good year, he comes in and wants to renegotiate."

In the evening, a subdued Nettles handed out a printed statement:

> The problem I have is a personal one. I now realize it should be settled at the conference table, and not on the field. I want to apologize if I have caused any embarrassment or inconvenience to the Yankees. All I want to do now is get ready for the upcoming season.

He had come back, he said in answer to the question, because it was the right thing to do. Was leaving the wrong thing to do, then? "I don't think I did the wrong thing in leaving."

Chambliss signs a five-year contract, starting at $150,000 and going up progressively. Chambliss had said all along that there was nothing to worry about, because after what the Yankees had paid the free agents, they couldn't afford not to sign the players who had won them a pennant. Chambliss is twenty-nine years old.

Ron Blomberg's leg is in a cast.

April 1. Sparky Lyle comes into the game against Baltimore in the seventh inning, in relief of Catfish Hunter, who had pitched very well for six innings. Lyle takes two warm-ups, and grabs his elbow. Consternation. When trainer Gene Monahan gets to the mound, Sparky's arm is drawn up against his chest and shaking uncontrollably. "Gene," he groans, "I popped something in my elbow." He can't straighten it out, that's how bad it hurt. He is still groaning as the trainer puts his arm around his waist and helps him back toward the bench. And then he isn't groaning. He's smiling.

April Fool!

Jackson lines out two doubles and a single as DH, and runs wind sprints in the outfield between his turns at bat.

April 2. In perhaps the most astonishing day of the entire training season, nothing happens! Nothing that is reported, anyway.

April 3. The Yankees have won six straight, and Billy Martin, in a suddenly expansive press conference, lets it be known that Steinbrenner's concern about winning in spring training is ridiculous. He won last year, he reminds the writers, and he could win again if the owner let him alone. "Without me, they could win," he says, "but there would be a lot of problems." There were players, in fact, he was keeping from going after each other. "I want to stay the Yankee manager as long as I can. This is it, as far as I'm concerned. But I'm going to do my own thing. Nobody tells me what to do as long as I have this uniform on."

Does he expect to be fired before the three years on his contract are up? "Yeah, with him here." And then he smiles his Billy the Kid smile. "He might do it just for the publicity."

When Billy runs off his litany of complaints against Steinbrenner, you can almost bet there has been a fight, and that Billy is expecting to be fired momentarily. He has given it all to them: How Steinbrenner phoned him in the dugout after last year's opening-day ceremonies to tell him he wanted Munson fined for not wearing his cap, and Billy told Steinbrenner he didn't like phone calls on the bench. "He didn't call me no more." How he once ripped his office phone off the wall when Steinbrenner called down after a tough loss. How he stood up to George when the owner came bursting into his clubhouse, screaming at him, after the loss to the Mets in St. Petersburg.

This time, the shouting match had come after Billy informed George that Chambliss was going to bat fourth on opening day and Reggie was going to bat fifth. Steinbrenner had been willing to settle for having Reggie bat third. Not a chance. Like Billy said, nobody tells him how to manage. And if George wanted to fire him, let him fire him.

April 4. New X rays show that Blomberg has torn cartilage in his knee, and is out for at least half the season. As a result, the Bucky Dent deal is suddenly not so sure.

Martin announces his opening day line-up, with Jax batting fifth, and perhaps to help George look on the bright side, bats Jackson sixth against the Mets. As Blomberg was making his sad departure, he told Jackson he'd be back in two months and batting right behind him. "Then you're going to be awfully far down in the line-up," said Reggie.

Nevertheless, Jax tried to be a good soldier. He had never been moved around the way he had been this spring, Reggie said, batting everywhere between second and sixth. "I've never had to think about where I was going to bat when I came to the ball park. Maybe I'm going to have to get used to it."

Before they left the park, Martin called Jackson in to explain why he was going to bat Chambliss fourth, give him a lecture on team offense, and assure him that when he was swinging a hot bat, he'd bat him fourth.

To the press, he put it a little stiffer. "The guy has had his way all along. He's not used to playing the way other people want him to. But it's no big deal."

During the game, Chambliss had two singles and drove in the winning run. Reggie had nothing. "How about that number-four hitter," crowed Martin. "He'll come through like that all year. We're not playing egos, we're playing pennant. What's best for the club."

What surprised the players most of all was that he had used Carlos May as DH instead of Oscar Gamble. Billy knew that Oscar Gamble, who still hadn't signed, was not going to be with them in another day.

April 5. On the day the Yankees were breaking camp, they finally acquired Bucky Dent. The deal had been off and on for more than four months. Oscar Gamble, who had become expendable from the moment Jackson was signed, had been part of it from the beginning. The wheeling and dealing between Gabe Paul and Bill Veeck had been entirely on what else the Yankees were going to put into the deal. Veeck had asked for $700,000, which quickly became $500,000, plus a pitcher or two. When Guidry was injured, Veeck tried for him. "Over my dead body," Paul said. Okay, said Veeck, if he couldn't have Guidry, he'd take Lyle. Paul was willing to let him have him. Steinbrenner wasn't, and Martin certainly wasn't. So they had settled back and waited to see whose need was going to be the greatest at the end of spring training.

Veeck needed the money to open the season, which is about as needy as you can get. All he got by way of extras, were two minor-league pitchers of no particular value. He didn't even get the $500,000. In knocking down the Vida Blue sale nine months earlier, Bowie Kuhn had set a $400,000 limit on the money that could be passed in a trade. The theory, presumably, was that beyond that sum, the value should be expressed in players. Veeck didn't get another player, or a better player, or a different player. He just didn't get the extra $100,000.

He almost didn't get a deal at all. With Blomberg out, Gamble had become less expendable. The Yankees had Birdie Tebbetts following Dent all through spring training, and his reports weren't really that ecstatic.

Dent was "the best shortstop available," he reported. Dent had slightly more range than Stanley, he said, and he hit a little better. With Gamble having acquired a new value, Paul believed the price had become too high. His vote went against making the deal. Between Stanley with Gamble, and Dent without Gamble, Billy Martin infinitely preferred Stanley. Steinbrenner, with that dream of fielding an All-Star team, still wanted Dent. He also didn't want any unsigned players. He asked Paul two questions: "In your opinion, is Dent better than Stanley?"

The answer was yes.

"In your opinion, is Gamble still expendable?" Expendable meaning, could they win without him?

The answer was yes.

Make the deal, Steinbrenner ordered. And, you know, he was right. When you're talking about shortstops, *this much* difference in range can be *the* difference.

The Yankees had broken camp, and were on the bus ready to roll when Paul called Gamble off to tell him he had been traded. "Mr. Paul, you've made a big mistake," Gamble told him. "You know I'm a better ballplayer than Reggie Jackson."

Reggie leaving spring training was not the same man as Reggie arriving.

Two weeks after the braggadocio of the Ward interview, Reggie was groaning to Steve Jacobson of *Newsday,* "I don't know if I'm going to fit in, man." The straw that stirs the drink was talking more like the cream in Billy Martin's coffee. "It's my job to blend into the team, not for the club to blend with me. If I have the leadership ability, physically and mentally, it will show itself."

Reggie was being an astonishment again. "I am a myriad of personalities," he had said. He is also an emotional kaleidoscope. Shake him, and he comes out different. Where had he gone, the Reggie Jackson who stood on the podium and announced that he had considered his course carefully ("the sociology and all that") and been charmed by Steinbrenner's warmth and persistence?

The way he saw it now, Steinbrenner had pressured him into making the wrong decision. "I didn't have time to consider my personality," he told Jacobson.

"Where I'd fit in best socially, what sort of players I'd fit in with. How do I come to a team with so much of its power left-handed?"

He longed for the days in Oakland when they had all been young and hungry together, and when he had real emotional support from Joe Rudi, the solid man, the good friend with whom he could weep openly when one of his fits of depression was upon him. And, yes, a manager, Dick Williams, with whom he could weep unashamedly, too. "When you have that relationship on a team, it gives you a feeling of being home. It takes a lot of the pressure off you; gives you a feeling of security, of sharing. Sharing—that's what man's all about."

He had turned Montreal down because Montreal was "foreign," and he was suddenly beginning to realize that New York was a foreign land, too. "Philosophically and socially, there is a difference between the East Coast and the West Coast. I'm a liberal guy, and the East Coast is not liberal. I don't think the East is used to the black man standing up and saying what he thinks."

That will come as welcome, if perhaps belated, news to Barry Goldwater. Now, it wasn't because Reggie was anxious to make a fool of himself that he was saying the most liberal section of the country wasn't liberal. What he was saying was that if he failed in New York, it wasn't because he couldn't hit any more, it was because he was an outspoken black man.

He was willing to admit to "a ray of doubt" about being able to perform. What if he did have a bad year? Jacobson asked. "I can play," Jackson answered quickly. "You know I'm going to hit." And then, pulling back, "Maybe I'm wrong. Maybe I can have a rotten year."

But, of course, even that was relative, wasn't it? He was going to be measured by a standard that had never been applied to anybody before. "Everybody thinks I'm going to electrify New York. So I hit thirty-five home runs. How do I turn that city on?"

He still could not bring himself to talk about the fear that was consuming him. He simply wasn't able to say *What if I've lost it, what if my body is about to fail me?*

Instead, he said, "How much will I have to deal with every day? I'm not allowed to have a headache, be tired, not allowed to have time to be with myself. That's the way it's going to be."

The best clue to his frame of mind was that he revealed the existence of a clause in his contract that gave him the right to demand that the Yankees trade him after two years. He hadn't played a game for them yet, and he was preparing an avenue of escape. "If I can't relate to the people off the field, then I'm not going to stay there. I'm not sure I want to play five more years, anyhow."

As hard as he had worked, he was just about where he should have been at the beginning of spring training. Nor had he been able to tell anybody, except the people who were closest to him, what dreadful shape he was in. It was as if it were some shameful secret, some weakness to be hidden from his enemies. "There are little things you can do for show, like running back to your position after you make a play. I played nine innings today. You think the owner doesn't like to see me play nine innings? He's up there watching, so I'll play three extra innings if it makes him happy."

For public consumption he dismissed his hard work and his hustle as no more than a psychological ploy. "They mean nothing, but they impress some people. It's all eyewash, and I've mastered it."

Well into spring training, Phil Pepe commented to him that he seemed to be playing an awful lot for spring training. "You're playing just about every day. What's the purpose?"

"Don't ask me," Reggie said, looking toward the manager's office. "I don't know what he's trying to prove."

Billy Martin almost came out of his chair. "He said that? I'll be a sonofabitch. He asked to play. He told me, when we had our meeting, he likes to play a lot of innings in spring training."

When Reggie came to New York to start the season, he told his close friends, "I'm not going to talk to the New York press any more. They scare me."

Writers are the people who report on who won, who lost, who succeeded and who failed.

3

TEN ROTTEN DAYS
IN APRIL

"I was reminded that when we lose and I strike out, a billion people in China don't care."
　　　　　—the Wit & Wisdom of Reggie Jackson

The fun and games of spring training were over. Fun as in funny farm, and games as in *Games People Play*. There was just too much talent on the Yankees, it was generally agreed, for the team to self-destruct.

Dock Ellis, the last of the Great Unsigned, wasn't so sure. "It's a hell of a club," he agreed. "But something is going to happen. You can see it. You can feel it." As far as Ellis was concerned, most of the trouble could be laid to Steinbrenner's insistence on interfering with the manager. (Or could it have been his insistence on underpaying a pitcher named Dock Ellis?) "Let him stay up in his box," Dock said. "Count the money, push buttons and stay the hell out of the clubhouse."

When Reggie Jackson entered the clubhouse for the light workout that was held the day before the opener, he was handed a uniform with a new number. In spring training, he had worn number 20, an undistinguished number devoid of personality. For the regular season, he was given number 44. Double cleanup. The number worn by Hank Aaron and Willie McCovey. For those who question the mystic powers of numerology, Aaron and McCovey tied for the home-run championship in 1963 with—guess what?—44.

It would have been more appropriate, Jackson all but said, if the number had been 55. What he did say was, "I'm batting fifth until they find out where everybody should be hitting."

On a scale of 55, Billy Martin would not be numbered among your greatest believers in clubhouse meetings. The only important ones, he has always believed, are the welcoming speech on the opening day of spring training and the unity speech just before the opening of the season. Needless to say, there had never been a season where a unity speech was more indicated. Billy's speech, delivered after the workout, ran to how he was going to treat the players like men and expected them to own up to their failings. "Constructive criticism," he emphasized. That's what the old Yankees used to have, that's why they had been winners. "When we were wrong we told each other, and when we were right we bragged on each other. But the opposition didn't know. We did it within." With a losing team, he said, it was called second-guessing. And then he held forth for a while on mutual respect and putting the troubles of the spring behind them and playing as a team, with the guys on the bench pulling for the guys on the field even when they believe they should be in the starting line-up themselves. Addressing Stanley directly, Billy told him that he knew exactly how he felt because he had ridden the bench himself with the old Yankees when he was sure he should have been playing. "You may not think so now, but you're going to end up rooting for Bucky Dent harder than for anybody else on the club. And when that happens, when everybody's rooting hardest for the man in his own position, we'll know that we're a team." And at the end he said, as he always does, in a sentiment so traditional that the old-time managers used to hang it on their office walls, "Whatever happens in this clubhouse stays in this clubhouse. We're not going to hang our dirty laundry out in public." If there was any dirty laundry, they could bring it into his office and they'd wash it out together.

Later in the afternoon, during a reception for the players at the mayor's mansion, Milton Richman of UPI asked Billy Martin whether anything of interest had occurred at the meeting. "I'll give you a little story," Martin said. "Reggie Jackson came over to me afterwards and said, 'In all my years in the big leagues, that's the best meeting I was ever in.' " Asked to confirm it, Reggie went absolutely cold. "Who gave you that?" he demanded.

With the best will in the world, Jackson *had* made an effort to reach out to Martin. With the best will in the world, Martin had seized upon an opportunity to let everybody know about it. And somehow Reggie was taking it as an act of betrayal. *He tells us not to talk and immediately runs to the press to repeat something I told him in confidence.*

There was no way it was going to work. Even when they tried, Martin and Jackson couldn't make contact.

And they weren't the only ones. In flat defiance of Dock Ellis' edict, George Steinbrenner came into the clubhouse on opening day and held a ten-minute meeting with Graig Nettles. Just a conversation about Nettles' contract, Steinbrenner said. "He had some questions about his deferred payment and we're working on it."

"If that's his story," said Nettles, "we'll leave it at that."

And, always, there were Reggie Jackson and Thurman Munson. Reggie had been assigned the second of the five lockers against the left-hand wall as you entered the clubhouse. It was almost as if the management were saying, "We know where the writers will be going after every game, so we're going to make it easy for everybody." To make it even easier, the first locker had been left empty and the locker on the other side of Jackson was assigned to the injured Ron Blomberg. After that came Elrod Hendricks, who was as much a coach as a player, and, at the end, just before you came to the shower room, Willie Randolph. For all practical purposes, Reggie would be flanked by an empty locker on one side and two empty lockers on the other.

"He's still basically an insecure kind of guy. He really is. His ego needs to be constantly massaged, and the way he does it is through quotes; he can get attention from the press even when he's not the focal point of the game. He goes 0 for 4 and the Yankees win and the pitcher pitched a hell of a game. You notice that a lot of the reporters go to him after the game, rather than the pitcher. That rankles a lot of the players. You're saying, Jesus Christ, what the hell did he do? Why don't you go over and talk to the guy who pitched the game? But the fact that peeks through is that Reggie is intelligent enough to do what he set out to do. He wants to get the attention."

—Yankee player's view

Thurman Munson had the end locker, right alongside the trainer's room. Good thinking. The trainer's room was where Thurman was going to be spending most of his time.

Opening day came up cool and windy but, somehow or other, it wasn't until Thurman Munson was walking by on his way out to the field that Reggie realized he didn't have anything to keep his neck warm. "Hey, Thurman," he said, as the writers' pencils began to move, "have you got an extra turtleneck dickey?"

"No," grumped Thurman. "You got an extra right-handed batting glove?"

Jackson reached into his locker. "Here's one. Just remember where you got it."

"How can I forget?" Munson said. "It's got 'Reggie' written all over it."

It's all in the tone. There was the sense that if Reggie had been able to get Munson to go back and get him the turtleneck, he would have been reducing him to the role of valet. Reggie was still trying to establish a kind of psychological superiority, and Munson had one-upped him two times in a row.

And then the game itself was great. Just great. A 3-0 win over Milwaukee in which the new players—plus Catfish Hunter—played a conspicuous part. The coaching staff had concentrated on Catfish all through

58

spring training, and after a terrible beginning he had started to come along. Despite the cool weather he had his control on Opening Day and, even, pretty good speed. After giving up a single to the first batter, he allowed just two more singles in seven innings, walking nobody and striking out five. There was, however, one thing that looked like nothing at the time: in the sixth inning, Von Joshua lined a shot back off the Cat's left instep, and after he had pitched another inning, the foot seemed to cramp on him. Sparky Lyle had to come in to complete the shutout.

The best defensive play by far was pulled off by Bucky Dent, who showed the 43,785 fans why the Yankees had wanted him by making a spectacular backhanded leaping catch of a line drive.

Jim Wynn, the right-handed DH they had been forced to settle for (the man who was thrilled to be a Yankee this late in his career), came to bat as leadoff man in the second inning and started the scoring for the season by hitting a gargantuan 450-foot drive into the center-field bleachers.

The new man, Reginald Martinez Jackson, was (need it be said?) the cynosure of all eyes. Reggie had come up for the first time as a Yankee in the bottom of the first inning with two men on, and as he set himself in the batter's box, a cheer erupted from the upper grandstand off to his right. A fight had broken out. Pure symbolism. He brought the inning to an end with a fly to center field, and it was going to be a long time before Reggie came up with two men on base again.

He did score the Yankees' other two runs, though, on his next two times at bat, after leading off both innings with a single. In the fourth inning, he went headfirst into third on a single by Nettles (after missing a steal sign), and slid under the catcher on a squeeze play. In the sixth, he came sliding in on a wild pitch. Lot of speed there, lot of hustle.

"Reg-gie, Reg-gie, Reg-gie," they chanted, as he came to bat again in the eighth. The cheering of a huge crowd as heard from the stands is one thing. From down on the field, it's something else. On the field you are at the bottom of a bowl, and the sound comes crashing down upon you from all sides. It's not even a sound, it's a wind of noise, a physical phenomenon that can be felt as well as heard.

Reggie lined a wicked foul ball into the right field bleachers, and the wind grew louder and stronger. They continued to cheer him even after he grounded out, and when he turned back at the dugout steps and waved, the crowd went mad.

"You hear that sound," Reggie said afterward, "and it turns on your adrenaline. You feel secure and you feel comfortable. It makes you feel loved. With fans like that, all I have to do is keep my cool and pop one in the air. They'll go crazy."

When it was mentioned to him that Jimmy Wynn's home run was the first ball ever hit into the center-field bleachers in the new Yankee Stadium, he gave the mob of writers his most prophetic look and said, "Stick around."

They had to stick around until his final swing on his last time at bat in the World Series, and then damned if he didn't do it. A good ten rows higher than the ball Jimmy Wynn had hit in the first game of the season.

But do you know who got the biggest cheer of the day? Last person you'd guess. Fred Stanley was sent into the game for Bucky Dent in the ninth inning and received a standing ovation that must have lasted three full minutes. Remarkable. Fred Stanley was the most anonymous member of the team, the one player who could have walked down the street in full uniform without being recognized. What were they cheering, then? A player who had lost his job? That happens all the time. No, the cheers were for the mediocre player, the player of limited talent who works hard and develops enough of the small complementary skills to make himself useful, necessary and—in Stanley's case for that one year—indispensable. The kind of player for whom, it seemed, there would no longer be a place on the Superteams of baseball's industrial age. The cheer was for the Good Old Days. A cup of kindness for *auld lang syne*.

And what did that constitute except a rebuke to George Steinbrenner and his whole Best Team Money Could Buy philosophy? Even though (if you can follow this) they want only a winner, will cheer only a winner, will reward only a winner.

During the pre-game ceremonies, there had been a benediction delivered by a good reverend who, somewhat carried away by the grandeur of his assignment, thanked God (whom he seemed to have confused with Santa Claus) for last year's pennant. Then, being an inordinately difficult man to please, he also asked for divine intercession that "from Your great heaven" the Yankees might be granted a World Championship in the coming year. Up in the press box, there was an understandable flurry of concern about how George Steinbrenner, magnified and sanctified be his name, was going to feel about all that credit going to the Great Interloper in the Sky.

The Lord moves in mysterious ways, His wonders to perform. The season opened on August 7, and by August 19, the Best Team Money Could Buy had the worst record in the major leagues. Worse than even the two expansion teams, Seattle and Toronto. If the world could have come to an end before dawn broke on August 20, twenty million baseball fans would have died happy.

You'd have thought it would have been easy. Even the schedule maker had seemed to be on the side of the Yankees. They were opening in New York with three games against Milwaukee (who had finished at the bottom of their division), going on the road to play Kansas City twice and Milwaukee three more times, and then coming back home again for a four-game series against Toronto. Ten of the first twelve games against patsies.

It didn't quite work out that way. Before the Yankees left town, Milwaukee had beaten them twice. In the first game, Reggie dropped a fly ball that led to all three runs in a 3-2 loss. In the ninth inning of the second, he was picked off first base with the potential tying run. That sound you heard crashing down onto the field wasn't *Reg-gie, Reg-gie, Reg-gie* any more. It was *booooo, boooooo, booooo*.

Except for Jimmy Wynn, nobody on the Yankees was hitting at all. In his first time at bat in that first loss, Wynn boomed one of the longest ground-rule doubles ever seen, a 420-foot drive which landed on the hard running track in the deepest part of left center and bounced high over the eight-foot fence. There wasn't another Yankee hit until the eighth.

In the second loss, Don Gullett, the $2 million pitcher, got his first start as a Yankee and lost, 2-1, on two home runs by Sixto Lescano, a $45,000 outfielder. The first one had tied the score, and the second one put the Brewers ahead in the ninth.

The Yankees came to bat in the bottom of the ninth, suddenly behind for the first time in the game, and Reggie led off against a left-handed relief pitcher, Bill McClure. (Chris Chambliss, Billy Martin's cleanup hitter, had gone out eleven straight times by then and pretty much converted Jackson into a leadoff hitter.) There are two ways to put it. One is that Reggie led off with a single. The other is that he was given three outs in the space of about thirty seconds. It started with Reggie chopping the ball into the dirt toward first, and McClure throwing the ball past the first baseman. Reggie rounded first, clearly intending to go to second, tried to double back when he saw that the second baseman had backed up the play, but got tagged out. Incredibly, the umpire gave him a life by turning himself into a mind reader and ruling that Reggie had not made a definite attempt to advance. Having been saved from one humiliating experience, Reggie immediately got himself into another.

The Yankees had never faced McClure before, but his reputation had preceded him. Not much of a pitcher, but he had the trickiest move to first base in baseball. A balk move which the umpires in the minor leagues had let him get away with. Martin had already warned his players about it, but to make sure that Jackson hadn't forgotten, the entire coaching staff leaped to the top step of the dugout to shout a warning. Jackson nodded to show that he understood, took one step off the base and was picked off.

Martin came out screaming at Val Voltaggio, the same rookie umpire who had ruled that Jackson hadn't rounded first base. Voltaggio had umpired in the Southern League while McClure was setting pick-off records. "It's legal there," he told the furious Martin, "and it's legal here." Actually, Martin had been screaming at him since the fourth inning, when Voltaggio ruled that a Nettles line drive that had been deflected off the Milwaukee first baseman's glove into foul territory had been foul when he touched it.

After the game, George Steinbrenner called Martin from his home in Tampa to find out why the Best Team Money Could Buy had a losing record. He was the owner, he had a right to know, and he wanted Martin to know he was going to exercise that right.

They hadn't lost two games, Martin told him. They had won one, lost one and had one foully stolen away from them by the umpires. And then, sitting absolutely naked in the clubhouse, surrounded by sportswriters, he rolled his eyes to the ceiling and let the man on the phone rail on. "I know that, George." "That's for sure, George." "Worse than that, George."

Reggie had no excuses. It is part of his character that he will almost always admit when he has made a mistake. He had known about the balk move. He had heard the warnings. Why he hadn't simply kept his foot on the base instead of taking one meaningless step off he didn't for the life of him know. "I wasn't invited into the kitchen," he said. "I walked in."

Same thing about whether he should have been called out when he rounded first. "If he had called me out, I couldn't have argued."

Milwaukee had started two left-handers in the three games against the Yankees, and when they got to Kansas City they faced two more. The Royals were the team they had beaten in the ninth inning of the fifth play-off game on Chris Chambliss' home run, and they expected to be meeting them in the play-offs again. The first game was also going to be the premiere of ABC-TV's *Monday Night Baseball* (Hi there, Howard), which made it a living cinch that Reggie was going to hit a home run.

Reggie hit a home run, and the Yankees lost their third straight game. This time it took thirteen innings. It was Reggie's first home run of the season, and it was also his first run batted in. With Chambliss running his hitless streak to 16, Reggie had been to the plate seventeen times, and fourteen of them had come with nobody on base. Against the left-handed curveballer, Paul Splittorff (remember the name), Martin had moved Jim Wynn, still the only Yankee who was hitting, up to the cleanup spot and dropped Jackson down to sixth.

To make matters worse, Martin's running game, the rationale for dropping Reggie Jax out of the cleanup spot from the beginning, was either nonexistent or counterproductive. Splittorff retired the last thirteen batters he faced. Then Mark Littell, who will always be remembered as the pitcher who threw the ball Chambliss hit *the* home run off, came in for four innings and allowed only two batters to reach first base, both on walks. Both of them, Blair and Rivers, were thrown out trying to steal. For Rivers, it was the third time he had been thrown out in four attempts.

Reminded that the game had been televised back to Tampa for Steinbrenner to enjoy, Billy Martin—ever mindful that to an old football man like the Coach every loss was a big one—stuck his head out into the clubhouse and shouted, "Full pads tomorrow."

Maybe it was to pacify Steinbrenner or maybe it was because nobody else was hitting, but with another left-hander, Andy Hassler, going against them in the second game, Martin shuffled his line-up again. Now Munson was batting second and Jackson third. They both struck out on their first two times at bat. The Yankees won anyway, 5-3, the most runs they had scored all season, but they did it on a collection of bloops and bunts and tricklers. And lots of luck. They scored the third run, to give you an idea, when Nettles got a checked-swing single, was caught cold at second on a broken hit-and-run play, ended up on third base when the throw went into center field and scored on Rivers' bunt single. For Rivers, it was his third hit of the game, and not one of them had reached an infielder.

The winning run came in when Martin let Bucky Dent bat for himself with two out in the eighth, instead of sending a pinch hitter in for him as he had been doing in that situation. Dent got the only extra-base hit the Yanks had all day, a long drive off the left-field wall. Given the choice between saying he'd had a hunch or proving what a great psychologist he was, Billy never hesitated. "Keep yanking him, and he's going to go down the drain," he said, sagely. Which didn't keep Martin The Sage from yanking Dent through the rest of the year. (Martin's psychology was right. Dent became so completely demoralized at one point that he was ready to jump the club. By one of those dramatic coincidences, the most explosive incident of the whole season broke around him just as he was ready to leave, and caused him to change his mind. Watch for it.)

The win in Kansas City may not have been very artistic but it was the only one the Yankees were going to get in the brief road trip. Having already surprised the Yankees by taking them two out of three in New York, Milwaukee swept them at home. Some series. It started with the first confrontation between Martin and Jackson, moved on to what might have been the most galling defeat of the season and ended—in the madness which enveloped the entire season—with the Yankees in the cellar of their division, but feeling happier and more together than they had ever been before or would ever be again.

The Martin-Jackson confrontation had its origins in the nonartistic victory in Kansas City. Having added three pop outs to the two strike-outs, Reggie had removed himself from the game in the ninth. As he should have. He had hurt his elbow again in the second game of the season by making a long throw to the plate, and it had become so painful that he knew he wouldn't be able to make another one if he had to.

With an off day coming up in Milwaukee, Reggie told the writers that his arm was going to be examined by the Brewers' team physician. It turned out to be nothing more serious than an inflammation, and Jackson came to the park for the first game of the series ready to play. His name wasn't in the starting line-up. "His arm is bothering him," Billy explained. "He told all the press that his arm is bothering him." A couple of days' rest, he said, and Reggie could come back strong. And then turning to Reggie, who was seated several feet down the bench, he snapped, "Right, Reggie?"

Reggie scarcely deigned to look at him.

Jackson, the $3 million hitter, sat on the bench while Don Gullett, the $2 million pitcher, was racked for seven runs in less than five innings. The pitcher who had always had the great won-lost percentage was now 0-2. To make it Black Friday on Millionaires' Row, Catfish Hunter had tried to warm up before the game and found his foot was hurting as much as ever. The first prognosis had been that he might miss one start. He had now missed two. Another set of X rays was ordered.

Winners sing one song, losers another. The way the game developed, Billy was given two chances to use Jackson as a pinch hitter and resisted both of them. In the eighth inning, the Yankees rallied for two runs to bring the score to 7-4 with two men still on base. A perfect spot for Reggie. A right-hander, Bill Castro, had been sent in to pitch to Jim Wynn, and he'd have to stay in there for one batter. Martin stayed with Wynn, and Wynn grounded out. In the ninth, with two on and one out, Martin sent Elrod Hendricks, a lefty, to the plate for Dent. Bill McClure, the man with the magic motion, relieved, and Martin countered with a right-handed hitter, Fran Healy, who hadn't been up all year. Healy hit into a double play.

Martin was uncharacteristically on the defensive. In neither instance, he admitted, had he asked Jackson whether he thought he could swing. "If I had asked him, he would have said he could, for the good of the team. He's that type of guy. He'd try to do it for the team." And maybe be lost to the team for the next two weeks.

When Jackson was asked whether he was disturbed by the way it had been done, he gave a firm "No comment." There are times, of course, when no comment is the most telling comment of all.

However: Yes, he could have hit. "I'm not mad because I didn't. He was trying to protect me. This is what I've been told, so I have no reason to think otherwise."

Had he volunteered?

"He didn't say anything to me. He never asked me anything. He communicates with the trainer."

Never mind. They managed to communicate for two and one-half hours that night at the hotel bar. The next day, Jackson was in the starting line-up as the Designated Hitter. "He's the type of guy you have to explain things to," Martin told the press. "I just wanted him to understand why I do certain things."

Like what?

"Like he didn't know I don't allow players to tell the press about injuries."

The press didn't even bother to ask him why he hadn't been honest about it on the previous day. The press already knew how Billy did certain things.

Asked about his return to the line-up, Jackson gave a noncommittal "I'm just glad to be here."

Asked about his relationship with Martin, he gave a great deal of thought to whether he wanted to talk about it. "I just don't know what's between us," he said finally.

Between the interviews, they were playing a ball game and, of course, losing. With Hunter out, Ken Holtzman, the number five pitcher on what was supposed to be such a tremendous staff, was finally getting his first start. And the Yankees went into the last of the ninth leading, 3-1. Jackson had scored one of the runs following a bloop double. The next time he came to bat, Mickey Rivers was on second with two men out. Astonishingly, Martin gave Rivers the sign to steal third base and Mickey was thrown out. A gratuitous insult. Jackson was the guy who was supposed to knock in runs, and with two men out it didn't make all that much difference whether the runner was on second or third.

Holtzman, pitching one of the best games he was to pitch all season, had allowed only three singles over eight innings, but when the leadoff man in the ninth inning singled, Martin brought in Sparky Lyle. Can't argue with that. Holtzman had pitched so little that he could easily be tiring, and the tying run was at the plate. That's Sparky Lyle country, and Sparky had been very effective all season.

Not today. It took a great play to get one out, then Cecil Cooper hit a hanging slider deep into the right-field stands. Just like that, the game was tied. Sal Bando sent a long drive into the alley in right center for a triple. But Lyle struck out Don Money, and Yogi

67

Berra ran out to tell Lyle not to give Steve Brye anything to hit. The winning run was on third base, and another base runner meant nothing. Giving him nothing good, Lyle got two good sliders on the outside corner for two strikes, tried for another, hung it, and Brye lined it into right center to win the game. The winning hit on an 0-2 count, the cardinal sin for a pitcher. But that's the way it goes, when everything is going wrong.

The Brewers, who were in first place where the Yankees were supposed to be, acted as if they had just won the World Series. The Yankee clubhouse was deep in gloom.

Then, just like that, it changed. And, of course, it was Reggie Jackson who changed it. Reggie, who can achieve extraordinary depths of gloom, had retreated into total silence. But a couple of friends were traveling with him and during a long talk that night they did what friends are supposed to do: They advised Jackson to take the first step in setting things right with his teammates.

Having reached his emotional nadir, Reggie came in the next morning in high spirits. To buttress that mood, there was the Sunday morning chapel session which is always conducted in the clubhouse for anybody who wants to attend. Jackson had become a born-again Christian and he is deeply religious, hardly surprising in such an introspective man. After the sermon, he had a long private talk with the preacher. "He took me out of myself. I was reminded that when we lose and I strike out, a billion people in China don't care." Reggie at his best. If he could remember that more than once or twice a season, he'd be a happier man. After the sermon, he went right for the two main sources of hostility. He began by cutting a picture of a fat man out of a magazine, wrote an inscription on the bottom ("To George, Best Wishes. Thurman Munson"), and pinned it to Munson's locker.

And then he called Graig Nettles, who had shown an open distaste for him from the beginning, to look at it.

From there, he went into the trainer's room to join in the kidding and horseplay.

The message was writ bold and clear: I am joining the team.

During early batting practice, Thurman Munson went to the outfield to welcome him. The gist of what he said, as relayed to the press by Jackson, was, "I didn't realize you were so sensitive and emotional. Don't let it bother you. Go after them. We need you."

For the first time all season, the bench was alive, with everybody up and shouting encouragement. And with the Yankees putting thirteen runners on base, they had plenty of opportunity to give their lungs an airing. Unfortunately, all thirteen of the runners remained on base. Billy Travers, who had lost the opener to Hunter on a shutout, turned around and shut the Yankees out, 2-0, dropping them—kerplunk—into last place. The third straight loss. Six losses in seven games. Their record for the season was 2-6. In six of the eight games, a left-hander had been started against them, and in one of the others the winning pitcher had been a left-handed relief pitcher.

But that was all right. The New York Yankees were leaving Milwaukee feeling, for the first time all season, that they were a team. "All that junk from spring training is cleared away," said Thurman Munson, who had led the cheering. "Everybody was pulling for everybody, and this is the first day that happened. Sometimes the heads are screwed on right, you just have to tighten them a little bit."

They were going to be home for only four days. Four games against Toronto. To change their luck—you really have to be desperate to need a change of luck against an expansion team—Billy Martin shaved off his mustache. After the game, he hid both himself and his newly shorn upper lip in the Players' Lounge. In other words, they lost again. Against Toronto, a team of rejects, the Yankees managed to collect four singles. They also committed four errors.

With right-hander Dave Lemanczyk, who had never been able to make it with Detroit, going against them, Martin had packed six lefties into the batting order. Half of the four hits came from Willie Randolph, a right-handed hitter.

Everything was still going wrong for them.

On the same day that Hunter was placed on the disabled list and sent home, Ed Figueroa was hit on the right instep by a line drive, stayed in there for another inning (just as Hunter had), and was hit by a line drive on his pitching arm.

Jackson hit a line shot back at Lemanczyk which literally took his glove off. Unfortunately, the ball and the glove landed only a few feet apart, and Lemanczyk threw him out.

Nettles, given a questionable error on a tough chance, gave the finger to the official scorer.

Reggie, booed lustily on his final time at bat, struck out and was booed even more lustily. That was okay, he said. When you were 2-7 and in last place, you were supposed to get booed. "They weren't booing the team. They're just saying, 'You should be doing better, dummies.' " -

Otto Velez, who had been picked up from the Yankees, hit a home run for Toronto and knocked in another run with a single. Him, they cheered.

Mickey Rivers, who had come into camp asking to be traded, was asked to comment on a story that he was going to be traded to Oakland along with Dock Ellis. "If they want to trade me, just trade me. Nobody wants to play with all those things on their mind. Let *him* make the decisions."

"Him" was Billy Martin. And guess who agreed with him? Reggie Jackson, still being a force for good within the community, was pleading that Billy Martin be given a chance. "He doesn't swing the bat. He doesn't make the errors. If this ball club doesn't win, I quit." And then, significantly, "Just as long as the bosses stay cool, we'll be all right."

Reggie Jackson was in communication with Steinbrenner, make no mistake about that. All year. Don't completely dismiss the possibility that it was Steinbrenner, from his perch in Tampa, who had arranged that meeting in the neutral territory of the hotel bar. And do not—repeat, do not—discount the possibility that it was Steinbrenner, not Jackson's traveling companions, who had told him to make his peace with everybody so that in the event it became necessary to let Martin go, Reggie wouldn't be blamed. Not that

George wanted to fire Billy. He didn't. He was very anxious to make it work for Billy, if only to prove that he, George Steinbrenner, had been able to pull Billy through. But managers who keep losing have an increasingly short life expectancy. George's primary interest was to protect Reggie Jackson, and how could anybody blame Reggie when he was right there, on the record, taking Billy's part against the bosses?

And where was Billy Martin while his fate was being debated? Billy, minus his mustache, was still in the Players' Lounge, where a sign above the door read, "Yankee Players Only." The traditional sanctuary for the players was the trainer's room. The difference between that sanctuary and this sanctuary was that this sanctuary came equipped with a television set and game boards.

After forty-five minutes, Billy sent the stadium manager to his office with the following message for the waiting writers: "Mr. Martin will not be in. He has no comments."

Billy had already got the word that George Steinbrenner was going to be in the next day to chat with him. Which made it a very good idea, Billy may well have decided, to keep his mouth shut.

Nobody was pushing the panic button yet, George told Billy, but he knew as well as anybody else that any manager's tenure was determined by his won-lost record. If he'd stop playing games with Reggie, he'd be doing himself and everybody else a favor, George said. And if he'd realize that when George and Gabe offered advice, they weren't trying to hurt him, they were trying to help.

"If you'd stop agitating for Reggie and tell him to subordinate himself to the team instead," Billy told him, "that's how you could help. This way, you can only hurt."

After he had talked to Martin, Steinbrenner called in a select group of newspapermen to defend himself against some charges that had been made against him. Better that he hadn't. There could be little doubt that he was responding to a Murray Chass article that quoted an unnamed player—who was probably Dock

Ellis—as saying that Steinbrenner had better stay off Martin's back because Martin had most of the players in his corner. The article quoted another unnamed player—who was most certainly Dock Ellis—as saying that "the more we lose, the more often Steinbrenner will fly in. And the more he flies, the better the chance there will be of the plane crashing."

"If anybody says I've been on Billy Martin's butt, he's a liar," Steinbrenner roared. "I've had no conversations with Billy Martin about the ball club since spring training. If Billy does his job, he's not going to get any riding on his back from me."

Made you wonder what they talked about when George called the clubhouse. Hardly a day went by . . .

Steinbrenner also wanted the press to understand that Billy was going to make it or break it on what the ball club did on the field. "It's like the president of a company. If you produce earnings, you don't have to worry. I have every confidence that Billy is going to turn it around. This club is going to win. An acorn doesn't make a fall."

While he was willing to admit that down in spring training he had made some suggestions about the batting order, he was quick to add that he wasn't going to try to stick any line-up down his manager's throat. What that meant, of course, was that he knew by now that Billy wasn't going to let him.

And then there was the Bucky Dent deal. Steinbrenner had been accused of making that deal just because he wanted a team of All-Stars. Not true, he said. The Yankees had made the deal not because George Steinbrenner wanted Dent but because Billy Martin wanted him. "Billy came to me five days before the end of spring training and said, 'You gotta get me Bucky Dent.' The Bucky Dent deal was dead until Billy said, 'I have to have him.'"

Whatever Billy may—or may not—have said five days before the deal was made, Steinbrenner was the man who wanted Bucky Dent. And he wanted him because of that dream of a team of All-Stars.

The trouble with Steinbrenner is that once he starts talking he can't stop, a problem he shares with his manager. When he gets defensive he begins to mouth off and lose control of what he is saying, a trait he also shares with his manager. It can make for a very difficult relationship. Each accused the other of being a liar many times during the season, and nobody was disposed to argue with either of them.

Steinbrenner was not going to trade Dock Ellis. "I like Dock Ellis, he's a good pitcher. No one's going to trade Dock for spite."

What that meant was that Finley had been asking too much to suit Gabe Paul, and they were going to have to start all over again.

Not that Steinbrenner denied everything. No, he accepted the blame for not describing the players' injuries accurately. "I'm the offender on those. It won't happen again." That was big of him. Everybody in the room knew it was a policy which predated him by decades, and that it was Martin who was the principal culprit.

"I'm not Little Red Riding Hood, and I didn't just ride into town on a load of pumpkins either. I'm learning . . . I've ridden people both in sports and in business. There are times to exhort; there are times not to exhort. And this is one of those times."

Whereupon George went into the clubhouse to do some exhorting.

Having talked to the press about his relationship with Martin, he told the players they shouldn't talk to the press about his relationship with Martin. He wanted them to know there were no differences between himself and their manager, and that the players could only create differences by talking to the press. Although he didn't mention the trade rumors directly, he did tell them the team was intact. "The players in this room are the players we'll be finishing the season with." Well, maybe that wasn't putting down the trade rumors either. Dock Ellis wasn't there. "I'm not going to listen to that High School Charley shit," Dock had said.

No wonder George liked him.

And then George went into the pep talk. The pride of the Yankees. The great players who had worn the pin stripes. The glorious tradition of winning. "Let me tell you something, the first time you win is easy. It's

73

winning the second time when everybody is looking for you, that's the mark of a true champion."

"It's like a college rah-rah-rah, that's what it comes down to. We come back from batting practice and George walks in, and Billy says, 'Well, George would like to speak to you.' And George would give you a Knute Rockne type talk. It's like shish-boom bang, rah-rah-rah. Well, we pay you real well to play baseball; if you don't play baseball we've got other people down in the minor leagues who want to play baseball real bad."
—Yankee player's view

"Most people don't understand this, but the players like George. But George's background is not base-ball. He doesn't know what it's like to play the game. I don't need nobody coming up to me and telling me, Boys, you should be proud to wear the uniform of the New York Yankees. If he thinks that makes an impression on how you go out and play the game, he is mistaken. The player has to motivate himself."
—Yankee player's view

Thus inspired, the Yankees went out and lost another game to the Blue Jays. Just losing to a team called the Blue Jays is embarrassing enough. To get battered by the Blue Jays is humiliating. The Blue Jays battered them 8-3. For the second day in a row, the hitting star was Otto Velez. Instead of yelling, "Reg-gie, Reg-gie, Reg-gie," the Yankees fans were chanting, "Vel-lez, Vel-lez, Vel-lez."

Thurman Munson, playing one of the worst games of his life, had two errors plus a passed ball to go with the two wild pitches thrown by his pitchers. The Yankees' pitching was in such disrepair that Martin had been forced to start Gil Patterson, who had just been called up from Syracuse to take Catfish Hunter's place on the roster. As the first number one draft choice of the Steinbrenner era, Patterson had become Steinbrenner's pet project. Patterson lasted less than four innings, before Ron Guidry came in and got plastered for five runs in less than four innings. Just as he always seemed to get plastered when Steinbrenner was watching. The previous day, against Lemanczyk, Martin had packed the line-up with left-handed hitters. With a twenty-one-year-old left-hander, Jerry Garvin, going against them, he packed it with all right-handers except for Rivers and Nettles. The boss had come in to agitate for Reggie Jackson, and Martin replied by benching him again. But, you will note, he also benched Chambliss. (Can't you just hear Steinbrenner telling him during their meeting, "You bench Jackson against left-handers because you say he isn't hitting, but you keep playing Chambliss and he's hitting even worse.") One for me, George, and one for you. A very nicely modulated defiance. For all the talk about Billy's suicide drive, he had a very keen sense of survival.

Before the game came to its dismal end, Billy picked his next day's line-up from out of a hat. Reggie Jackson, who was just sitting around not doing much, anyway, did the picking. Reggie picked himself third. Or so we were told. Which also let Steinbrenner, and everyone else, know that Jackson was going to be playing the next day, didn't it?

Off the field as well as on, the team was in complete disarray. Martin was railing against the umpires again, because of an incomprehensible rule interpretation that had gone against them while the Yankees were still in the game. Follow this, if you can. With Wynn on third base, Piniella doubled. But the third-base umpire had called a balk on the pitch and ordered Wynn to stay right where he was. There was a new rule covering that kind of thing, and it had been instituted precisely so that a pitcher would not be rewarded for having committed a balk. Nevertheless, the interpretation of the new rule, as applied to this particular situation, went like this: If Wynn had scored, the balk would have been nullified and Piniella's double would stand. Since Wynn hadn't scored, it was a balk and there was no double. Which meant that Wynn scored on the balk and Piniella had to bat again. The reason Wynn hadn't scored was that the third-base umpire, the same umpire who had called the balk, had told him to stay where he was.

You figure it out.

In addition to railing against the umpire, Billy had to explain to the writers why he had ducked them a day earlier. He could do it with Billy the Kid charm or he could do it with ill grace. With his back to the wall, Billy did not opt for charm.

Was there anything in particular that bothered him about the losing streak?

"Yeah, the losses." And the rotten stories they had been writing.

Did he think the writers were against him?

"I'm not taking it against me. Against the ball club."

Had the stories affected the team?

"I think they have, yes."

Were the stories the reason the team was losing?

No, he hadn't said that.

Was he worried about the tension on the club?

"There's no tension. No tension! That's just the way it is when you lose."

Was he relaxed right now?

"Oh, yeah. Awful relaxed." He shot a look at the questioner. "Would you be relaxed if your house was on fire?"

Was his house on fire?

"No," snapped Billy Martin.

In the clubhouse, it was so tense that even Roy White, usually the most calm and gracious of men, barked at a reporter who asked him for an opinion on Garvin. "You've got eyes! What do you think?"

A TV reporter who wanted to interview Dock Ellis refused to identify himself, and so Dock shouted that he wouldn't be interviewed. "The little TV shit is trying to screw someone," he screamed to the room at large.

Lou Piniella, the most candid and obliging of players, was explaining the balk call to a group of writers when Graig Nettles, who had knocked in zero (0) runs in the ten games, screamed at him not to talk to Bob Kurland of the Bergen *Record*. Kurland, as official scorer, had given Nettles the error the previous day. Then Nettles proceeded to shout a vilely insulting word at Kurland over and over and over. While he was about it, Nettles had a few words to say to another reporter who, as today's official scorer, hadn't given him a hit he thought he should have had.

Well, with luck, Reggie Jackson might have been able to put it all in perspective. Didn't it sound like something from the good old days with the Oakland A's?

"No," Reggie said. "Nice try, but no."

Up in the Yankee offices, where Steinbrenner was holding a meeting with his top personnel, Gabe Paul suddenly felt faint and found his tongue growing so thick that he could barely speak. They rushed him to a hospital. He had suffered a cerebral spasm.

4

OUT OF THE HAT

"You don't trade your future away as 'something more.' "

—Gabe Paul

The next day, Martin started his out-of-the-hat line-up and thirteen games later the Yankees were in first place. So you can just forget what you might have heard about the meek inheriting the earth. Martin's thinking was the thinking of the gambler. A reshuffling of a cold deck. It loosens everyone up and, as Martin was quick to point out, if nobody's hitting it doesn't matter where they're batting.

The first name out of the hat had been Willie Randolph. A lot of people thought Willie should have been batting first anyway. Then it was Munson, who hates batting second but is an excellent second batter because he will take the ball to right as well as anybody in the league. And who did Jax pick third but himself, Reggie Jackson, which led those incurable skeptics up in the press box to do a little investigating. ("If the manager says I picked it out of the hat," said Reggie, "then I picked it out of the hat.") Nettles was fourth, which wasn't the worst spot in the world for a man who had just led the league in home runs. Rivers was number five, clearly not the spot for him but he batted in two runs anyway. And then it was Roy *White and Carlos May (where he had been anyway* when the Yankees had had to use a left-handed DH). Chambliss was down to eighth. That left Bucky Dent right where he had been, at the bottom of the line-up.

Not a bad line-up at all. Randolph opened the game by doing what Rivers almost never did. He drew a walk. (He also had a home run, equaling his entire output for the previous year, and two singles. Some leadoff man.) Munson went down the right-field line for two bases, and Jackson singled them both home, lifting his total RBI's for the season from one to three. A couple of walks loaded the bases and Chambliss brought Jackson in with a scorching line drive to right field. Before the day was over, the Yankees had hit in every inning, 14 hits in all, with everybody having at least one hit except Carlos May.

Don Gullett finally won his first game, struggling all the way and giving his fielders a chance to shine. Bucky Dent showed why they had wanted him by getting a good jump on a hard shot into the hole, planting his foot and gunning out the runner. That's the play that separates the shortstops from the Short-stops. Nettles made things official by making *his* play, a diving catch on a wicked line drive to his left. That's a play he makes as well as anybody who ever lived, and which he must have made two dozen times during the year.

The next day, the out-of-the-hat line-up had 13 hits. Chambliss, the number-eight hitter, knocked in five runs with a homer and two doubles. Nettles, the clean-up man, finally knocked in his first run of the season and made two diving catches of line drives, one to his right and one to his left. (Two games later, in Cleveland, Chambliss knocked in six runs, on a bases-loaded double and a three-run home run.)

What did it all mean, these glorious victories over an expansion team? Naturally, the press went to the resident philosopher, Reggie Jackson, to find out. For Reggie, it was an opportunity to minimize the influence of his admittedly divisive presence on the team's poor start. "The magnitude of the story," he said modestly,

79

"was worth printing. But the magnitude in here was too much. The undercurrent of dissension, that was going too far."

Mickey Rivers, with that incisive mind of his, went to the heart of the matter. "Everybody's saying, the Yankees got a great team on paper, so why are they losing? We were losing because we weren't playing good ball."

Since Billy Martin's philosophy was a basic don't-fool-around-with-a-good-thing, he announced that as long as the Yankees kept winning, the batting order wouldn't be changed.

The out-of-the-hat line-up won six straight games, and you just have to look at the scores to see how awesome the hitting was: 7-5, 8-6, 9-3, 10-1, 7-1, 9-6. In the sixth one, they went so far as to defeat a left-hander, Baltimore's Ross Grimsley. That wasn't the story of that game, though. The story was the return to Baltimore of Reggie Jackson.

Play was started in the rain, quite fittingly, after a delay of more than an hour. It continued to rain all night. Reggie's name was booed loudly when the line-ups were announced, boos followed him wherever he moved, and all manner of things were thrown at him, including a hot dog (relish and mustard) which almost hit him when he came to the plate for the first time.

Anybody who had followed the tempest-tossed career of Reggie Jackson knew that he was going to shove it back down their throats. In the first inning, he doubled and scored a run, and returned to his position in time to watch himself being hanged in effigy. Signs were hanging all over the place by then. Some of them, like *Reggie Is A Bozo,* were funny. Most of them weren't.

And then the situation became not at all funny. The Orioles got their fans excited by scoring four runs in the bottom of the fourth to take a 5-4 lead. Top of the fifth, Reggie steps up with Munson on base and hits a mammoth home run into the right-center field *stands.* Normally, Reggie has a powerful, forward-leaning stride as he runs around the bases. *Not this* time. Having remained at the plate initially to watch the ball in its majestic flight, he slowed down after he had rounded third and literally strolled the final 20 feet home.

Ho-boy. Everything was thrown at him for the rest of the game. Hunks of glass, nuts and bolts, ice containers, paper airplanes with darts in them. Just when it looked as if things were going to settle down, Reggie came up again, hit another double and scored another run.

As he came running toward the dugout at the end of the game, something hard and shiny went whistling by his ear, and Reggie went rushing to the stands to point the culprit out to the park police. Unfortunately, the park police already had more than they could handle, just trying to keep the rampaging customers away from the Yankee dugout. As one guy came bouncing off the dugout roof, Graig Nettles, the quiet man who always seems to be there when there's a brawl, leaped upon him and threw him to the ground. Nettles ended up with an injured hand.

That wasn't the only Yankee injury of the night. Don Gullett, with that talent of his for strange injuries, had fallen off the wet mound in the fourth inning, landed on his elbow and had to be taken out of the game. Gullett was in traction, with a sprained ankle and neck.

Reggie's post-game comment would have been very odd for anybody except Reggie. It wasn't the booing or the verbal abuse he minded, he said. It was those funny little paper airplanes that stuck in the ground. "If I get booed and have a horrible night, they win. If I have a good night like tonight, I win."

It was Rudy May who had the good night the next time they took the field. May, who had been the key player for Baltimore in the June 15 deal for Ken Holtzman, brought the out-of-the-hat line-up's streak to an end. He did it by getting Reggie to fly out weakly late in the game, in a spot where a home run would have tied the game. By Reggie's reckoning, the fans had won. There is nothing in the records to indicate any wild celebration along the banks of Chesapeake Bay.

Before they went home from Baltimore, the Yankees had begun another winning streak (Reggie drove in the winning run in the ninth inning with a long fly) and had also completed a trade on which they had been working since the early days of spring training. A trade which went under the code name of "See You Later, Dock."

Steinbrenner had made it clear from the beginning that he was not going to have any unsigned players on the team. Certainly, he wasn't going to have an unsigned player who talked about how good it would be for team morale if a plane crash occurred, starring their beloved owner.

The logic of an Ellis-for-Torrez trade was that Charles O. Finley was every bit as eager to get rid of Mike Torrez. The difficulty of trading an unsigned player for anybody except another unsigned player in the New Era should be obvious. A signed contract had become an integral part of a player's value. Charlie Finley, whose foul-up on Catfish Hunter's contract had opened the door to the New Era, had fouled up again. Finley had sent Torrez a contract, which he really didn't expect him to sign, raising his salary from $83,000 to $100,000. After taking the precaution of consulting Marvin Miller of the Players Association, Torrez had signed it and whipped it back. The new Player Agreement, which the owners had just ratified, allowed a player to declare himself a free agent after six years, and Torrez was going into his sixth year. Since Mike had already announced that he was going to play out his option, a one-year contract was meaningless. What Finley should have done (you've got to be a lawyer to operate a ball club these days) was to send Torrez a multi-year contract and then cut the prescribed 20 percent from his previous year's salary when he refused to sign. Instead of paying him $100,000 for the year, he'd have been paying him $66,400.

Once he realized his mistake, Finley suggested to Torrez that he be a man about it if he didn't intend to come back, and at least take the 20 percent cut on the hundred grand. Finley didn't understand the new order at all. Players don't give, they get. They get, and they get, and when somebody else is out-getting them, they get mad.

The sticking point to an Ellis-Torrez trade was that Finley wanted the Yankees to put in something extra.

There is an almost ritualistic exchange that takes place in this kind of thing. "Okay," Finley would have said, "but Torrez is better than Ellis. If you were sitting where I'm sitting wouldn't you want something more?" All Finley wanted was one of the Yankees' young pitching prospects—preferably Gil Patterson—and with the Yankee pitching not so young any more (look at it!) Gabe wasn't about to give up any of his good young pitchers.

If Dock had been able to keep his mouth shut, he probably would have been able to make a deal with the Yankees for something like $400,000 for three years. He had pitched very well in his three starts, even though he had only one victory to show for it, and with Oscar Gamble gone he was more valuable than ever in the clubhouse. He had even made a conciliatory gesture of sorts by sending a letter to Gabe Paul, through his agent, announcing that he was calling off his war until the club, and particularly the pitching staff, got straightened away.

The "plane crash" line, which was kind of kidding on the level, put an end to any possibility of Ellis's staying. With Steinbrenner anxious to re-activate the talks, Finley came up with a new proposition. They could balance the Torrez and Ellis swap by exchanging their center fielders as well: the speedy Mickey Rivers for the speedy Bill North. Steinbrenner was more than willing. The way he looked at it, he'd be getting rid of two of his problems at the same time. Rivers' financial troubles had become even more complicated because of the break-up of his marriage (that was the personal problem Mickey had alluded to in spring training), and as George had come to know only too well, Mickey's financial problems very quickly became George's problems.

Gabe Paul was able to talk Steinbrenner out of the deal. "Mickey Rivers *ignites* this team," he told him, for perhaps the hundredth time. "The New York Yankees cannot win the pennant without him." Mickey Rivers could go down to first base faster than anybody he had ever seen. Once he was on base, he demoralized the other team. His instincts were faultless, he was baseball-smart. To an old pro like Gabe Paul, real talent was so hard to find that when a great player like Mickey Rivers came along, you handled whatever problems came with him. There's another Branch Rickey axiom which Gabe is wont to quote: "Problems are the price you pay for progress." Did Steinbrenner remember their first year in New York? No problems then, were there? You could go to sleep from the lack of problems. You could also go to sleep watching the ball games.

When Steinbrenner told the gathering of reporters that he wasn't going to trade Ellis out of spite, it was because Gabe Paul had just talked him out of dealing Mickey Rivers away.

Before that day was over, you will remember, Gabe was in the hospital. And so, Finley, who is a pretty shrewd cookie, very quickly came up with another proposition. His "something more" would be Ron Guidry and Mickey Klutts. To Steinbrenner, that was giving up nothing. He had never been able to understand why everybody was so high on Guidry, and how could you blame him? Every time he had seen Guidry pitch, the kid got clobbered. He had just seen Toronto, with all those Triple-A league hitters in their line-up, knock the kid's jock off. And, Jesus, he was such a skinny little kid that a good breeze would probably knock him over. Klutts? Klutts had a broken hand. Now that they had Dent, who needed Klutts?

Well, when you're lying in the hospital after having had the kind of scare Gabe had just had, you tend to become philosophical about such mundane matters as destroying a ball club. "Guidry is going to be the best left-handed pitcher in baseball within the next two years," Gabe told George. It was a matter of talent again. Rivers could run faster than anybody; Guidry could throw harder than anybody. Never mind what George's eyes told him. Guidry had been out for 61 days at the end of the previous season, he hadn't touched a ball all winter, and he had been thrown off again by the injury early in spring training. His confidence in himself had undoubtedly been shaken a little, but he was also just coming around to shape. "Where do you find an arm like that?" Gabe asked. The answer was, "Nowhere." When you found an arm you could find nowhere else, you hung on to it. Regardless.

As for Mickey Klutts? Well, the hot rookie at the moment was Oakland's Mitchell Page, who was merely leading the league in everything. Did Steinbrenner think that Page was a good hitter? Playing in the same league with Page last season, Klutts had outhit him by 25 points. He had also hit two more home runs than Page, and knocked in practically the same amount of runs.

You didn't trade your future away, Gabe said, in the further education of George Steinbrenner, as "something more." And you didn't put too much "something more" into what was a reasonably even trade to begin with. Finley needed everything. When he saw that he couldn't get what he wanted, he'd take what he could get.

A couple of days later, Finley agreed to take the unsigned Marty Perez, whom the Yankees wanted to unload anyway, and a minor-league outfielder. But do you know what clinched it? Steinbrenner had a three-year-old horse, Steve's Friend, which had won an upset victory in the Hollywood Stakes a couple of weeks earlier, and was eligible to run in the Kentucky Derby. Finley, who's a card, stipulated that George would also have to enter the horse, give Finley two tickets to his box on Derby Day and, in the event that Steve's Friend actually won the race, allow Finley to lead the horse into the Winner's Circle.

You think about it, and it almost seems as if there was an unseen hand hovering over the Yankees to protect them from making any irreversible mistakes. The three pitchers who won the pennant for them in the end were Lyle, Guidry and Torrez. If Guidry had lived up to his advance billing in spring training, Lyle would have been traded away and Guidry would have remained in the bull pen. If Gabe Paul's cerebral spasm had been a stroke, as originally feared, Guidry would have been given away as "something more."

To close the circle—or perhaps complete the triangle—it was Torrez' tardiness in reporting that gave Guidry his chance.

Maybe the guy who delivered the opening-day benediction knew something.

The trade was announced on a Wednesday, there was an off day on Thursday, and then the Yankees opened a home stand against the western clubs with a weekend series against Seattle. The open day on Thursday was fortunate, because it gave Torrez a good 48 hours to fly to New York, meet his new teammates and be ready to pitch. With Gullett's neck in a brace, Hunter still on the disabled list and Ellis gone, the pitching staff was so thin that Martin didn't have anybody else. Thursday came and went. No Torrez. Friday morning, Friday afternoon, Friday evening. Where was Torrez? An hour before the game, Billy Martin came to Guidry's locker to tell him he was going to be the pitcher. In the first inning, Seattle loaded the bases on Guidry with one out, and it looked as if it were going to be the same old thing again. But then Guidry got his darting slider going, struck out the next two batters, and for the next seven innings the Mariners couldn't touch him. All Martin had wanted out of him was five decent innings, and Guidry gave him eight and one-third before Lyle had to be sent in, with two men on, to complete a 3-0 shutout, and move the Yankees into second place. Okay, it was only Seattle, and Martin was making no effort to hide the fact that he had gotten away with something: "Tidrow's going tomorrow, and Sparky on Sunday. I'm putting all the starters in the bull pen." But for the first time, Guidry had shown what Tebbetts' scouting report was all about.

Not to keep you in suspense about Torrez, it was Monday night before he arrived in New York, and Tuesday before he pitched. The first word was that he had gone to Montreal to be with his wife, who was in the hospital because of complications following the birth of their first child. Mike's brother, who answered the phone at Mike's home, said that he had just come back from the hospital himself and that Mike was in northern Arizona, fishing with his agent. His agent was Gary Walker, the agent who handled Reggie Jackson. Mrs. Walker said that Torrez and her husband had indeed gone fishing, and that she didn't know when they'd be back. Billy Martin said he was thinking about fining Torrez $5,000 a day, which shows that Billy was also having a little trouble adapting to the new order of things. You don't take money away from ballplayers any more, Billy, you throw money at them. Any fine over $100 has to go to arbitration, and the ball clubs' record of success in that kind of thing puts it under the heading of "Why bother?"

The way the Yankees were going, it didn't matter.

They beat Seattle two more times, making it ten out of eleven, and moved to within a game of first place. Figueroa, who had been their best pitcher all season, won an easy 7-2 game, and Holtzman, who had been hit hard on his previous two starts, won a very difficult 5-2 game. It just goes to show you. Seattle had 13 hits off Holtzman and an equally ineffective Sparky Lyle, and had about a half-dozen more taken away by the Yankee infield. Four double plays, a diving catch of a line drive by Nettles, a diving catch of a line drive by Randolph, a diving catch of a line drive by Chambliss. To show how it was going, the score was only 4-2 in the eighth inning, when the first two batters singled off Sparky. The next batter bunted in the air toward first, Lyle lost the ball in the sun, and with Munson screaming for him to throw to first, Sparky, still blinded by the sun, whirled around and made a falling throw in the general direction of third. And got the runner. The next batter hit a ground ball up the middle, Dent got to it behind second and flipped it backhanded on the run to Randolph, for the start of a double play. All the things that had gone wrong earlier were now going right.

"I had my worst stuff of the year," said Sparky. "I had nothing." Since Sparky was going to get married the next morning, he could be forgiven. Or could he? "For me, getting married is like coming in to relieve with the bases loaded," he said. "I've been there before."

To show the kind of crowd Sparky travels with, his friends had a 1936 fire engine, complete with bells and sirens, waiting outside the church to drive him and his bride through the crowded streets of Manhattan.

That maroon Rolls Royce parked behind the fire engine belonged, of course, to Reggie Jackson. "Maybe

I ought to charge Sparky my usual three grand for a personal appearance," Reggie said, while he graciously signed autographs.

Mike Torrez, making his belated start, allowed the California Angels only one hit in five innings before he had to come out with a blister on his finger. And that gave Catfish Hunter, making his first appearance since the opening day of the season, a chance to pitch them into a tie for first place by beating his old Oakland club. Would you believe that the first batter he faced, Bill North, hit a line drive off his left instep? North, a former teammate of Hunter's, was so upset that he slowed down in the base line to ask the pitcher if he was all right, and got himself thrown out at first.

The Cat was all right. After a shaky start, he went the distance. But Oakland's Vida Blue was even better. The Yankees still weren't hitting left-handers, and so the Yankees were still in second place.

But the Cat was back. Or so it seemed. And Gullett was ready. For the first time all season, the pitching seemed to be in great shape.

So was Reggie. He had said that if he played in New York they'd name a candy bar after him. The folks down at Standard Brands, known to us all as the makers of Baby Ruth and Butterfinger, had held a fancy press luncheon at "21" that afternoon to let the entire chock-full-of-tasty-goodness world know that among his myriad talents, Reggie had been blessed with the gift of prophecy. Between you and me, they must have had some uneasy moments there for a while. As it was, they had waited until Reggie hit his first home run at Yankee Stadium, a mammoth blow into the right-center field bleachers, before they sent out the invitations.

The candy bar was going to be called "Reggie, Reggie, Reggie," a name which had come to the executives of the company in a flash of inspiration while listening to the chant of the crowd on opening day. Lucky that was the day they were there, the commercial possibilities of a candy bar named "Boo, Yabumya" being somewhat more limited.

To show what it means to be a certified folk hero in these days of the merchandisable celebrity, Jackson has a ten-year deal, according to which he will receive $250,000 a year as an absolute guarantee, against one percent of the gross sales. If the candy bar catches on at all, he will be able to make half a million a year out of it, easy. And if it does catch on, you understand, the deal won't be for only ten years, it will approximate perpetuity.

To take the curse of sordid coin off the proceedings, the company announced that it would be contributing $500 to a worthy community group for each Jackson home run ($1,000 for a grand slam), and was also buying tickets for 140 children (selected on a daily basis by their friendly local police precinct), in a sequestered section of the right-field stands where they would be known to one and all—if one and all should want to know—as Reggie's Regiment.

For those who wanted to see some money on the table —like, say, photographers—two certifiably ongoing charities each received a check for $500. Any remaining malcontents would just have to take Reggie's word that "I'm not doing it for what I can get out of it."

It was also educational. Reggie's original candy-bar statement had been made under the misconception, shared by all of us, that the Baby Ruth candy bar had been named for Babe Ruth. Uh-uh. Take it from the copyright owners, Baby Ruth had been introduced to the pubescent palate during Grover Cleveland's memorable administration, and had quite probably been named after the President's daughter. Which brings up the distinct probability that it was Babe Ruth who was named after the candy bar. I never did buy that story about one old Oriole saying to another, "Here comes Jack Dunn with his new babe."

Whether there were any escape clauses in the contract based upon Reggie's performance, longevity or mortality was not divulged. Who wants to introduce negative vibrations into such a deeply moving, charitable and educational occasion?

Not Billy Martin, certainly. In honor of Reggie's first New York home run, or maybe in honor of the candy bar, he had moved Jax into the cleanup spot against Vida Blue that night. Reggie really must have been swinging the bat well for him to have done that, huh?

Well, I don't know. The previous night's game had been rained out, sparing the Yankees the necessity of batting against Frank Tanana, who was not only the best left-hander in the league but probably the best pitcher in baseball. Far from batting Reggie fourth against Tanana, Billy had moved him completely out of the line-up.

But that was the night before the luncheon at "21." Could it be that Steinbrenner had whispered in Billy's ear that he wanted Jackson in the line-up, and batting cleanup, Vida Blue or no Vida Blue? And, just this one time, no bullshit about it, please. Naw, that couldn't be.

Reggie remained in the cleanup spot for the three remaining games at home, and the Yankees continued to win. On Saturday, May 7, they went into first place by pulverizing Charlie Finley's A's, while Charlie Finley sat with George in his box at Churchill Downs and watched George's Derby horse finish far up the track.

The Yankees, having rushed to the Players' Lounge after the game to watch the Derby on TV, debated the possibility of promoting a match race between George's horse and Mickey Rivers, a prospect Mickey found far more exciting than the three-run homer he had just hit. Home runs had never thrilled Mickey. "Once in a while is okay if it wins a game," he said. "Stealing bases is what turns me on."

The Yankees had run their streak to fourteen out of sixteen, and were leaving town in first place by half a game. During that stretch, the team batting average had gone from .232 to .284. Munson's average had leaped from .131 to .337. Thurman had hit in all sixteen games, for a batting average of .424 (28 for 66), belted five home runs, scored 18 runs, and knocked in 16. And nobody was even offering to name a stick of gum after him.

Before they left, the Yankees were supposed to play the Mets in the Mayor's Trophy Game, an annual affair which is played for charity and the bragging rights in New York City. Billy Martin was feeling so chipper that he was telling the press, "George really wants to win this game badly. He says it's a big one. *Dada ditda ditditdit.*"

The game was rained out. When they finally got to play it, six weeks later, the Yankee fortunes were at their lowest ebb and Billy Martin, having barely survived his worst two crises of the season, wasn't feeling the least bit chipper.

5

THE HENDRICKS FLAP

"I'm like a submarine being attacked by depth charges.
Complete silence, and I'm cruising on all batteries."
—the Wit and Wisdom of Billy Martin

A seven-game trip to the West Coast was all it was.
Against Seattle, California and Oakland, the same
three teams they had just beaten seven out of eight
times in New York. Seattle, an expansion club; Oakland,
which wasn't much more than an expansion club after
Bowie Kuhn and his brigands had picked Charlie
Finley clean; California, which had Rudi, had Grich,
had Baylor, and had a worse record than Oakland. The
trip started with Reggie Jackson hitting a two-run home
run in his first time at bat in Kingdome Stadium, the
eighteenth major-league park he had hit a home run in,
and ended with Sparky Lyle crawling off the mound
in Oakland on his hands and knees after completing
the longest relief stint of his career.

In between, there wasn't a hell of a lot that you
could say. Figueroa and Gullett pitched consecutive
wins over California, 3-0 and 4-1, the fourth straight
complete game for Figueroa and the best performance
of the year by far for Gullett. Ron Guidry, pressed into

a starting role again, pitched another classy eight and one-third innings. That's the good news.

The bad news was that the Yankees lost four of the seven games. The infield, which had been nothing short of spectacular throughout the winning streak, became unbelievably bad, and the outfield wasn't much better. Mickey Rivers was taken out of two consecutive games for loafing in the field, and after that home run on his first time at bat, Jackson had one hit in twenty-five times at bat, an infield single. And, oh, yeah, Billy Martin was almost fired the third day out.

They started by losing both games to a Seattle team which was coming off seven straight losses. Jackson's first-inning home run was all the Yankees could write in the first one, against the combined pitching of fellows named Abbott, Laxton and Romo. With any kind of defense, it would have been enough. The Yankees fell behind in the sixth inning on errors by Randolph and Holtzman and Roy White's weak throwing arm, and lost the game irretrievably in the next inning when Mickey Rivers and Bucky Dent got their signals crossed and let a high pop fly fall between them. The outfielder has the right of way on that kind of play, and Rivers willingly took the blame. Billy Martin put the blame on Dent anyway, an indication that he had reason to be concerned about his moody center fielder's personal problems.

What really seemed to be bothering Martin was that he had not had a left-handed pinch hitter to send to the plate when the Yankees had runners on first and third base with one out in the seventh, and were behind by only a run. "I want Elrod Hendricks," he fumed. "I need three catchers plus a left-handed pinch hitter. I've been asking for Elrod for a week and a half. But George and Gabe think I'm kidding. Why are we going with twenty-four players? Are we that bleeping great? It cost us tonight's game, as far as I'm concerned."

Well . . . Elrod Hendricks was a thirty-six-year-old catcher from the Virgin Islands, with a lifetime average of .218. And Billy did have a left-handed hitter on the bench in George Zeber, his switch-hitting utility infielder.

No, the issue wasn't a left-handed pinch hitter. The issue was control. Billy wanted Hendricks because he wanted Hendricks. He had objected to Hendricks' being sent out during spring training, and had got him back after Blomberg was injured. In addition to being a spare catcher and pinch hitter, Hendricks was, to all practical purposes, another coach. Billy Martin's coach. Hendricks had come to the Yankees as one of the five players in the Holtzman deal, after playing on all the Baltimore championship teams. In addition to being a good baseball man, he had a happy, sunny personality that made him extraordinarily valuable as Billy's emissary in the clubhouse. He had such value in that capacity that Earl Weaver had advised him to play out his option with the Yankees so that he could come back to Baltimore as a player-coach, a galling reminder to Martin that Weaver, his archenemy, had powers in Baltimore that Billy did not have in New York.

The front office had sent Elrod Hendricks back to Syracuse after Don Gullett's injury, to clear a place on the roster for Ed Ricks, a pitcher they were bringing up. To make it worse, they were taking Elrod away from Billy at precisely the same time they were trading away his other clubhouse emissary, Dock Ellis. Whether by design or not, Billy had never used Ed Ricks. After Gullett came back, they had kept Ricks around only to pitch in the Mayor's Trophy game, when, as it happened, Gabe Paul returned to the Stadium.

In the course of a long telephone conversation with Gabe that rainy afternoon, Martin had asked for the return of Hendricks. Gabe had other plans for filling that spot. From his home in Tampa, he had been working on a two-for-one deal with Texas which would have solved four different problems, the least pressing being the need for a third-string catcher. The next day being an open date, Gabe told Billy to come to the office before the team left, and they'd try to get the Hendricks thing settled.

Billy hadn't shown up. Instead, he had seized upon a situation that had arisen in the very first game to carry his battle to the press. The next day, he picked it up again.

After the opening loss in Seattle, Reggie Jackson

had taken the broad philosophical view. A regular David and Goliath story. Great for the Seattle fans. "I don't like losing, but it's good for baseball. The fans in New York will laugh about it and we'll come out tomorrow and score ten runs."

Not exactly. It was the Mariners who came out and scored the runs. Eight runs in the first three innings, aided in no small part by five Yankees errors. If the Yankee fans weren't laughing about it, the Yankees were; that's how bad they had been. The first error, coming after two outs in the first inning, had been followed immediately by back-to-back home runs off Catfish Hunter. "I didn't need any help," said Hunter, who had allowed eight hits and three walks in two and one-third innings. "I was going to be bad enough myself."

Munson's throw into center field in the second inning helped score another run, and the bases were loaded and another run in before Ron Guidry came to the rescue. Guidry threw three straight ground balls, and the infield made three straight errors. "They reminded me," said Hunter, "of me trying to get my legs out of the way of shots hit back to me."

For the Catfish, it was the earliest he had been knocked out of a game in six years, encompassing more than two hundred starts. As the year went on, it was going to get earlier and earlier. All the careful work of spring training had been wiped away by that shot off his foot on opening day, plus the practically forgotten drive off the same spot immediately upon his return. He never did quite regain his natural pitching motion, and by pitching unnaturally, he put a further strain on his sensitive shoulder.

The only bright spot of the game, the Yankees agreed, had come in the fourth inning, when Munson's warm-up throw to second collided with Nettles' practice throw to first. "I've been trying to do that," said Nettles, "for eight years."

Munson wasn't laughing about anything. In addition to the error, there had been three stolen bases against him, and he had left the game in the seventh inning with a cramp in his calf after a weak effort at running out an inning-ending double play. "His legs have been bothering him for a week," said Martin. "I need him for the whole year, not for one game."

That's right, he was back to Elrod Hendricks again, and this time he had Munson to help him. Since the Yankees were behind, 8-3, when Thurman took himself out, you can't ignore the possibility that he had merely wanted to underscore the need for another catcher. "I can't visualize a major-league team without three catchers," Thurman said. "All I know is, I'm not thrilled with what's going on. We have so much talent, we ought to go out and just love to play. Sometimes a millionaire will magnify your problems because he's frustrated all the time."

Whether the millionaire he was talking about was George Steinbrenner or Howard Hughes, he didn't say.

Question: Since Fran Healy, the second-string catcher, almost never got into a game, why was it so important to have a third-string catcher?

Billy Martin had the answer to that one before it was asked. A year earlier, when he'd had three catchers, Martin had been able to give Munson a chance to rest his legs by using him as the DH on occasion, or even by playing him in the outfield. If he used Munson as the DH with only two catchers and then had to pinch hit for Healy, Munson would have to go back behind the plate and, the way the Designated Hitter rule was written, the pitcher would now have to bat for himself. Big deal. In the first place, Healy wasn't that bad a hitter. He was certainly a better hitter than Elrod Hendricks. In the second place, there was nothing to prevent Martin from using a pinch hitter for the pitcher if the unlikely situation he was describing ever came up.

Billy was making an issue. His history showed that he always made his stand against the front office over a player of almost no consequence. He had fought Gabe Paul during the off-season over the trading of Sandy Alomar, a utility infielder who was eminently replaceable. The break with Minnesota had come when he attacked the farm director for sending a minor-league pitcher, Dick Woodson, to a Double-A farm club after Martin had told him he was going to be sent to Triple-A. He had lost his job at Texas in an identical dispute over a third-string catcher, Jack Egan. Billy had told Egan he'd be brought back. The front office wouldn't do it.

What is it about him? The conventional view is that Billy has a death wish. Maybe so. But if you're fighting the front office for control, who is there to argue about except the marginal players? But that isn't the only explanation. Billy believes that one of the basic tenets of leadership is that you can't have loyalty unless you give loyalty. He wants his players to know that he will fight for them. On the field, with the press, and with the front office. If he will risk it all to fight for the least among them, how can any of the others doubt that he will also fight for them?

George Steinbrenner, who also has very definite ideas about leadership, disagrees with him completely. "The trouble with you," Steinbrenner keeps telling Billy, "is that you want to be loved by your players. That's wrong. That's a weakness. They respect you as a manager because they know you're a hell of a manager. Whether they like you or not, they'll screw you just as soon as look at you, the first time they think it's to their advantage. Every one of them."

It wasn't just in popping off about Hendricks that Martin was challenging the front office. Don't forget that this came hard upon the breaking of the appointment with Paul. It wasn't the first time Billy had violated his contract by failing to show up for a meeting with Gabe Paul or George Steinbrenner, either. Not by a long shot.

Conferring with the general manager is part of a manager's duties. Martin's purported idol, Casey Stengel, had always been more than conscientious about coming in early and conferring with the general manager, George Weiss. Same thing with Leo Durocher, whom Martin resembles in so many ways. The days when a Leo Durocher could throw a Larry MacPhail out of the clubhouse were gone, but on the famous occasion when Leo did throw MacPhail out, his parting scream was, "If you want to talk to me, *send* for me!" That's exactly what Leo meant. He'd be there, in MacPhail's domain, whenever Larry wanted to talk to him, so what was Larry doing busting into Leo's domain, the clubhouse, to scream at one of his players? You didn't have to send for Leo. The Brooklyn offices weren't even at the ball park—they were in downtown Brooklyn, and Leo never went to the park without stopping off at the office first. Same thing when he was managing the Chicago Cubs. Leo always stopped at the Wrigley Building in downtown Chicago to see Mr. Wrigley before he went to the park to see the general manager.

The difference here was Billy's smoldering resentment about the clauses in his contract that put him on permanent probation. They didn't want him to do anything except manage the team between the base lines, so that's all he was going to do. He came to the park in time for the ball game and he left when the game was over. ("And," as one of the front-office people says, "in between he takes a drink.") Billy didn't even spend any time in New York City. He lived in Jersey City. He'd drive over the George Washington Bridge to the Stadium and turn around after the game and drive back. Why they had signed him to a contract for what he was, and filled it with clauses that tried to make him somebody else, was something Billy had never been able to understand. But if that was the way they wanted it, that was what they were going to get.

So here you had two things together: the old Billy and the new Billy. Think about it a little. In talking to Gabe over the phone for two and a half hours, Billy had discovered that there was still a noticeable slur in Gabe's speech. And that may have fooled Billy. It is not entirely impossible that Billy had mistaken the slur for a sign that Gabe had not recovered as completely as was supposed. Possibly even that he was never going to function at full capacity again. Gabe, after all, was 67 years old. If Gabe wasn't going to be able to hack it any more, there would be a power vacuum in the Yankee front office, and Billy may well have been moving in to assert his claim.

If so, it was a very serious miscalculation. Almost a fatal one. Gabe Paul could see the old familiar pattern developing, and he had the old familiar solution: fire him. Get rid of him now. As anyone who knows him can tell you, Gabe Paul's basic operating principle is,

"You ask yourself is it right or wrong for the team, and if it's right you have to be strong enough to do it."

Gabe had never believed that the Jackson-Martin mix was going to work. His prediction of disaster had been borne out from the first day of spring training. Since you couldn't fire Jackson, the only thing left was to fire Martin, and Billy had handed them a golden opportunity to fire him on the old familiar grounds before the situation got completely out of hand.

Steinbrenner said no. As far as he was concerned, they had anticipated that this kind of thing would happen when they hired Billy. Martin, you have to remember, was Steinbrenner's manager, just as Jackson was Steinbrenner's $3 million man. If the Yankees didn't win with them, he was going to look like the fool of the universe. He wanted it to work for Martin. He had been boasting publicly that he was going to do what nobody else had been able to, pull Billy through to a second successful season. Make a man out of him. If the failure would be Steinbrenner's failure, the success was going to be Steinbrenner's success.

The compromise they agreed upon was to hand out the stiffest fine ever levied by a team against its manager. If, indeed, any team had ever fined its manager before. Billy had tried to humiliate them? All right, they would humiliate him. And maybe Billy would learn that as much as it comforted him to tell his bosses where they could go, it was going to be a losing battle all the way.

Gabe Paul's phone call found Billy Martin in the lobby of a hotel in Anaheim, across from the wonderful world of Disneyland. And the message Billy got, slurred though it may have been, brought forth an anguished, "Gabe, if you want to have a winner, you've got to leave me alone. You've got to stop harassing me."

Gabe then called publicity man Mickey Morabito (who was catching all this flak in his first year on the job), to dictate a statement for the press. It started as a routine announcement that Dell Alson, a left-handed-hitting outfielder, was being brought up from Syracuse, and went on to make the point that Alston was hitting .338 with eleven stolen bases in nineteen games, while Hendricks was hitting .105. And then it stopped being routine: "Certain comments directed at Mr. Steinbrenner, the club's principal owner, by manager Billy Martin, concerning the alleged failure to add a twenty-fifth player, are totally inaccurate and unfounded."

And went on to say, in part:

"Martin was asked to report to my office on May 10th prior to the club leaving for Seattle, and at such time the determination of the twenty-fifth player was to be made. He agreed to be there. However, Billy failed to show up for the meeting with me. If we had had that conversation as scheduled, the twenty-fifth player would have been added and the matter would have been settled then and there.

". . . Frankly, if we have to depend on a player batting .105 at Syracuse to enable us to beat an expansion team, with the kind of talent that has been provided, we are indeed in bad trouble. The reason for the two losses in Seattle was strictly a matter of too many errors in the field and inconsistent pitching."

The $2500 fine was never officially announced. It just kind of leaked out from both coasts. Reggie Jackson, having apparently counted the $100 bills in his wallet and found them all present and accounted for, said, "I'll pay it for Billy."

Catfish Hunter's comment was, "This reminds me of the Oakland clubhouse. There are going to be some fights soon."

Martin was still being mildly defiant. "I should know what the needs of the ball club are a lot more than Gabe Paul." His principal need, he said, was to protect Thurman Munson.

"A lot of clubs have gone with two catchers," Paul pointed out. "Cincinnati went with two all last year and they had a pretty good season." If anything happened to Munson, Hendricks was only twenty-four hours away.

"I've got no recourse," Billy said. "I'll just accept it. It's their team. I'll manage what they give me."

By the time he had got to the ball park, he had retreated to, "For the good of the Yankees, no comment." By then, of course, he just might have received a call from George Steinbrenner, telling him that if he embarrassed the ball club one more time, he was through.

But Billy is irrepressible. When Dell Alston arrived the next morning, Billy had his no-comment sharpened to the point of a serpent's tooth. "I'm like a submarine being attacked by depth charges. Complete silence, and I'm cruising on batteries."

Since somebody up there had ordained that no issue was going to die silently on the 1977 Yankees, Munson got hit with two foul tips the next night, one of them leaving his left foot all puffed up and the other bruising the back of his right wrist. To make it even more pleasant, he had to drag his battered body back to the park for a Sunday afternoon game. "They" wanted him to play, he snarled, after he had got himself patched up and had taken a couple of pain-killing pills. "Don't I always play? But I'm not going to kill myself. If they think I'm going to catch a hundred and sixty games, they're crazy."

He was only playing, he let it be known, because with Frank Tanana pitching against them, they were going to need all the right-handed hitting they could get. He was right about that, and he was also wrong. As bad as the Yankees' record was against lefties (3-8), it was a lot better than Munson's almost unbelievable 0-for-31 against Tanana. The figures shortly became 3-9 and 0-34. Munson struck out twice, but on one of those turns at bat he barely missed a long home run when the ball went foul, and on his third time at bat he hit a long drive to the warning track in the deepest part of center field. Tanana had no trouble with anybody else, either, and when the Yankees fell behind, 7-1, after five innings, Martin sent Fran Healy into the game to give Munson a rest. He could have just as easily taken him out after the first inning when Mike Torrez, suffering his first loss as a New York Yankee, got ripped for four runs.

To keep the western swing from being a total loss, Martin found himself in Oakland on May 16, his 49th birthday. For the first time since he became a professional ballplayer, he was able to spend his birthday with his mother and sample some of her homemade ravioli.

In honor of Billy's birthday:

1. Munson gave himself the day off. The game wasn't three minutes old when Fran Healy threw the ball into center field, trying to catch the leadoff man stealing.

2. Billy gave Willie Randolph the day off, to let him rest his knee.

3. Mickey Rivers was given the last three innings off after showing a marked disinterest in his work. The same thing had happened the previous afternoon. In Anaheim, Billy had explained that Mickey just didn't hit Tanana very well. In Oakland, he rasped, "I wanted to use Blair. Period. I don't have to explain why I use guys."

4. Kenny Holtzman was given the last eight and two-thirds innings off, after allowing five runs in the first inning. Like Catfish Hunter in the Seattle game, Kenny got more help at being bad than he really needed. Three of the four Yankee errors were committed while Kenny was in there, giving them a grand total of fifteen errors in the six games.

5. Reggie Jax made his first appearance in Oakland as a member of the independently rich. A Family Night crowd of 32,400, probably the largest of the year at Oakland Stadium, came out on a cold, blustery night to boo everything he did. What he did mostly was strike out. Three times. Which gave him ten strike-outs on the road trip in twenty-six times at bat. Jackson, obviously distressed at such an unfriendly greeting in the city where he had been a hero over so many years, booted the first ball hit in his direction.

6. The Yankees were stopped cold by a left-handed relief pitcher named Bob Lacey, who had just been called up from the minors, bringing their record against left-handers to 3-10.

7. Boston and Baltimore both won, dropping the Yankees into third place, albeit only one-half game behind both of them.

Happy birthday, Billy.

Speaking of left-handers, Thurman Munson was back in the line-up for the final game of the road trip, to face Vida Blue. Reggie Jackson wasn't. If the Yankees won, they would be going home with a not entirely disgraceful record of three wins and four losses. If they lost, it was a disastrous two and five. Ron Guidry was the Yankee pitcher. His first start had come because Torrez didn't show up. He was getting his second start, twenty days later, because Hunter's shoulder hurt.

It turned into a tremendous ball game, a classic pitchers' duel. Vida Blue gave up four hits and two runs in the first inning, and pitched no-hit ball for the next nine. With Guidry, it was the other way around. The skinny left-hander went into the ninth inning with a three-hit shutout, retired the first batter and was rocked by monumental home runs off the bats of two of the Athletics' gray-beards, Manny Sanguillen, who had never hit a monumental home run before in his life, and Dick Allen, who had hit them by the ton. Just like that, the score was tied, and just as in Ron's first start, Sparky Lyle came in to relieve him after eight and one-third innings.

Vida Blue continued to set the Yankees down for four more innings before he called it a day. Sparky Lyle, who really hadn't signed on for this kind of thing, kept coming out, inning after inning giving up a hit an inning, but allowing no runs. In the top of the fifteenth, the A's sent out their veteran curve-balling right-hander, Joe Coleman. Billy Martin, looking down the bench for a left-handed hitter to bat for Bucky Dent, bypassed Reggie Jackson and sent Dell Alston to the plate for the first time in the major leagues. Alston hit a soft fly ball which fell just inside the right-field foul line for a double, and was singled home by Chris Chambliss. Sparky Lyle had actually pitched six and two-thirds innings, and when the game was over, he dropped to his knees and began to crawl toward his teammates, who were rushing out of the dugout to congratulate him. "How do you feel?" Yogi Berra asked him. "The same as when I went in," Sparky told him. "Horseshit."

With Boston and Baltimore both losing, the Yankees were coming back to New York in exactly the same position as they had held when they left, in first place by half a game. And who were they going to face right off the bat but Baltimore and Boston?

After the final game in Oakland, Billy Martin had insisted that he didn't care whether the press said that

Dell Alston had made Gabe Paul look pretty good. But he had also made it clear that he wasn't backing off anything he had said about the need for another catcher. "I'm not out to prove points. I'm out to win. I don't make comments to hurt people. I make comments to help the club."

Fine or no fine, the Hendricks issue wasn't dying. In fact, it took exactly two games to come back to life. In the second game against Baltimore, Big Lee May came barreling into home plate with the go-ahead run just as Munson was reaching for the low relay throw. A second later, Munson was flat on his back with a badly jammed hand and a sliced index finger. Nevertheless, Munson remained in the game long enough to come to bat in the last of the inning. Thurman was on another hitting tear. In the opening game at home, he had knocked in four runs with a homer, a triple and a single. In this one, he already had a double and two singles to run his streak to six out of seven. He made it seven out of eight by pounding out another double, and then retired to have three stitches put in his hand.

Fran Healy came in to replace him. Wouldn't you know that the Third Catcher Theme was about to come rising out of the orchestra pit? The music started when Dell Alston, a conscripted member of the cast, came to the plate as a pinch hitter with one out in the bottom of the eighth, and promptly got himself another double. The next batter was Willie Randolph, with Mickey Rivers and Fran Healy waiting in the wings. On the mound for Baltimore was a right-hander, a necessary ingredient in the drama. Can you see it developing? Randolph grounds out, and the scene is set. Earl Weaver, fully aware that Martin cannot pinch hit for Healy, deliberately violates one of the basic precepts of managing and orders his pitcher to put Rivers on base with the potential winning run. And naturally, Fran Healy grounds out.

"I'll tell you this," Weaver said afterward. "If Elrod Hendricks was sitting there, we woulda found out what Rivers coulda done."

Billy Martin, dealing with the same question, was as discreet as it is possible for Billy Martin to be. "The last time I said anything about that," he answered, "it cost me money. No, I don't want a third catcher." And lifted his eyes to heaven to be forgiven for telling such lies.

Gabe Paul sent an immediate wire to Syracuse for Elrod Hendricks. Elrod was in the clubhouse the next day. "He's not on the roster," was the way Mickey Morabito put it. "He's in a holding pattern."

If he were needed, he could be activated instantly. In the meantime, he could function as Martin's unofficial coach and all-purpose factotum. Which, as it happens, was pretty much the solution that Gabe Paul had worked out for the meeting Martin hadn't bothered to come to.

6

THE STRAW
THAT STIRS THE DRINK

"I can't wait to pick up the paper every morning to
see what's happening. It's like *Mary Hartman, Mary
Hartman*."

—Bob Lemon

I don't care what anybody says, there is no rivalry on
the face of the earth that can compare with the Yankees
versus the Red Sox. There is something special that
happens when these two teams meet, a shiver in the air
as the home team comes bursting onto the field that
turns their uniforms whiter against the greener grass.

There is a history there that speaks of sleeping heroes
and future glories. Joe DiMaggio versus Ted Williams.
Williams-Doerr-Pesky-Dom DiMaggio and Joe DiMag-
gio-Berra-Henrich-Rizzuto. Old dog-eared Casey Stengel pulling his first pennant out of the hat. Joe Mc-
Carthy, come out of retirement to manage the Red Sox
on the other side of the field, losing two years running
to Stengel on the last day of the season. Joe DiMaggio,
Ted Williams and Carl Yastrzemski coming off the
bench in the final innings to win important games with
pinch-hit home runs . . .

And, to bring it up to date, Lou Piniella barreling

into Carlton Fisk, precipitating a brawl which ended with Graig Nettles throwing Bill Lee down on his shoulder to ruin the 1976 season for the Red Sox, and almost end Lee's career.

It's everything a rivalry ought to be. Us against them, Home and Away, New York against New England, the people versus U.S. Steel. The spacious expanse of Yankee Stadium versus the looming monster of Fenway Park. And don't think it doesn't communicate itself to the players on the field. The playing is crisper, the batting is firmer, the ball comes off the bat with the fresher, cleaner sound of the first day of spring training. Baseball becomes again what baseball is supposed to be, a game of shifting fortunes within a series of steadily rising climaxes. An excitement.

The Red Sox versus the Yankees.

The schedule makers had done their work well. Ten of the fifteen games they would be playing during the season were packed into a thirty-four-day period; a pair of two-game series a week apart, to be followed by a pair of three-game series two weeks later. And then it was going to be eighty grinding games, half the entire season, before they would meet again for the five games that could very well decide the pennant.

The first meeting came on the thirty-ninth game of the season, during what had become another time of trouble for Reggie Jackson. The wall of ice had come down over him after he was benched in Oakland against Vida Blue. ("Yeah, I'm a mediocre ballplayer, and I'm overpaid. That's what the press says, isn't it?")

Back in the line-up for the opening game against Baltimore, he struck out his first two times at bat, to make it nine strike-outs and no hits in seventeen times at bat—broke out of it the following day with a slashing double against Jim Palmer (the same game in which Munson was injured), and was sent sprawling by Palmer's first pitch on his next time at bat—glared down at Palmer before he started to move toward first base after four straight balls, and then stopped again just before he reached the base to glare some more. "What are you looking at?" Palmer shouted. Reggie's only answer was a sour smile. "He should have been happy just to be on base," Palmer said, afterwards. "He's just mad because I said he was an average outfielder."

To make it a winning three days for him, he was benched on Saturday afternoon, in NBC's *Game of the Week*, even though Thurman Munson, with his newly stitched finger, wasn't going to be in the line-up either.

Through it all, the only thing he would say to the press was, "I'm not talking."

He wasn't the only one. After the Saturday afternoon game, the writers had found an empty manager's office with a "No Interviews" sign pasted to the door. The Yankees had lost, 3-2, in twelve innings, to fall out of first place, and Billy had a lot not to talk about:

Mike Torrez would have had a 2-0 shutout if Jim Wynn, who was playing right field in Reggie's place, hadn't slipped going after a catchable fly ball with two out in the seventh inning.

For the second straight day, the winning run had been knocked in by Eddie Murray, a twenty-one-year-old rookie who had remained with the club only because they were so desperate for anybody who looked like a hitter. The two winning hits were Murray's only hits in his last 24 times at bat.

The umpires had refused to allow Willie Randolph to advance to third base with the potential winning run after he admittedly had been interferred with. The ruling was (get this) that he should have kept running, and allowed himself to be tagged out instead of scrambling safely back to second.

Mickey Rivers had been pulled out of the game for failing to run out a ground ball.

Although Elrod Hendricks was there in civvies, Billy still didn't have a third-string catcher. So he had been unable to pinch hit for Healy in the bottom of the ninth, with the winning run on second base and nobody out.

And, possibly—just possibly—he had seen the June issue of *Sport Magazine* which was just beginning to make the rounds.

When Dick Young of the *Daily News*, the premier sports columnist in the country, transgressed upon the sacred confines of the Players' Lounge, where Billy was skulking, Billy screamed that he had no right to

108

be there, started to throw a punch, but was able to retain just enough control over himself to convert it into a heartfelt shove.

The next day, Earl Weaver pinned a sign on his own door: "Press-Media welcomed at all times." There's good old Earl for you. Always willing to help a buddy out in a pinch.

With Reggie Jax on the bench again, and Rudy May once again handling the Yankees with ease, the Orioles made it three in a row by taking the first game of the Sunday doubleheader. For the third game in a row, it was Eddie Murray who knocked in the winning run.

Martin called upon Ron Guidry in the second game to keep them from falling two and a half games behind. This time, Guidry went into the ninth inning with an 8-1 lead, got the first batter again, gave up a home run again, gave up a walk and was taken out after (all together now) eight and one-third innings.

Reggie Jax had played the second game and gotten himself a couple of hits, yet he still wasn't talking. "Save your breath, fellows," he said to the successive waves of reporters who came to his locker. As he was leaving, though, he turned back and said, "You better ask the coaches and manager. They don't even think I can hit."

Reggie had more than that to worry about. The Robert Ward article, the time bomb that had been ticking away since the first week of spring training, was just about to explode. The advance copies of the June issue of *Sport Magazine* had begun to filter around during the Baltimore series, and the front office had alerted Thurman Munson that he wasn't going to like it.

Wouldn't you know that the magazine would hit the stands on the same day the Red Sox were coming to town? The schedule makers had planned even better than they thought. Three or four copies were brought into the Yankee clubhouse, and wherever they landed there would be a small group of players huddled together, reading. First in utter amazement, and then in utter rage. "That prick!" they'd say, glaring over at Reggie's locker. "Why, that dirty sonofabitch!" Reggie, off in his own corner, got into his uniform as quickly as he could and went out to the field, but not before his shoes and equipment bag had been kicked by players who just happened to be strolling by.

After Munson had read the article, he went into the sauna in the trainer's room and settled himself alongside the player who was already there. "All right," he said, in a kind of shock. "I can see if he knocked me for one page. *But three pages!* I couldn't find enough adjectives about myself to fill three pages." And then, as if he were listing the things he could find to say about himself: "I just go out every day and play. I helped the Yankees win the pennant. I was MVP. What's so bad about that?"

The *Sport Magazine* article is one of the most astonishing magazine articles ever written because Jackson is . . . well, a constant astonishment, and because Ward wrote the hell out of it. But there are two things that have to be kept in mind. The interviews took place at the end of the first week of training, at a time when Reggie was worried sick about his sore elbow, and struggling desperately to get into shape. Once that has been said, it is also necessary to say that from the time Reggie signed with the Yankees, he had been telling his friends that Munson was a crude, overbearing, wholly unlikable guy (which was, in fact, the general view of Munson around the league; Thurman is a mean, tough competitor). As a ballplayer, in Reggie's view, Munson was a good hitter but an overrated catcher. As a leader, Reggie looked upon him as a joke. All he was going to have to do, Reggie had been telling them, was walk into the clubhouse and take over.

Reggie can get into one of his wildly boastful moods when he is either elated or fighting off a fit of depression. Ward had caught him at a time when he was trying to keep from being overwhelmed by the terrible fear that he was going to come into New York, with the eyes of the nation upon him, and be the greatest flop of all time.

Added to that, Reggie has this image of himself as a stand-up guy, and if you're a stand-up guy you have to say exactly what is on your mind. One of the things very prominently on his mind at that moment was that far from walking in and taking over, he had been frozen out.

"I've got problems other guys don't have. I've got this big image that comes before me, and I've got to adjust to it. Or what it has been projected to be. That's not 'me' really, but I've got to deal with it. Also, I used to just be known as a black athlete, now I'm respected as a tremendous intellect. . . ."

When Reggie begins to talk about the stupendous encounter between himself and his intellect you know that he is in an emotional turmoil, which may be why the word "black" will always be found nearby.

"You know, this team . . . it all flows from me. I've got to keep it all going. I'm the straw that stirs the drink. It all comes back to me. Maybe I should say me and Munson . . . but really, he doesn't enter into it. He's being so damned insecure about the whole thing."

So why not talk it out with him? Because, Reggie said, he wasn't ready for that yet. He didn't even know he felt that way. "He'd try to cover up, but he ought to know he can't cover up anything from me. Man, there is no way . . . I can read these guys. No, I'll wait, and eventually he'll be whipped." There would come the moment when Thurman Munson would know that Jax had won. "And then I'll go to him, and we will get it right."

"Listen," Ward said, in some astonishment. "Do you want this printed?"

"Print it," said Jackson.

"You see, this is the way I am, I'm a leader, and I can't lie down. But 'leader' isn't the right word . . . it's a matter of *presence*. . . . Let me put it this way: No team I am on will ever be humiliated the way the Yankees were by the Reds in the World Series! That's why Munson can't intimidate me. Nobody can. You can't psyche me. You take me one-on-one in the pit, and I'll whip you . . . The way the Yankees were

111

humiliated by the Reds, you think that doesn't bother Billy Martin. He's no fool. He's smart. Very smart. And he's a winner. Munson's tough, too. He *is* a winner, but there is just nobody who can do for a club what I can do . . . That's just the way it is. Munson thinks he can be the straw that stirs the drink, but he can only stir it bad."

Once again, Ward asked, "Are you sure you want me to print that?" Although Ward's style is to turn an interview into just this kind of boozy bull session, Reggie was giving him so much more than he had bargained for that he wanted to be sure he wasn't taking advantage of what Reggie may have thought to be a purely social situation. He had come to like Reggie. Writers always like subjects who give them good quotes, and Reggie was at the top of his game. Why wouldn't he be? This was Reggie putting forth the scenario he had obviously fantasized before he came to camp.

"Yes, print it," said Reggie, the stand-up guy. He tapped the bar peremptorily. "I *want* to see that in print. I want to *read* that."

Through it all runs a consistent note of deference toward Billy Martin. Yes, Billy had a presence, too. But Reggie was going to make it easy for him. "He won't have to be 'bad' Billy Martin fighting people any more . . . I'll open the road, and I'll let the others come thundering down the path!"

And, do you know, it isn't that there wasn't a certain amount of truth in everything he was saying, it was the distortion of the truth that made you uneasy. The distortion of the relationships. Monumental insecurity, sure. But more than that, a man who lives such a rich fantasy life that he has lost the line between the reality and the fantasy. A man who manipulates everybody—friends, allies, opponents, enemies—into turning the fantasy into reality by forcing them to react to it. That's where the writers come in. When Reggie saw Ward again the next day he wanted to know what the other players had been saying about him. When you live that kind of fantasy life, what people say about you is of vital importance. People who say bad things about you are enemies you have to protect yourself against. People who say good things may become the allies you have been searching for. That's why journalists are looked upon as allies. They project his words to the public, proving to him that he is alive and well, and they are also the ambassadors who go forth to bring the word back.

It's Munson he's interested in, of course, and Munson had denied there was any problem, any struggle for leadership, any jealousy. "You see," says Reggie, "it's a pattern." The guys who were giants, like Catfish Hunter, the guys who were really secure, weren't worried about him.

"But guys like Munson . . . It's really a comedy, isn't it? I mean, it's hilarious. Listen, I always treat him right. I talk to him all the time, but he is so jealous and nervous and resentful that he can't stand it. If I wanted to, I could snap him. Just wait until I get hot and hit a few out, and the reporters start coming around, and I have New York eating out of the palm of my hand . . . he won't be able to stand it."

Perhaps, Ward suggests, it's Reggie's verbal ability that puts other players off. Makes them feel inferior. That was true. Reggie had been through that before.

"But you know, the rest of the guys should know that I don't feel that far above them. I mean, nobody can turn people on like I can, or do for a club the things I can do, but we are all still athletes, we're all still ballplayers. We should be able to get along . . . I'm not going to allow the team to get divided. I'll do my job, give it all I got, talk to anybody. I think Billy will appreciate that."

Although people were saying that either he or Munson would be gone within two years, Reggie didn't want that. "Because, after all is said and done, Munson is a winner, he's a fighter, a hell of a ballplayer . . . but don't you see . . . Don't you see that there is just no way I can play second fiddle to *anybody?* Hah! That's just not in the cards. There ain't no way!"

Two weeks later, his fears had overwhelmed him and

he was pouring his heart out to Steve Jacobson for an article which was as remarkable in its own way as Ward's. No longer was Reggie taking over from Munson, or opening up the road for Billy Martin. His job, you will remember, was to blend with the club, not the other way around. He wasn't sure if he was going to fit in. He was the problem on the team; he caused problems just being there. If it got to a show-down between him and Munson, he would back off. If he did well, he was supposed to. "If I come short of it, if we don't win, it will be my fault." Nothing he could do would be enough to turn New York City on, anyway.

For the remainder of spring training and into the season, his new motif was the mistake he had made in signing with New York. Within that context, he had always singled out Thurman Munson as the most supportive of the Yankee players. It didn't matter. The interview may have taken place ten weeks earlier, the magazine was coming out *now*. And Reggie is always so goddamn quotable. "I'm the straw that stirs the drink . . . Munson thinks he can be the straw, but he can only stir it bad." Wow.

"In spring training, when we'd be riding on the bus from the hotel to the training field and back, I'd notice that Reggie would be taking out a notebook . . . not a notebook really, it was more like a writing pad. He'd jot something down and then put it away. I thought to myself, that's Reggie for you, always looking for another way to make a million bucks. He was keeping a kind of diary, I thought, and was going to find out after the season how much they'd pay him to write a book. So when that article came out, I figured he had all those good lines written down and, being Reggie, there was no way he was going to be able to keep them to himself."
—Yankee player's view

Normally, when a player of Reggie's stature takes batting practice, the other players stop whatever they are doing and watch. When Reggie took his early swings before the Boston game, there was suddenly nobody around the batting cage. Reggie swings so hard that

114

from up in the stands he seems to have a heavy, sledge-hammer stroke. You have to be watching from field level to realize how sweet and smooth a swing it is. Drive after drive went into the right field stands . . . plunk . . . plunk . . . plunk . . . while out in the field, and along the sidelines, his teammates ignored him.

The Red Sox had a one-man side show of their own to present on their first visit to New York. Billy Martin's friend, Bill Lee, who had last been seen in those environs holding on to his left arm as he was being helped from the field, was making his second start of the season. Although his recovery from the shoulder separation had been very slow, he was the only left-hander on the Red Sox staff—the *only* one—and that meant he had been penciled in to open against the Yanks.

The reporters didn't go to the Yankee dressing room to talk to Reggie, who wasn't talking anyway. They gathered around Space Man Bill Lee for whatever words of wisdom he wished to impart about last year's fracas, the coming ball game and the state of the universe.

"We have polluted our planet beyond repair," Lee said, warming up. "Everything that has gotten specialized has become extinct. The dinosaur got specialized and became extinct. Baseball will become extinct. It's just a game. It'll be extinct before it's a holy war. The weather is going to change before then, and we'll go into a glacier age. The earth will go on, and we as a species will become extinct. The designated hitter, Astroturf and concrete stadiums instead of the quaintness of a Fenway Park or a Wrigley Field. The system's view of baseball. We're moving toward Rollerball."

Rollerball. Violence in sports. The workings of Bill Lee's mind are wondrous to behold.

Was he out to revenge himself against Nettles?

"I had a dream the other night, a vision of the Ghost of Christmas Past. It came into my room, and it had Steinbrenner's face and Billy Martin's body. I don't like Steinbrenner's politics. His illegal campaign contributions. I don't like the way he handles his shipping business. I don't like him personally. He tries to use his economics to gain superiority. I dislike Billy Martin and his archaic baseball. There's a part of him that functions perfectly, and a part of him that's not screwed on. It's Martin's system. His win-at-all-cost type of ball. You have to have limits. That's what civilization is founded on. I don't like the way he tries to master his players through fear and intimidation. They were all robotized for the fight. They were other people, they weren't themselves."

Lee's own limits clearly do not inhibit him from calling people Nazis because he doesn't like the way they do business. But then, as the Great Yogi may well have said from his perch high atop the Himalayas, "One man's civilization is another man's rock 'n' roll concert."

The New York Times heading on the game read:

RED SOX TOP
YANKEES, 4-3;
GAME QUIET

By which the guy who writes the heads up there seems to mean that nobody took a punch at anybody. Otherwise, it is a game that goes into the great book of unquiet Yankee-Red Sox contests, under the subtitle: Reggie and the Unhandshake, a production of *ABC Monday Night Baseball*.

The early going featured consecutive home runs by Boston's Dwight Evans and rookie third baseman Butch Hobson, and the catch of the year by Paul Blair on Fred Lynn's long drive to the concrete wall in right center. At first it didn't seem possible that Blair could get there, and then it seemed as if he would get there just in time to splatter himself against the wall. And then he was catching the ball over his head, right where the sign reads, "417 feet," and, by some miracle of footwork, bringing himself to an instant halt.

Reggie got one of the runs back in the second inning on a line-drive double and an error. On his next time at bat, his scorching ground ball down the first-base line was turned into a double play. In the seventh, he teed off on one of Lee's sinkers and hit a tremendous home run to tie the score. A ball hit so powerfully that he stood at the plate once again to watch it disappear into the stands. And maybe do a little thinking about Brotherhood, the meaning of life and the Neilsen ratings. Reggie doesn't loiter in his home-run trot, he runs with a powerful forward thrust, as if he were being swept along by a wind at his back. As he headed for the plate, his teammates gathered in the well of the dug-out for the ritualistic handshakes and backslapping. Reggie came toward them and then, ignoring the out-stretched hands, veered off sharply toward the far end of the dugout.

What you have to understand is that there was nothing insincere about the congratulations that were about to be tendered. Once the bell rings, personali-ties are forgotten. Nobody is a winner unless the team is a winner, and without a productive Reggie Jax, they were not going to win. Everybody on the team knew that. Nobody knew it better than Reggie, who genuinely admires any player who can rise to the occasion when the pressure is greatest. This is a man, remember, who still has his boyhood collection of bubble-gum cards.

It was a shaken ball club that took the field when the inning was over. Reggie himself immediately played Hobson's legitimate single down the right field line into a double by completely overrunning the ball. Den-ny Doyle laid down a bunt, and Willie Randolph—who never makes that kind of mistake—was so upset that he didn't cover first base. Before the inning was over, both runners had scored, and it was Doyle's run that proved to be the winning one.

The Yankees got one of them back in the last half of the inning. Jimmy Wynn, who was in a terrible slump, led off with a walk, and eventually scored when George Scott (who is probably Reggie's closest friend in baseball) dropped the throw to first on Munson's two-out ground ball. Whereupon Bill Campbell, who had come in after the walk to Wynn, picked Munson off first base. *Thurman Munson, the smartest base runner on the team.*

The ninth inning had its moments, too. Chris Cham-bliss started things off with a single, but Mickey Rivers, who was sent in to run for him, was thrown out try-ing to steal. Roy White flied out, and that left it all up to Reggie Jackson. With one swing of the bat, he could tie up the game and give himself another chance to either shake his teammates' hands or give them a re-run of his other-side-of-the-dugout routine. Reggie ended the game by flying out.

That was game number one of the Yankee-Red Sox series. There were still fourteen games to go.

"When that incident happened, I think it solidified a lot of their hostility and animosity toward Reggie, it really did to a lot of guys. Whatever he did . . . it seems to me, a lot of players were waiting for one incident to happen that would justify their not liking him. And that was one thing. No matter what Reggie did it for. I didn't think it was to slight the players as individuals. I remember hearing a lot of comments around the clubhouse saying, 'Son of a bitch, if that's the way he wants it, fuck him.' I remember hearing that. That was no secret either. . . ."

—Yankee player's view

"I don't know whether Reggie tried to create events himself. In other words, the intent of a player not shaking hands with other players on his team normally would mean that he just hates the guts of every player on that team, and would fight any one of them in a minute. That's not what happened. It seems to me that it might have been, I'm not saying it was—*might* have been—a spontaneous thing, but which is premeditated to get some attention for himself, knowing that there is going to be publicity over it, and there was going to be an uproar. I can tell you about Reggie that he's out for the recognition and the publicity first. He just wanted to see, I guess, what would happen."

—another Yankee player's view

"The way it happened almost proves to me that it was premeditated. Being in that it was just reported about the rift between him and Munson. Then you read for three days where this was the main topic and everything else was subordinated. The game was subordinated, believe me. He could have been 0 for

4 for those three games, and the focal point of those games was still going to be Reggie."

—a third Yankee player's view

"What's so hard to figure out about that? That was Jackson reacting predictably. Fuck me, huh? If they're going to take that attitude, fuck them. That's how I read it."

—sportswriter's view

When the writers got there after the game to ask Reggie the obvious question, they found him at the sandwich table in the center of the room. "I had a bad hand," was all he would say.

"Maybe Reggie was mad at me because I didn't play him a couple of games against left-handers," Martin said. "Go ask him. I'm sure he'll have some answers for you. Ask him about the ball that got away from him at the start of the eighth. He probably forgets about those things."

"I'm not going to talk no more," said the untalking Reggie. "Write whatever you want. You've been doing that all year."

Munson fended off the reporters at first. "I'm just glad to be here," he kept saying, putting on a goofy smile. But he couldn't contain himself forever. Told about Jackson's "bad hand," he said, "He's a fuckin' liar. How's that for a quote?"

Why did he think Reggie had done it? "I don't know. I'm just happy to be here. I wish George would buy *me* a Rolls-Royce."

Had he been surprised? "That's unquotable. Hey, don't make it just me. There's twenty-three other guys on the club were waiting to shake his hand."

Up until then, Munson had acceded to front-office pressure to remain quiet about the *Sport Magazine* article, but now that he was talking, he didn't duck the questions about it. "I'll kiss your butt if the New York fans think anybody likes to play baseball more than I do . . . for a man to think Thurman Munson is jealous of anybody else in the world, he has to be ignorant or an imbecile. I've got three of the cutest kids and a lovely wife and everything I need. I could go home tomorrow, and I don't need material things to make me jealous of someone." In fact, Munson said, not without truth, he had tried to make Jackson feel at home. "I've probably talked to him more than anybody else."

When it was suggested to him that Jackson, "in a less troubled mood," probably would acknowledge that, Munson snapped, "From here on in, he won't."

Even if Jackson came to him and apologized?

"It's not that important," Thurman said, putting an end to it. "Not as many people read the retractions."

There was only one thing wrong with what Thurman Munson said. He was at the top of his profession, he was the MVP, he had a lovely family and he was a wealthy, or at least potentially wealthy, man from his real estate investments. He was also insanely jealous of Reggie Jackson. Reggie had read him right on that. There was no reason for him to be jealous. Thurman Munson is a Hall of Fame player, the one thing that Reggie Jackson would rather be than anything else on earth. Reggie doesn't have a chance: His fielding eliminates him. The only thing that had changed in Munson's feeling about Reggie was that where he had merely disliked him before, he now hated and despised him. Thurman Munson is a truck driver's son from Canton, Ohio, and he has a truck driver's code. He wants the part of the road that belongs to him.

When he walked out of the clubhouse, the magazine was sticking out of his hip pocket for all to see. "I'm going to go home," he said pointedly, "and read it again."

He wasn't the only one who read the article that night, or had at least read about it. When Thurman came to the plate against the Red Sox the next day he received the greatest ovation of his career. Jackson was greeted by a mixture of boos and cheers, with the boos easily predominating.

The first game had come around to Reggie Jackson in the seventh inning. This one came around to Thurman Munson. Or, to look at it from the other side of the field, it came around to Luis Tiant. Going into the seventh inning, the Red Sox were leading, 5-2. Graig Nettles and Carlos May, the first two batters, hit home runs on consecutive pitches and suddenly it was 5-4, and the Stadium had come alive. Under normal conditions, this is where you bring in a relief pitcher. Especially when you have Bill Campbell, who had been practically unhittable for three weeks.

For Don Zimmer, the Red Sox manager, there was something else to be considered. The Yankees weren't the only team whose season was being affected by the turbulence arising out of the Re-Entry Draft. After the Red Sox had ushered in the new era by signing Bill Campbell for $1.5 million (over five years), Luis Tiant, who had been practically their entire pitching staff for five years, had refused to report to training camp until the Red Sox sweetened the pot for him. It took so long for the Red Sox to appreciate the force and brilliance of his logic that Luis, who was thirty-six going on fifty, was still trying to pitch himself into shape. Without a Luis Tiant who could be counted upon to go the distance, the Red Sox had very little chance of winning. Zimmer, hoping that Luis' time had come, stayed with him. Bucky Dent immediately singled, and now the tying run was on base. And still Zimmer stayed with him. Willie Randolph laid down a perfect sacrifice bunt, the tying run was in scoring position, and now you have to bring in the fresh arm. Zimmer came to the top of the dugout steps—and hung there. He was going to let Tiant pitch to Mickey Rivers.

Rivers slashed a line drive down the left-field line. The game was tied, and Mickey was obviously going to be carrying the go-ahead run into scoring position. This is what it's all about. Nobody is better than Carl Yastrzemski on this play; racing over, scooping up the ball and making a strong, accurate throw to second base. Nobody is faster than Mickey Rivers between home plate and second base. An eight-second filmstrip. Yaz makes the play to perfection, Rivers goes diving in—baseball, the game of inches—and Rivers is there.

The winning run is on second base. The batter is Thurman Munson. Having blown the chance to get Tiant out of there while he still had a lead, Zimmer decides he might as well give Tiant a chance to pitch out of the inning and perhaps still win the ball game. ("Butchered it up," he said afterward. "I'll take the blame for this one.") Munson hits a soft liner into center field for a single, Rivers comes roaring around third base, keeps going after he has crossed the plate, and goes hurtling into the arms of the assistant trainer in the dugout like a sprinter into the padding at the end of the runway. They wanted hustle. Mickey would give them hustle.

Steinbrenner was back in town. Martin had gone up to talk to George, and had then called Rivers into his office. And, what do you know, Mickey Rivers didn't seem to have any problems any more.

Reggie Jackson had problems. He was continuing to maintain, rather plaintively, that he hadn't read the *Sport Magazine* piece or seen a newspaper or watched any television news show, because he knew it would only get him upset. As soon as the questions became more specific, he showed how much it had got to him, first by mumbling unintelligibly, then by repeating the writers' questions back to them, and finally by answering in Spanish. When the questions kept coming, he turned to Carlos May and said, "My face hurts. I haven't smiled this much in a month and a half."

It had started to get to him from the time he had walked into the clubhouse. Before the game, Martin had called him into his office—as he had told the writers he would—for a closed-door meeting with Billy and his coaches. Martin's version of the meeting went: "This is me thinking, but when a guy wants to do so good so badly, the guy gets down on himself. Reggie said he had no reason for what he did, that it just happened. Which I accept."

You can believe that if you want to. In the first place, Billy Martin knows everything that is going on in his clubhouse. Everything. He tells the players in his pre-season meeting that he has to have that kind of information so that if there is anything brewing, "I can nip it in the bud."

In the second place, Reggie, the stand-up guy, does not duck that kind of question. "Every player on this team hates and despises me," Reggie told him. Billy not only knew the depth of the feeling against Reggie in the clubhouse, he shared it. Nevertheless, Billy had him there to get across the message that whatever anybody's personal feelings might be, everybody on the team, including the manager and the coaches, was rooting like hell for him to do well.

He had no complaints about Reggie's hitting. He was in a slump, he'd get out of it. He did have complaints about his fielding. It was hurting the team because it was bad, and it was hurting the team because he wasn't hustling. Information had come to him that Reggie had been complaining about being taken out in the late innings. "I'm the manager, and I will do what is best for the team." Until Reggie's fielding and attitude showed a great deal of improvement, he was going to continue to take him out in certain situations, and when he did, he expected Reggie to root like hell from the bench. Reggie did have a position on this ball club, Billy wanted him to know, and that made it all the more important for him to be a cheerleader in that kind of situation. With Reggie continuing to maintain that he was hustling, even if it didn't look that way, Billy said, "Look in the mirror, and that's what you're looking at. If you lie to that mirror, then you're in trouble."

Altogether, a depressing day.

There were to be four more depressing days at the Stadium before the club went to Boston. A twi-night doubleheader against Texas, and three games against Chicago, the only two teams they hadn't faced. When Reggie came into the half-filled clubhouse before the twilight game, he was handed a freshly cleaned uniform by one of the clubhouse men. As Reggie hung it on the hook and opened the top buttons of the shirt, it could be seen that there were no pants on the hanger. Just a hunk of adhesive tape hanging down from the cardboard crossbar. SUCK MY ASS, it said.

"This is what I have to put up with," Reggie said to the writer who had come in with him.

After a couple of minutes, he called over to Willie Randolph to find out what time they were going to hit. Willie, sitting on the other side of the two empty lockers, didn't answer.

"What time do we hit, Willie?" Reggie said, raising his voice.

Willie just sat there, leaning on his chin and looking straight ahead.

"Willie, *what time do we hit?*"

He shouted the question out three or four more times, and Willie Randolph, the greatest kid alive, kept looking straight ahead, giving not the slightest indication that he had heard.

The writer was Roger Kahn, who was doing a stint as a columnist for *Time*. When Kahn had approached him a day earlier, Reggie had informed him that he wasn't giving interviews. But *Time* Magazine is *Time* Magazine and Kahn is the author of *The Boys of Summer,* and that was a combination which Reggie, whatever his frame of mind, could not bring himself to let go. "I'm not being difficult," he said quickly. "I just mean, don't make me the center of the story. And don't count on me to say something controversial."

Giving up on Willie Randolph, he turned back to Kahn. "Did you ever see anything like this? Thank God I'm a Christian. This stuff doesn't bother me."

To prove how little it bothered him, he asked, "Do you think I ought to call a team meeting to apologize to these guys?"

Why not, answered the astonished Kahn. "It can't hurt."

"Do you think I ought to do it now?"

"Yeah, get it over with."

Reggie took a couple of steps toward Martin's office and looked back over his shoulder. "You know," he said, "I don't have to do this. I'm going to make $1.3 million this year."

Whatever happened in there, this is the official version, according to Martin: "I didn't want to have a meeting. I explained my reasons, that everybody understood what he's going through and his emotions, and everybody respects him. He's a competitor, and he can do it all by himself. I told him, if you want to say anything on a man-to-man basis, do it, but you don't have to have a meeting to do it."

Steinbrenner's attitude, expressed after the game, was that Reggie had shown his class by offering to apologize, and that was all that was necessary.

Steinbrenner ought to know. He was there. Within a minute after the door had closed behind Reggie, Steinbrenner came out of the trainer's room and headed directly for Martin's office.

Whether it was Steinbrenner's decision or Martin's, you have to wonder why. With Reggie in a mood, at last, to have a meeting of the minds with his teammates, there was a strong possibility of clearing the air. But then, there was also the possibility that it would degenerate into an exchange of grievances. The one thing that is clear is that as soon as Billy heard Reggie wanted the meeting, he called George.

If Billy knew the depth of the feeling against Reggie, George knew the state of Reggie's emotions. Reggie and George spent a lot of time together when George was in New York. George had got Reggie an apartment only a few blocks away from the Carlyle Hotel, and they would have breakfast together. Reggie would come to the Stadium early so that he could have a drink with him up in his office and maybe second-guess the manager a little. (Listen, everybody second-guesses the manager.) And when Reggie was really feeling low, he would make late-night calls to George in Tampa. If Reggie had told Martin that every player on the team hated and despised him, think how many times he would have said that to George. When George would advise him just to keep his mouth zippered and let his bat do his talking for him at home plate, Reggie would say, "I'll take it, but I won't eat it."

Either George couldn't see anything to be gained by a meeting which would have to end with Reggie either eating it or refusing to eat it, or—as he says—Billy just didn't see any necessity for a meeting.

Whatever it was, when Reggie emerged from the office, he was clearly unhappy. He looked at Elston Howard, and pointed to Kahn, the man he had just asked for advice on how to conduct his life. "Look at them," he sneered—although Kahn was the only "them" there. "Waiting to hear if I have anything to say."

During the twenty-five-minute period before the game when the press is barred from the clubhouse, Reggie went around and apologized to everybody. A couple of the guys who had been in the bull pen said, "What are you apologizing to me for, I wasn't there." Reggie knew that. "I just want to tell everybody I'm sorry for not shaking their hands after I hit the home run."

Munson listened to him, and said nothing. A lot of them listened to him, and said nothing.

"Can you believe this?" the neutral players were saying to each other. "This is becoming a bleeping circus."

The White Sox' manager, Bob Lemon, who had been the Yankee pitching coach a year earlier, pinned it down to perfection. "I can't wait to pick up the paper every morning to see what's happening," he said. "It's like *Mary Hartman, Mary Hartman.*"

He was not alone. When Lou Piniella's wife left New York to go home to Florida, she insisted that the New York papers be sent to her every day. Like any soap opera, it had become addictive. Miss a day, and you might miss the best part.

This was the ball club that was asking the question: "Now that Reggie has apologized for not shaking Thurman's hand, will Thurman be willing to shake Reggie's hand?"

Hit a home run, Reggie, and we'll find out. First time Reggie comes to bat against Chicago, the Yankees are behind 5-0. Two of the runs have come in on a Richie Zisk double off the webbing of Reggie's glove, the others on a three-run homer by Oscar Gamble, the man Reggie has replaced. Believe it or not, Reggie tried to get on with a bunt, fouled it down the base line, and naturally hit a 450-foot home run on the next pitch. This time, he came running into the dugout with both hands extended, grabbing every hand in sight. Munson managed to emerge with his hand ungrabbed by taking it down to the other end of the dugout. Okay, let's try it the other way. Before the inning was over, Munson had tripled in two runs and scored the tying run on a Chris Chambliss single. He might have shaken Jackson's hand amidst the forest of hands that were thrust at him as he came into the dugout, Thurman said. But if he had, it had not been because he wanted to.

In the final game of the series, Chris Chambliss hit a two-run home run with Munson on base. Jackson, who was coming to the on-deck circle, extended his

126

hand to Munson. Munson ran past it, whistling a merry tune. "Chris shook my hand," Jackson pointed out to the always inquisitive reporters. Yeah, but that wasn't what they had asked. What about Munson? "I don't think he saw it."

"I saw it," said Munson.

Back to Jackson for his views on their relationship. "I'm just trying to be a good Christian," Reggie said.

It had been the kind of a day that would have tried the patience of St. Francis of Assisi. Having no left-hander to call its own, the White Sox had brought one up from the minor leagues, Ken Kravec. Jax struck out three straight times against him, and as soon as the Yankees took a lead, Martin got him out of the game.

Reggie couldn't see what Ken Kravec—24 hours out of the minors—had to be so proud of. "Because he struck me out? Anybody can do that. That's no big deal."

His fielding, which had always been the weakest point of Reggie's game, was breaking down completely under the pressure. After the first game, he had admitted that he should have caught that double by Zisk. In the second game, Zisk hit a line drive down the right-field line with the bases loaded, a legitimate double, and ended up on third when Jax (1) let the ball bounce under his glove, (2) misread the carom off the wall and (3) dropped the ball a couple of times before he could pick it up. It was more than just the errors. He wasn't getting any kind of a jump on fly balls, line drives that should have been caught were falling in front of him, and he was fighting balls that he had to go back for.

As the Yanks got ready for the trip to Boston, Martin was intimating that he might be giving Reggie a lot of rest in the late innings for a while. "I don't know how he's going to like it," he snapped, in answer to the obvious question. "Why don't you ask him? I'm just trying to win ball games."

Reggie didn't like it, but at least his sense of humor was beginning to return. He wasn't looking so bad out there on purpose, he wanted everybody to know. "I'm trying, so I can face myself in the mirror. But it's a struggle. The way I'm going, it shows people it's not always easy. And if it doesn't show people, it shows me."

On the plane to Boston, a couple of the writers asked Munson what he'd do if he hit a home run. In other words, would he shake Reggie's hand? Initially Munson took the attitude that there wasn't a chance. But as the writers began to argue that it was his job as captain to bring the team together, not to widen the breach, he grew increasingly pensive, and admitted they had given him something to think about.

It was the Yankees versus the Red Sox for the second straight week on *Monday Night Baseball*. The last time America had seen Reggie Jackson swing a bat, he had hit a home run off Bill Lee, and gone off to a corner to sulk about it. It's national TV again, it's Bill Lee out there again . . . it's . . . yes, it is . . . you *know* it is . . . it's out of here, America. And when Jax gets to the dugout, Munson is there to shake his hand.

In the fourth inning, Jackson singles in another run, putting the Yankees in front, 3-2, and when Jim Wynn doubles him home, Munson is there to shake his hand again.

In the end, it was Munson's game rather than Jackson's. Starting in the fifth inning, when Thurman drove in what proved to be the winning run on a fielder's choice. Jax gave the run back in the last of the inning by bobbling a ground ball, Carlton Fisk hit a home run in the eighth, and as the Red Sox came to bat in the last of the ninth, the score was 5-4. With one out, Butch Hobson attempts to steal second, and Munson's throw to Bucky Dent has him cold. Dent starts to put on the tag before he catches the ball—and never catches the ball. Denny Doyle hits a line single to center field. Short center. Mickey Rivers is the only center fielder in the major leagues they'd send the runner home on in that situation. Mickey's throw is perfect. Hobson, a former quarterback and safety for the 1972 Alabama Orange Bowl team, is caught ten feet up the line. His only chance is to knock the ball out of Munson's hand. Munson tucks himself in like a turtle to absorb the force of the crash, flips Butch over his shoulder, and reaches back to tag him out.

Jackson, who had been removed from the game by then for defensive purposes, was out on the field as soon as the game was over to congratulate him.

It was the second runner Rivers had thrown out that night. He had also thrown out two runners against the White Sox two days earlier. Four assists in three days. How did he account for the sudden strength in his arm?

"More money," said Rivers. "You throw better when you make more money. You do a lot of things better."

The Yankees and Red Sox had played three great games. The fourth one looked easy on the scoreboard, as the Red Sox won, 5-1, behind Reggie Cleveland, who had been making a career of it. He had beaten the Yankees three straight times in 1976, and had a 6-1 lifetime record against them. It wasn't that easy. He won it by getting Reggie Jackson out with men on base. Seven runners, Reggie left on.

The month of May had ended. The Yankees were still one and a half games behind Baltimore, but they were a game ahead of the Red Sox. And everybody knew that Baltimore wasn't going to stay up there.

7

A QUIET LITTLE TRADE

"You better stop bleeping reading and writing, Jackson, and start bleeping hitting."

—Mickey Rivers

The Yankees' besetting problems through the first two months of the season were their almost disabling weakness against left-handed pitching, and the disorganized state of their own pitching staff. As the season approached June 15, the trading deadline, their record was 10-15 against left-handers, compared with 25-11 against right-handers.

What made the weakness even more glaring was that the American League had a remarkably weak crop of left-handers. The outstanding ones were Frank Tanana, who was injured halfway through the season, and Vida Blue, when he was in a mood to pitch in his peculiar status as the Prisoner of Oakland, and perhaps Paul Splittorff. Baltimore was able to do so well against the Yankees because they had a strong crop of left-handers: Rudy May (whose seventeen wins made him the winningest left-hander in the league), Ross Grimsley and Mike Flanagan, a rookie who began to come along after a slow beginning. Other than that, the Yankees had all the good left-handers themselves: Gullett, Guidry and

Lyle. Even the relief pitchers. Except for Tippy Martinez, of Baltimore, and Sparky Lyle, every other team's ace relief pitcher was a right-hander.

The Yankees had not only been losing to left-handers, they had been losing to lousy left-handers.

One of the contributing factors, certainly, had been the failure of Jim Wynn as the right-handed DH. Jimmy Wynn was a small man (five feet, nine inches, one hundred and seventy pounds), with a big, sweeping swing which, as Gabe Paul should have suspected, was not at all suited to intermittent playing. After his burst of hitting during the first two weeks, he had stopped dead.

But, then, from the beginning, Jim Wynn had been considered purely a stopgap. Immediately after the free agent sweepstakes ended, Paul had gone after Tony Perez, who was on the market to open up first base for Dan Driessen. The Yankees were sure they had him, up to the day they read in the newspaper that he had gone to Montreal.

At the time of the Hendricks Flap, Gabe Paul had been working on a deal whereby the Yankees would trade Ken Holtzman to Texas for John Ellis, a right-handed-hitting catcher, and Ken Henderson, a switch-hitting outfielder, whose main strength was from the left side of the plate. Since Ellis could also play first base and Henderson was a considerably better-than-average outfielder, the Yankees would obviously be solving a multitude of problems.

And the beautiful part of it was that they would be giving up a pitcher for whom they had very little use, since Billy Martin had made it abundantly clear that he did not hold Ken Holtzman in high regard.

Ken Holtzman had a no-trade clause in his contract, which meant he had the right to approve the deal. It was a mistake. When Holtzman came to the Yankees in June, 1976, he was unsigned and eager to try his luck in the free-agent market. Along with Catfish Hunter, Holtzman had been the clutch pitcher for the Oakland A's in their three championship seasons. He and Hunter had the best World Series records of any active pitchers, four wins against one loss. It was for that reason specifically, Steinbrenner told him, that the Yankees wanted him. To pitch in the postseason games.

To show Kenny how much confidence he had in him, Steinbrenner offered him a five-year contract at $165,000 a year so that he could play out the rest of his career as a Yankee.

That kind of pitch is hard to resist. It occurred to Kenny that since George wanted him to spend the rest of his days with the Yankees, and Kenny wanted to spend the rest of his days with the Yankees, George could hardly object to writing a no-cut provision into the contract.

Unfortunately, Holtzman's pitching was so uneven that when it came to the postseason play for which he had been signed—the play-offs and the World Series—Billy Martin passed him by. Whether it had anything to do with Holtzman's role in the Players Association, or a basic disagreement over his ability, Billy clearly didn't like him. The only explanation anybody can give is, "I don't know, it's just a quirk." Billy has always said that he would play Mussolini and Hitler if they could help him on the field. He means it. But whether Mussolini could help is a subjective consideration, isn't it?

The general view that Holtzman was never given a chance by Martin in 1977 isn't completely accurate. As the number five pitcher in the rotation, Holtzman was given his regular start. He started on April 16, 21, 26, May 5, 11, 16 and 24.

Breaking it down, he had missed his first start because of the two open dates in the first week of the season, which is what usually happens to the number four and number five pitchers. Then he had started three straight times in turn, missed a turn because of two rainouts and an open date, and pitched in turn three more times. He didn't do the job. Kenny complained that he had to pitch every four days to stay sharp, but all pitchers say that. Figueroa and Torrez were pleading for a four-day rotation. Both of them are sinkerball pitchers, and it is an article of faith in the pitchers' union that a sinkerball pitcher can't be effective unless he pitches with a "tired arm."

Even after Kenny's place in the rotation had been taken by Guidry, Martin gave him a final chance by starting him against the Red Sox. (That was the game in which Zimmer left Luis Tiant in too long.) Kenny had to be taken out in the fourth inning, trailing, 4-1.

A week before the trading deadline, Holtzman's old teammate, Darold Knowles, informed him that he had been crazy to veto the deal, because Texas was a great place to live and raise a family. Holtzman, who had already given the Yankees permission to trade him to Milwaukee or either of the Chicago teams, immediately added Texas to the list. The Rangers were no longer in a position to put John Ellis in the deal, which is possibly another way of saying that Holtzman was no longer that attractive.

With only a few days left, Paul set his sights on Cliff Johnson of Houston, whom he had been chasing almost from the time he came to the Yankees.

Cliff Johnson was a big guy who hit a long ball consistently enough to have one of the best home-run ratios in baseball. Most notably in 1975, when he played enough to have 20 home runs in 340 turns at bat. He had been a catcher, for the most part, in the minor leagues. Since the National League does not have the DH rule, Houston had also used him at first base and in the outfield. Tal Smith, the Houston general manager, had been Gabe's assistant during his first year in New York, and so Smith had been on both sides of these calls. As the first week of June was coming to an end, he told Gabe that with Houston off to such a miserable beginning, Cliff Johnson could be had. "But it's going to be expensive." All he wanted were the two top prospects in the Yankee chain.

Not unexpectedly, the talks wound down to the trading deadline. On the afternoon of June 15, Gabe told him that he could give him one of the players he wanted, Dave Bergman, but that in place of the other he'd have to take two lesser players, Mike Fishlin, a shortstop, and Randy Neimann, a lefthanded pitcher. Houston was playing a night game against Atlanta, and then taking a plane to New York to play the Mets. After the game had ended, Smith told Paul that he still hadn't made up his mind but would call him from the airport with a definite answer.

An hour or so later, he called and said, "It's a deal." There was one minor complication. Since it was going

133

to be impossible for the Yankees to get waivers on Bergman, they were going to have to announce it as Fishlin, Neimann and "a player to be named later." The next morning, Paul went to their hotel to meet Smith and draw up the memorandum on Bergman. As long as he was there, he picked Cliff Johnson up and took him to Yankee Stadium to introduce him around. When they got to Steinbrenner's office, Johnson said, "In all fairness, I think I should tell you people I have a bad ankle."

"What!" Steinbrenner screamed. It amounted to nothing. Johnson had two, small, bone chips, but they didn't affect his maneuverability at all. Cliff Johnson was everything Gabe Paul had hoped he would be, and more. He had twelve home runs in 142 turns at bat, and knocked in 31 runs. His slugging percentage, .606, was better than the league leader's. And as icing on the cake, he was a far better catcher than anybody had a right to expect.

The deadline deal for Cliff Johnson was a prime factor contributing to the pennant. And still, Steinbrenner groused all year about the deal Gabe had made for an injured player. Despite the invaluable contribution Johnson made, despite a successful operation on the ankle during the winter, Steinbrenner never stopped trying to get it cancelled.

The team Johnson joined on June 16 wasn't in bad shape at all. The Yankees had survived a brutal road trip, which had taken them into five different cities in eleven days. Starting with those two games in Boston, and going on to Minnesota (which was a hot team), Chicago (another hot team), Texas (a hot team) and Milwaukee. They lived out of suitcases, and were always on buses that either got lost in the airport or trapped in traffic. After the opening game in Chicago, the bus got caught in an impossible traffic jam, and tempers began to fray. Reggie Jax finally hollered out, "Bussie, you're the only guy I've seen all season going worse than I am."

For Reggie, taking part in the bus humor signaled a change of mood. During one of the earlier road trips, he had abandoned his customary place in the front of the bus to join Mickey Rivers, Lou Piniella, Carlos May and

Catfish Hunter in the humorist's section. As a man of words, Reggie doubtless felt that he could hold his own with ease. Well, intellect is one thing, and the give-and-take of baseball humor is something else.

Everybody's favorite Mickey Rivers story goes back to the spring of 1976, when Mickey and Carlos May were insulting each other, clubhouse style. "I got a higher I.Q. than you," said Mickey, which as insults go isn't bad.

"You can't even spell I.Q.," answered Carlos.

Although nobody has ever accused Mickey of having more intelligence than he really needed, he has a withering street humor and a sharp native wit. "Reggie bleeping Martinez Jackson," Mickey said, bringing one exchange to an end, "you got a white man's first name, a Spanish man's second name and a black man's third name. No wonder you all bleeped up, man. You don't know what the bleep you are."

A few days later, the bus was passed by a truck with a black driver. "There goes Rivers in five years," Jackson said. "Driving a truck."

"Yeah," said Rivers, dead on target again. "But at least I'll be a happy truckdriver."

"Listen to me," Reggie said, "arguing with a guy who can't read or write."

"You better stop bleeping reading and writing," said Rivers, "and start bleeping hitting."

Reggie was doing some bleeping hitting. He had 14 for 31 on the trip. And with power. In that opening game in Chicago, he had two doubles and a four-hundred-and-forty-foot fly to the center-field fence. In the final game in Chicago, he hit a ball into the upper center-field bleachers, an exotic land into whose bourn only one or two balls had traveled. In the first game in Texas, he hit two home runs. In the next one, he hit another.

The great exception among the starters was Ron Guidry. He didn't want to go every fourth day. He preferred every sixth day. In the minor leagues, he had been used to blowing the opposition out for one or two innings. Nine innings was a long way for him to go, which may have been why he had never been able to get there. "My arm still doesn't know whether it's start-

135

ing or relieving," he would say. Guidry is from the Cajun country of Louisiana. In the eyes of the older reporters, he had very quickly established himself in the mold of the old Yankees. The Yankees of class. He kept himself away from the turbulence in the clubhouse, said nothing except when he was asked, and had a quiet sense of humor about himself.

After he had broken the Baltimore winning streak against the Yankees, he got bounced around by the White Sox, the one team that was going to give him nothing but trouble all year.

In Minnesota, he took a 3-1 lead into the ninth, and this time he altered the pattern slightly. He got nobody out. The first two batters singled, a double-play ball took a bad hop over Nettles' head, and Lyle was in again. Sparky got two outs. It still takes three. Rod Carew got up with the bases loaded, and drilled a Carew single into left.

Nine days later, having lost a start while Martin was testing Gil Patterson, Guidry got another crack at Minnesota. The Yankees were leading, 4-1, into the ninth. The Twins had scored on two singles and an error in the first inning, and Guidry had positively overpowered them from there on, striking out eight men. A single, an out and a walk, and Guidry was out of the game again after eight and one-third innings.

"Next time, I'll shoot for eight and two-thirds innings," he said.

The Yankee front office, convinced that it had the stopper it was looking for, was rooting desperately for Guidry to pitch a full game. June 16, the day after the trading deadline, he was up to pitch again against Kansas City. After the game, the Yankees would leave for Boston, for the first of the six games the two teams would play in the next ten days. The Red Sox were leading the Yankees by a half a game. Guidry went into the ninth with a 7-0 lead. Another overpowering performance. Seven strike-outs, and he had allowed only three hits. He walked the first batter. He got the next three. "I kept telling myself it was the seventh inning," he said after the game. Was he still strong at the end? "I felt so good," he said, perfectly deadpan, "that I

136

could have pitched the eighth and even the ninth if I had to."

The Red Sox lost to Chicago. The Yankees were going to Boston in first place.

8

CRISIS IN BOSTON, CRISIS IN DETROIT

"The great thing about baseball is that there's a crisis every day."

—Gabe Paul

Rick Burleson hit Hunter's second pitch into the screen on top of the wall, the first of only three home runs he would hit all year. Fred Lynn hit a 3-2 pitch into the bleachers in right center. With two out, Carlton Fisk and George Scott boomed shots over the wall, over the screen, over everything. Four home runs before the inning was over, and Hunter set a new record for himself in precipitate departures. Catfish didn't take the loss, though, and Lee didn't get the win. The Yankees came back with three runs in the second, tied it up in the third, and would have gone into the lead if Dent hadn't missed the pitch completely on an attempted squeeze play. The losing pitcher was young Ken Clay, who also happened to be the only Yankee pitcher who was effective. Clay pitched a good four and one-third innings, but allowed the tie-breaking run in the fifth on, of all things, three singles. Dick Tidrow came in, and got things back on the track by giving up monster home runs to Yastrzemski and Fisk.

Six home runs, a humiliation.

Before the Saturday afternoon game, Reggie was in a conspicuously happy-go-lucky mood. Maybe it was because it was another *Game of the Week*. In the five games in which he had been on national television, he had hit .363, with four home runs. He had a hitting streak of thirteen consecutive games going. It was a hot, sunny day, and a crowd of 34,603 was gathering, the largest afternoon crowd in Boston in twenty years.

Reggie was out on the bench early, sitting alongside Bucky Dent, when Billy came over to tell Dent not to worry about yesterday's busted squeeze play. "I thought it was a good play," Billy observed to Reggie. "What do you think?"

"If you really want my opinion," Reggie told him, "I think he feels like you take the bat out of his hand making him squeeze in the second and third inning."

Came the ball game, and it was the same thing all over again. The Red Sox had five more home runs: two more by Yastrzemski, two by Carbo and one by Scott. Making it eleven home runs in two games. But that wasn't the story.

The Red Sox were leading, 7-4, in the sixth inning. With Fred Lynn on first base, Jim Rice hit a checked-swing pop fly out to short right field. At first, Reggie seemed to be under the impression that Willie Randolph was going to be able to make the play without any difficulty. Be that as it may. Then he started slowly, showed no great enthusiasm about going after the ball once it had fallen in, and made a weak throw in the general direction of the pitcher's mound as Rice went wheeling into second.

As Martin left the dugout to replace Mike Torrez with Sparky Lyle, the player sitting next to Paul Blair said, "Get ready to put your glove on, Paul. He's going to pull Jackson out of there."

He wasn't wrong. Billy was still out on the pitching mound waiting for Lyle to come in when he told Munson, "I'm going to go get that sonofabitch."

The crowd saw Blair before Jackson did. Reggie was leaning against the bull-pen fence, talking to a couple of the players in there, and it was the roar of the crowd that made him look around. When he saw Blair, he took one step toward him and then kind of rocked back against the fence in confusion and disbelief. Blair waved him in, and when Reggie got to him, he asked, "You coming after me?"

"Yeah."

"Why?"

"You got to ask Billy that." As Reggie came running in, with his purposeful stride, to do exactly that, the center-field camera—that other scorekeeper—followed him every step of the way. Martin had been leaning forward from the edge of his dugout seat, waiting. Jackson spread his hands out in an expression of total bewilderment. "What did I do? What did I do?"

Martin came off the bench at him. His chin jutted up, combatively. "What do you mean, what did you do? You know what you did!"

Reggie continued on down the steps, and it was as if he hadn't heard Billy. He still only had one thought in mind. "Why did you take me out? You had to be crazy to embarrass me in front of fifty million people."

Elston Howard had moved in front of Jackson, interposing his body between him and Billy. Martin spat a curse. Jackson spat one back. "You showed me up in front of fifty million people," Reggie said. "You're not a man." He turned his back and began to walk away. "Don't you ever dare show me up again, you motherfucker."

Martin, who was at hair-trigger anyway, maybe just looking for an excuse, let out a bellow and went after him. "I'll show you whether I'm a man or not!" Howard tried to pin him against the pole, but as soon as he realized that Billy wasn't going to be held gladly, he let go. Dick Howser grabbed him just long enough to stop his charge, and Yogi Berra wrestled him to the bench. As Reggie turned back, Jimmy Wynn wrapped his arms around him. "You never did like me," Reggie shouted. "You never did want me on the ball club. I'm here to stay, so you better start liking me."

It was a roundabout way of saying it, but Reggie had laid it out for everybody to hear. *I'm here to stay, so you better start liking me.* If one of them went, he was saying, loud and clear, it was going to be Billy, not him.

And all of it had been caught by the TV camera in

center field. There was another camera right on the scene, too. A mobile camera situated right there alongside the dugout, right in front of the box where Gabe Paul was sitting, apparently overhearing the whole thing. The guy who was running the camera had wheeled it around and moved in on top of the scene. Before he could activate it, another cameraman of sorts—Ray Negrone, who runs for the Yankees the same kind of closed-circuit video camera that football teams use—was screaming at him to get the camera out of there. Negrone is a former Yankee bat boy and minor-league ballplayer. He had been hired for the job at the beginning of spring training through the intercession of Billy Martin. He had also become very friendly with Reggie Jackson, possibly because they both speak Spanish. He had reason to admire, and be grateful to, both of them, and what was happening was so painful to him that almost before he knew what he was doing, he had screamed out and tried to throw a towel over the camera. For some reason, the mobile cameraman recalled afterwards that it was Martin who had shouted to him to get the camera out of there. Not so. If Billy worried about things like that, there wouldn't have been any dugout brawl to begin with.

To keep it from becoming a clubhouse brawl, Elston Howard told Jim Wynn to go in after Reggie, and try to talk him into leaving. Mike Torrez, who had become one of the "allies" Reggie had been looking for, was still sitting at his locker. Mike had gone back to the clubhouse just in time to catch the blow-by-blow of the fight coming over the radio. Wynn tried to tell Reggie that the wisest thing for him to do was to take a shower, go back to the hotel, and try to forget what had happened. Relax. Go out. Have a good time. Torrez urged Reggie to take Wynn's advice. But Reggie was in an emotional whirl. He was the one who had been humiliated. He didn't see why he should run. Torrez went to the trainer's room to soak his arm, and Wynn kept talking until he felt he had got through to Reggie.

Shortly after Wynn left, Fran Healy came running in from the bullpen to give Reggie the same advice. Healy had become Reggie's other close friend and ally.

The relationship between Reggie and Torrez is easy enough to understand. Torrez had come in from the outside, they had the same agent, Gary Walker, and they both spoke Spanish. Healy is not so easy to understand (if, indeed, it is necessary to try to understand why any two men become friends). Initially, almost everybody believed that Healy had been assigned to Reggie by Steinbrenner.

"Whenever Reggie was having a low period, he was the guy over consoling him. I thought, shit, he's the twenty-fifth ballplayer on the club and they've given him a job to do, and that's to keep Reggie's dauber up; in other words, to keep him from sinking out of sight when he got into one of those demented, tortured states. Apparently, it wasn't the case. Apparently, Fran really had a feeling for the guy, really liked him. He's a nice guy, Fran."
                                        —sportswriter's view

Healy has the kind of competence that allows him to move very easily into any situation. As the second-string catcher, he was as close to Munson as he was to Reggie. And also friendly enough with Billy Martin.

Healy found Reggie in the trainer's room with Torrez. He also found Bucky Dent. Bucky had been removed for a pinch hitter in the Yankee half of the sixth, and he had come back to the locker room, steaming. It was bad enough that a pinch hitter was being sent in for him routinely, any time the Yankees were behind late in the game. Now Martin was taking him out with the game half over. Bucky had grabbed the phone just outside the clubhouse, made a reservation for a flight to Chicago, and then called his wife to tell her to pick him up at the airport. Bucky Dent, having had enough, was jumping the club.

Between phone calls, he had heard the Boston announcer talking about the shouting match in the dugout but, preoccupied as he was, it hadn't sounded serious to him. (To Torrez, on the other hand, it had sounded more serious than it was; the way it sounded to Torrez, the announcer had been trying to let the audience know that punches were being thrown, without actually saying so.)

Bucky, who was already fully dressed, intercepted Healy at the doorway to the trainer's room. "Fran," he said, "I'm leaving."

"What?"

"I can't take any more of this," Dent said. "I'm hooking it. I'm jumping the club."

Healy could only stare at him. Wondering, I suppose, whether to point first to Jackson and then to Dent, and say, *"You* go . . . *You* stay!"

He gave Bucky the kind of look that told him he was going to have to wait his turn, and went on in to tell Reggie what everybody else had been telling him. "For the good of everybody concerned, don't stay around and give it a chance to start up again."

With three of his teammates there, one of whom had actually seen the play, Reggie wanted to explain why he had played the ball the way he had, and to ask Healy whether he thought he had loafed. Bucky Dent was watching and listening from the doorway, and the more he heard, the less important his own problem seemed to be. By the time Reggie had showered and dressed, Bucky Dent had called his wife back to tell her to forget about picking him up at the airport, he had changed his mind.

If he hadn't changed his mind—which also means, if Healy hadn't come running into the clubhouse— Billy Martin would never have survived the next forty-eight hours. Of that, there can be very little question.

George Steinbrenner had left Boston after the game on Friday night to attend a funeral in Cleveland, but he had seen the whole thing on television. No sooner had the shouting ended in the dugout than a call came to the Fenway Park press box for Phil Rizzuto. Since there is no phone connection between the press box and the radio booth, Bill Crowley, the Red Sox publicity director, assumed he had a nut on the line, and hung up. Immediately, the phone rang again. A flustered operator demanded to know who had hung up, while behind her, a heavy voice shouted, "This is George Steinbrenner." Upon hearing Crowley tell the operator that there was no way of putting the call through to Rizzuto, Steinbrenner asked to talk to Mickey Morabito. That, Crowley could do for him.

Whatever else Steinbrenner may have had to say to Morabito, he most certainly instructed him to have Gabe Paul call him. The inning had come to an end, and Gabe had just exchanged a few smiling words with Billy Martin from his box seat when Morabito came down and passed the message to him. Gabe strolled up the aisle and disappeared from sight.

Steinbrenner wanted to fire Martin out of hand. It had been an absolute disgrace, the man had lost complete control of himself on national television. What kind of example was that to set for American youth?

There were other factors that had to be considered, Gabe cautioned him. Like whether you could fire Martin over this without making it seem as if Reggie were running the team. He would talk to both of them and take a reading. Meanwhile, the best thing to do was let things settle down. They would be in Detroit on Sunday night, and George could meet them there. He did talk to both Martin and Jackson after the game. Not together. Separately. Martin in the clubhouse, immediately after the game. Jackson in his hotel room, shortly afterward. Both of them were still badly shaken. Billy Martin took the attitude that, goddamnit, he was the manager, and nobody was going to tell him how to handle his players. Reggie's nature is such that the more he brooded over his humiliation, the more emotional he became. Rather than have a meeting that night, as he had suggested to Martin, he set it up for breakfast the next morning.

With Jackson gone, Billy had the post-game rehash all to himself. He couldn't have been more open about his motives. "I ask one thing of a player," he said, "and that's hustle. If any player don't hustle, and shows the team up, then I show the player up. I don't care if it was seen all over the world. I'm not going to let television run my team. Does television win games for you?"

He admitted that he had cursed Reggie. "Words were said that I didn't like." But he saw no reason why the situation couldn't be repaired. Not that he seemed to be losing any sleep over it. "We won without him last year, didn't we?" he said, for perhaps the hundredth time. The players were solidly behind him. One player, identified only as a "Yankee regular" (guess who?), said, "It was a ridiculous play by Jackson. This was a big game. The Red Sox are in first place. Where does he come off, trotting after a ball when we're losing? I'm glad that Billy took him out. Maybe that will shock him into losing his superior ideas about himself. I was there busting ass all day. I would've liked to take a swing at Jackson myself."

To a man, they were behind him: "People were giving Reggie the benefit of the doubt," another unidentified player said. "He can play, but if you don't want to, what good is it? . . . He forgets the other half of the job is to hustle and play defense."

When the unanimity of the feeling against him was relayed to Reggie by Steve Jacobson, a writer he trusted, Reggie went beyond a defense of the particular play into what he believed to be the real issue. "I can't win here. I am alone."

Somewhere around eight o'clock, either Reggie invited Paul Montgomery of *The New York Times* to his room to hear his version of what had happened, or Montgomery phoned to ask if he could come up. There is also the possibility that it was George Steinbrenner who made the initial call to set it up. Having made the decision to fire Billy Martin, Steinbrenner would have a vested interest in protecting Reggie from the fallout. At any rate, Montgomery had barely arrived in the room before Phil Pepe of the *Daily News* called Reggie, to ask if he could come up and talk to him. Montgomery very generously agreed to share the interview.

It was some interview. Reggie was sitting on the floor as they started, bare-chested except for a gold cross and two gold medallions. A blonde was in the shower. Mike Torrez was sitting next to Reggie with a bottle of white wine. Reggie had asked Torrez to come in for a very specific reason. "If I go too far," he told Torrez before he began, "stop me." He was wound so tight that he seemed to have only the most fragmented memory of the disputed play. He took

145

the position that he had charged the ball the way he thought he could play it best. "If Martin feels I didn't hustle, I'm sorry for him. You know, in this game the manager is always right, and I'm just a player."

The refrain seemed to be stuck in his head, almost as if he had been programmed. The phone would ring, and still another reporter would be on the line. "I have nothing to say," Reggie would answer. "The manager is always right."

His memory was that he hadn't said anything when he came back to the dugout, but had merely held his arms open in a "What did I do wrong?" motion. "The man took a position today to show me up on national TV. Everyone could see that."

He'd had three cortisone shots since spring training, he informed them. "With my bad arm, I'm not going to take a chance throwing to second, so I fired home. I didn't want the run to score." Not only was that not the way it had happened, it didn't even make sense. At one point, Reggie sat on the bed and read the Bible for while. He had been a born-again Christian for three years, he told them, and often went to the Bible for solace.

And then he was back on the floor. "I don't know anything about managing, but I'll take the heat for whatever the manager says." He played right field when "they" let him. He hit wherever they put him. "I do anything they tell me to do." All he wanted to do was to go out and play to the best of his ability.

Suddenly, it became the fault of the press. "If the press keeps messing with me, I'll get thirty homers and maybe ninety ribbys." If they left him alone, he'd have 40 homers, 120 ribbys and hit .300. "And the Yankees would be running away with the pennant."

And then he began to speak with real emotion. "I'm just a black man to them who doesn't know how to be subservient. I'm a black buck with an I.Q. of one sixty, and making $700,000 a year. They've never had anyone like me on their team before." Except for Steinbrenner. "I love that man, he treats me like I'm somebody."

His voice broke, and he came up on his haunches. "The rest of them treat me like I'm dirt." The tears were running down his cheeks. "I'm a Christian," he screamed, "and they're fucking with me because I'm a nigger, and they don't like niggers on this team." The Yankee pin stripes were supposed to be Ruth and Gehrig, DiMaggio and Mantle. "I've got an I.Q. of one sixty, they can't mess with me . . ." He was a man in torment, a man so clearly on the slippery edge that Mike Torrez, who had been watching him with great concern, stood up and told the writers, "I think you'd better leave."

When Jackson and Martin came to Gabe Paul's room for breakfast, they were both still bristling. In no time at all, it got worse. Reggie insisted that he hadn't loafed. He had been playing deep because you had to play Jim Rice deep, but once he had seen that Randolph wasn't going to catch it, he had charged the ball. And Martin said, "Boy, what you think you're doing and what my eyes tell me you're doing are two different things."

In his hypersensitive mood, Reggie chose to take the "boy" as a racial slur. You can imagine his reaction. Billy assured him that there had been nothing racial about it. Gabe Paul assured him there had been nothing racial about it. But there were five or ten very hairy minutes before Reggie was willing to accept it—or, at least, to drop it.

After that, the breakfast went about as well as could be expected. If there were no vows of perpetual friendship exchanged, there was a meeting of minds.

The Red Sox completed the Boston Massacre by hitting five more home runs as they defeated the Yankees, 11-1. To rub it in, it was the weak-hitting Denny Doyle who broke the game open with a three-run home run, the first home run he had hit in two hundred and four games. (When he saw the umpire twirling his upraised fingers, said Doyle, "I figured either he was trying to show me some seagulls, or it was a homer. And I didn't see any seagulls.")

One of the casualties was Reggie Jackson's fourteen-game hitting streak. Not that the pressure had gotten to him. Against Ferguson Jenkins, a top pitcher who had his good stuff, Reggie had hit three smoking line drives. Unfortunately, they had all gone right at somebody.

147

Where the pressure buckled him, as always, was in the field. He stumbled around badly under a couple of fly balls, and made a miserable throw to the cutoff man for an error.

If the carnage was awful, the casualties were many. Dick Tidrow, for instance. Dick Tidrow came into the game in the seventh inning, and Bernie Carbo, the first batter he faced, hit a home run. Jim Rice hit one in the eighth, and two pitches later, Yaz hit one over the bull pen and into the bleachers. For Yaz, it was nine for fourteen on the series, with four home runs and ten RBI's, and the message was flashing on the scoreboard that the Red Sox had tied the all-time record for home runs in three consecutive games. With two out, George Scott, the league-leading home-run hitter, came to the plate. The fans were screaming for the record breaker. One of the inviolable rules of hitting is that you're never going to hit a home run when you're swinging for one. The Boomer boomed one into the center-field bleachers, the most distant part of the field.

For Tidrow, it was the sixth home run he had given up over five innings. One longer than the other. It left him shell-shocked for two months.

Ed Figueroa had been making his first start in a week after straining his back, and you could almost see his back stiffening up on him after three innings. When you can't bend your back, the ball stays high, and when the ball stays high, it's Goodbye, Charlie. Once every two hundred and four games or so it's even Goodbye, Denny. In the clubhouse, after the game, Figueroa, normally the most quiet of men, was furious. Not about his back, but about the happy-go-lucky attitude of his teammates. "Look at them," he said. "Last year everybody played hard. Now they all have three-or-four-year contracts and they don't care." They had been horsing around in the shower, he said, and they'd be drinking and playing cards on the plane to Detroit. "In Detroit, they will drink and play cards again. They don't give a bleep. Go ahead and write it. I'm not afraid to say it. It's the truth."

That's what Reggie Jackson had been accused of, wasn't it? Not caring enough. Figueroa was accusing everybody. Most of all, he was pointing the finger at

148

the manager, Billy Martin, who was still running the most lackadaisical clubhouse in baseball. "They're all thinking we got such a good club, we're going to win it later. Maybe they will start trying when they are nine or ten games behind, and maybe it's going to be too late."

Over in the manager's office, Billy Martin was, indeed, being his optimistic self. Not defiantly optimistic, that doesn't enter it. Undiscouraged and undiscourageable. "If this was September," he was saying, "I'd be worried. This is June. We'll be in first place next Sunday." The Red Sox were a hot team now. When the Yankees got hot, they'd run away with it.

It had never entered his mind that he might be in imminent danger of losing his job because of the dugout battle with Jackson. Quite the contrary. After that game, he had been suggesting that he might hit Reggie with a fine. "A big fine. I'll see how he reacts, and what happens when we talk."

Before Sunday's game, he said, "We went over everything, and everything turned out fine. There is no problem. Yesterday is history."

Long after the game was over, he was sitting in the Boston press room, drinking with Gabe Paul and Don Zimmer. "The way you're drinking," Gabe told him, drily, "you'd think we won."

The players had no feeling that Billy's job was in jeopardy, either. During the plane ride to Detroit, the main topic of conversation was whether Billy had wanted to be held back, or whether he was so far gone that he'd have popped Reggie if he had been able to get at him. Most of the players, you have to remember, had been either on the field or out in the bull pen. The overwhelming consensus of opinion was that if Billy had been able to break loose, he'd have stuck his jaw into Jackson's face again and yelled some more. Billy's reputation as a fighter meant not a thing to them. To the players of a new generation, he was just another old-timer. It was, in fact, the consensus that if nobody had held Billy, he wouldn't have kept coming at Jackson. "Would you want to take on Reggie?" they asked each other. Noooo, they would answer. Reggie is one solid block of muscle.

By the time they woke up in the morning, they had something else to talk about. Milton Richman, sports editor of UPI, had a story on the line that Billy Martin was going to be fired within a couple of days and replaced by Yogi Berra, "as a result of the Jackson episode, coupled with the three losses in Boston."

Milt Richman's reputation along the sports beat is such that there wasn't a reporter or ballplayer with the club who didn't believe it. Richman has been around for a long time, he has sources right at top, and he has a remarkable record for being right. He'd had the story about the signing of Gullett before anybody else, and he'd had the story about the signing of Jackson. So you knew he had a pipeline.

But there was something interesting about it. Richman was in Tulsa, covering the U.S. Open, which meant that he'd have been out on the golf course all day Saturday and Sunday. He had also been on the phone throughout Saturday afternoon, getting sidebar material on Tom Seaver's first start in Cincinnati. On Sunday, there had been a series of conferences with USGA officials on the question of making public a death threat against Hubie Green, who was in the process of winning the Open. Whatever might have been going on in Boston could hardly have been of major concern to Richman.

And it hadn't been. Milt Richman had gotten back to his hotel after midnight, to find an urgent message for him to call his New York office. Just the kind of message you don't want to find at one o'clock in the morning. The tip had been phoned in to him, complete, and the tipster had identified himself only by his initials. You hear those initials and one name comes immediately to mind. Not the name of a baseball man, but the name of a very famous figure—a veritable Giant—in an entirely different field. The Giant's connections with baseball were such that Milt could see exactly how he could have come into possession of that kind of information. And Milt had spent a long night with him a couple of weeks earlier discussing the anatomy of a newsbeat. The problem was that if the story were true, there was no reason to believe that it was going to hold for another day, and Milt had no way of getting in touch with the Giant at one o'clock in the morning. There were other people he could get in touch with, though. He made some other calls, and by the time he hung up, he was convinced that Steinbrenner had indeed decided to fire Billy Martin.

He went with it. And by going with it probably saved Martin's job.

Gabe Paul had warned Steinbrenner that while he wasn't anxious to keep Martin as manager, the alternative at the moment could only be destructive. The Richman story gave them a rare opportunity to look at the consequences ahead of time. Steinbrenner and Paul met in George's suite at the Pontchartrain Motor Hotel, and Paul laid it out to him in person as he had been laying it out to him over the phone. Fire Martin and you're making Jackson the manager. The new manager is placed in a wholly untenable position, and Reggie Jackson's position in regard to his teammates becomes impossible. Whether the players liked or hated their manager was normally of no importance to Paul. Whether the players wanted a manager kept or fired was also of no importance. But every situation turns on its own events. The question that never changes is, "What is best for the team?"

There was also the racial factor, or (as Steinbrenner referred to it) "the black-white thing." It wasn't there in reality, but it was there because it's always there. And because Reggie Jackson, in his personal battle with Reggie Jackson, had put it there.

If Bucky Dent had jumped the club—if he had walked out without pausing to pass the word to Healy —there would have been adequate cause for saying he had lost control of the team as well as of himself. The way this situation had developed, they were not only going to have to live with Billy Martin, they were stuck with him unless the team fell completely apart.

George Steinbrenner had not marched into Detroit with his banners flying, in order to fold his tents and steal quietly away. There were meetings to be held with Gabe Paul, Billy Martin and the key players. But the Richman story had also put George in the position of defending a decision, rather than finding out what was going on. Thurman Munson, for one, had placed himself solidly behind his manager, and there were stories already going around that if Martin were fired over this, Munson was ready to walk away with him.

While everybody was shuttling in and out of Steinbrenner's suite, Billy was on the golf course with his old friend Phil Rizzuto. "I beat him for more than a hundred dollars," Rizzuto said. "He wasn't even looking at the ball. He must have sent me back to the clubhouse five times to make a call to see if anything was happening. I've known him twenty-eight years, and I've never seen him like that before."

Billy's meeting with Steinbrenner and Paul took place late in the afternoon. If George couldn't fire him, he could at least knock some concessions out of him. But, you know, it didn't even come to that. All George was asking Billy to do was to live up to the clauses already in his contract. Clauses put up there in the first place only to make more emphatic what every other manager took for granted.

Billy was by no means contrite. Frightened, yes. Subdued. When Billy is emotional there is a kind of bony look that comes over him, as of tightly drawn, highly spun nerves. But Billy is never contrite. He was not going to allow anybody to tell him how to manage, he said, for the umpty-eighth time. They weren't telling him how to manage, said Steinbrenner and Paul, for the umpty-seventh time. They were telling him that he was going to have to meet his responsibilities.

What was being demanded of him was discipline. "Because you can't have discipline on the ball club without being disciplined yourself."

"You do things without telling me," Martin said.

"How can we tell you things," Paul asked drily, "when we can't get ahold of you?"

All right, Billy said at last. What did he have to do?

He had to maintain contact. Contact and preparation. Those were the words Steinbrenner kept using. He was not only going to have to make every meeting that Paul called, he was going to have to come to the office every day and work harder on preparation. Preparation meant getting to the park earlier, not fifteen minutes but three hours before the game, and studying the charts and reports Steinbrenner sent down. That was the football man talking. The computer freak. And no more bad-mouthing the front office.

But it was all repetition of what was already in the contract. Billy could already be fired for acts of insubordination, failure to attend meetings, and publicly criticizing the front office.

And one other thing, something that wasn't in the contract: He had to be more "flexible" in his handling of Reggie Jackson.

After Billy had agreed to everything, George told him that the decision whether he stayed or left was to be made by Gabe Paul. George was going to remove himself from the scene. The goddamn club brought him more trouble and aggravation than all his other companies put together. "It's in Gabe's hands now," was the last thing he had to say.

The last thing Billy said was, "I just want to ask you one thing. Were you going to fire me when you came here?"

"I won't lie to you," Steinbrenner said. "You were gone."

But George wasn't quite ready to fade silently into the twilight. He wanted Martin and Jackson to go to the ball park together, and put on a display of unity for the world. So they took a taxi to the ball park, and walked into the clubhouse with their arms on each other's shoulders. "We are allies," Jackson announced. He quoted a passage from the Bible that instructed him to be obedient to his superiors, the same passage that Alvin Dark had quoted when Reggie was at Oakland, to explain why he was allowing himself to be humiliated by Charlie Finley.

George came to the clubhouse during batting practice and put on a show of his own. Otherwise known as voting his stock. He started by calling Munson into the manager's office, while Martin loitered outside. Then he had Martin in. Then he sent out to get Reggie, so that he could talk to them together.

And, for a grand finale, the pep talk. On this one, there was an extra ingredient. Despite all those meetings, some of the players hadn't even known that Steinbrenner was in town. Some of them had been away from the hotel all day. Some had stayed in their rooms. All of them had come to the park believing that Martin was about to be fired. For once, it hadn't been the reporters going to the players for information—it had been the players asking the reporters what they had heard. The writers hadn't heard anything. It was *Monday Night Baseball* with Howard Cosell, and George was holding his announcement of the non-firing for national TV.

"You guys are a finger-snapping away from firing your manager," George began. "If you love him so much, you guys had better get on the ball." That was how the players learned that Billy Martin was still their manager. For a while, anyway. George hit the Jackson situation rather obliquely by saying, "I think this ball club is prejudiced against certain individuals on the ball club." You've got to say this about George Steinbrenner: For a man who was supposed to be so concerned about "the black-white thing," he certainly did have a way with words. He said, "Everybody in every other city is trying to pull us apart. If you guys are pulling against each other, we don't stand a chance to win." From there, it was pretty much the standard pep talk from the Book of Knute, telling them how great they would be if they ever got around to playing ball.

The Coach had rallied the troops, and the troops went charging out there and lost their fourth straight ball game, 2-1. It was Mark ("Go, Bird, Go") Fidrych, *Monday Night Baseball* and 47,236 fans. Another full house. Billy Martin was greeted by a standing ovation as he brought the starting line-up to home plate. "Wasn't that super?" he said, when he returned to the dugout. He was positively aglow. "I'll bet George just loved to hear that."

Reggie must have loved it, too. It was another bad night for Reggie all around. He had driven in the Yankee run with a sacrifice fly in the top of the fourth inning. The Tigers tied it in their half. Disaster came in the last of the seventh, as Reggie came racing in for Mickey Stanley's line drive. Just as he reached for the ball, you could see that he had lost it in the glare of the Tiger Stadium lights, which a recent study had shown to be the brightest in the major leagues. The ball

154

went sailing over his shoulder, and the next batter singled in the winning run.

At the end of the inning, Reggie ran right through the dugout and into the clubhouse, looking as if he were about to break into tears. Billy Martin went back immediately to console him, and so did Dick Tidrow, who could not, by the wildest stretch of the imagination, be numbered among Jackson's admirers.

"He felt so bad," Martin said. "We told him not to fault himself."

Reggie was faulting himself, anyway. "That's probably the worst I've ever felt on a ball field. I ought to quit. Give up."

Not only was Martin not faulting him, he was willing to offer some friendly advice. Maybe, he said, Reggie ought to get his eyes examined.

Over in the other clubhouse, the Bird (so called because of a startling resemblance to *Sesame Street*'s Big Bird) had some financial advice for George Steinbrenner, whom he insisted upon calling "Steinberger." Listen, it's close enough. It was the Bird's fond, innocent belief that the Yankees were showing "Steinberger"—and presumably impressionable multi-millionaires everywhere—that "you can't go out and buy everything in life. If they finish second, that will prove it. They'll watch the World Series just like us."

The Red Sox, going along their merry way, had shut out Baltimore. The Yankees were now three and a half games behind.

After the next game, it was four and a half, but neither George Steinbrenner nor Gabe Paul was there to see it. The real crisis of the 1977 season didn't come on June 18, the day that Billy Martin and Reggie Jackson almost came to blows in the Boston dugout. It came in Detroit on June 21. That was the night that Gabe Paul dumped the ball club back in George Steinbrenner's lap, and went home.

After George delivered his stirring pep talk, Gabe Paul had gone up to the press box to read the following statement:

"There will be no change in our organization, regardless of what has been said. We don't feel there's

155

a better manager than Billy Martin, and we want the Yankees to have the best.

"There were some things that had to be straightened out, and they were straightened out. From the first pitch till the last one, there's no better manager in baseball than Billy, and he's the one we want."

Who had made the decision, Paul was asked.

"This was my decision," Paul said.

Earlier in the day, Steinbrenner had been telling the writers the same thing. Quote: "The decision is strictly Gabe Paul's. I'll stand behind him, either way he goes. He's the guy right now."

He had been saying that from the beginning. And also leading the reporters to believe that it wasn't so. After the Boston episode, he went on record that he had been watching the game on television, and didn't think that Reggie had dogged it. Beyond that, he had put forth the line that he had stayed away from the club from the time Dock Ellis called him a Lone Ranger, and in the current crisis had merely told Gabe (you could just catch the note of impatience under the chuckle), "Don't come to me now." Although, yes, he was going to meet the club in Detroit to find out what was going on.

And he kept it up. Publicly, everything was Gabe's decision. Privately, and off the record, he let it be known that the tension on the team was beyond anything Gabe seemed aware of, and that he was getting annoyed with being called whenever there was even a minor emergency.

After the announcement of Martin's retention, George got a little rambunctious, but that was mostly at the expense of his manager. At a press interview the next day, he went crazy, a veritable Louis Armstrong blowing his own horn, a veritable Heifetz of machismo.

Q. Who made the decision to keep Billy Martin as manager?

A. I did. It was my decision entirely. We were headed for complete collapse. Dissension on the team was terrible. We were getting no leadership and no fire. Something had to be done quickly.

He said that he had never had any intention of firing Martin, but that Martin "and others among the Yankees" had not been doing their jobs. "Billy was very subdued, and has promised to get in touch with me every day. I intend to keep in daily contact with the team." He had told Billy, "The next time you drive me to the wall, I'll throw you over it."

He denied categorically that he had always taken Jackson's side in disputes with Martin. He had warned Reggie that if he ever mentioned racism again, "I'll beat your head off."

And how had Jackson reacted to that? "Jackson listened and took it."

He had also taken Munson to task for failing to carry out his duties as captain. According to Steinbrenner, Munson had replied, "I thought Jackson was the captain."

"You are the captain," Steinbrenner told Munson. "When I want Jackson to be the captain, I'll tell him and you, too. You are the captain. Now be the captain."

He said that several players had told him that his pep talk had given them a lift. They had told him earlier, in the lobby of the hotel, that they wanted him to take a greater part in running the club. "We want you around," he quoted them as saying, "watching things, pulling for us."

Here are a few guidelines toward a better understanding of George Steinbrenner:

1. He does not get up in class every morning and pledge allegiance to the truth.

2. He has an ego bigger than all other egos.

3. He is a publicity hound.

4. It makes him very unhappy to realize that he does not get the credit he doesn't deserve for the trades that put the Yankees together.

5. He is jealous of Gabe Paul, who did make the trades that put the Yankees together.

Note: Items two through five are all the same thing.

George and Gabe had always had a very good relationship. They liked each other. George also had a very good relationship with Billy Martin, except when they were disagreeing about the ball club. By all accounts, George is a delightful person socially—lots of fun, and he can be counted on to pick up the check.

But he's a terrible guy to work for, attested by the fact that nobody who was with the Yankees when he came is still there, and neither is anybody who came in with him.

George's problem was that he needed Gabe, and he wished that he didn't. And so from time to time he'd make believe that he didn't. It wasn't a matter of who was making the decisions. It was George's ball club. Every decision was really his. George had overruled Gabe at the time of the Hendricks flap. He had then, incidentally, given it to Dick Young the other way around, following the shoving incident, to make it look as if he shared Young's dim view of Billy of the moment. What did Gabe care? He had even come out of it looking like a good guy. But in constantly stating that this was Gabe's decision, and then announcing that he had been forced to step in and do it himself, George had made Gabe look like a flunky. He was saying that Gabe Paul's name was his rag doll to punch around as he wished.

Gabe walked out of the hotel, and caught a plane home to Tampa. George was on a plane that same night. The next morning, he went to Gabe, hat in hand, and promised him that if he would come back it would never happen again.

9

BILLY MARTIN:
STUBBORN IS HIS NAME

"A leader has to remember that he is a leader, no matter what. He will be strong when you're going good, and when you're going bad. He will show his strength off . . ."

—Billy Martin

After it was over, Billy Martin maintained that the turning point of the season came in Boston when he pulled Jackson out of the ball game and got his team back. Well . . . that's kind of a self-serving way to put it. Taking Billy on his own terms, though, the recapture of his team was effected in two steps. The immediate result of the public humiliation of Reggie Jax, in point of fact, had been the public humiliation of Billy Martin. Not only had George Steinbrenner hung him out and made it seem as if he had been forced to beg and crawl, he had undercut him even further by passing the word that Reggie Jackson ("I am not a vengeful man!") had saved Billy's job by interceding with him on Billy's behalf.

The immediate question didn't seem to be as much whether Billy had won his team back, as whether he had given up so much of himself in the eyes of his players that he had lost his power to lead them. In point of fact, he had given up exactly nothing. But he had to contend with the appearance of being weakened, and when you are a leader you know that appearance is everything.

Billy Martin is a leader. And stubborn is his name. He had told them up in Steinbrenner's suite that he would continue to manage as he saw fit. It was now necessary to prove it to his players by taking the team back from George Steinbrenner.

The first thing Billy had to do was win. He had to turn it around, or he was gone. Never mind that Gabe Paul had told him that the determining factor wasn't going to be his won-lost record. Any manager who keeps losing is going to be fired, and should be. Since that meeting, Martin had lost two straight games. The next four were crucial. He had to break the losing streak by winning the final game in Detroit, then go home to a big weekend series against the Red Sox and reverse the disaster in Boston. And he had to do it with a pitching staff that was shot. A staff so far gone that he was shoveling for a pitcher to start the final game in Detroit.

With the most important four games of his life coming up, here is Billy's situation: His five starting pitchers are Hunter, Torrez and Figueroa, the unfortunate victims of the mayhem in Boston, plus Gullett and Guidry, who had pitched the first two games in Detroit. Hunter has been relegated to the bull pen and practically written off. Figueroa is out of action. The only pitcher in the regular rotation who can start is Torrez, who would be going with three days' rest. Nothing wrong with that. Mike not only can pitch with three days' rest, he wants to pitch with three days' rest. He has been begging to pitch with three days' rest. Billy is a disciple of the five-day rotation himself, but an emergency is an emergency.

But who will that leave for the really crucial three games against Boston? Even with an open date (thank God for those wonderful people who make out the schedule), he has nobody to start the first game except Ken Holtzman, who hadn't pitched for almost a month, or Ken Clay, who had been brought up from the minors when the other kid, Gil Patterson, developed a sore arm. Gullett would pitch the second game, with his customary four days' rest, and Ron Guidry, who really needs five days between starts but had pitched once before with four days and won, would have to start the third.

You're Billy Martin, and your life is on the line, so what do you do? You show your strength off. You don't play it safe. The Boston series is the one that counts, and he is not going to give the first game away. He's going to have to use Holtzman in one of the four games, anyway. He is going to have to find out, in fact, whether he can put Holtzman back in the rotation.

If you're Billy Martin, with your life on the line, you start Ken Holtzman against Detroit, and save Torrez for Boston.

Having made that decision, he shook up his line-up. With a left-hander, Dave Roberts, going for Detroit, he put Cliff Johnson in the field for the first time, playing him at first base instead of Chambliss, DH-ed Lou Piniella, sent Jim Wynn out to left field and put Paul Blair in center field for the slumping Mickey Rivers.

It was a line-up that got him three runs in the first inning. Thurman Munson knocked in two of them with a triple, and scored on Reggie Jax' infield out. Reggie's double and Piniella's single made it 5-1 in the fourth. Cliff Johnson hit a home run in the fifth, his first as a Yankee, to make it 7-2. A laugher. And then, it wasn't. Holtzman, not unexpectedly, ran out of gas in the sixth inning. Tidrow, in a repeat of his Boston performance, was rocked for two home runs and a double, and the Yankees came back to the dugout reeling. The score was 7-7.

Three more runs off Lyle in the seventh, and they were losing, 10-7. In the eighth inning, the Yankees came back. Graig Nettles tied it with a three-run home run, his first in eighteen days. Munson singled, Chambliss batted for Cliff Johnson and singled, and the wheel had turned, as it had a way of turning, to Reggie Jax. Reggie Jax, as he has a way of doing, put the Yankees ahead 12-10, with a line-drive double to the opposite field.

It wasn't over. Detroit made it 12-11 in the ninth, and had the bases loaded with two men out. Martin, who had stuck with Lyle for as long as he could, brought in the only pitcher he had left, Ken Clay. As he handed him the ball, Martin let his eyes swing around the bases. "They're not your fault," he said. "You didn't put them there." The batter was Phil Mankowski, who had come in as a pinch hitter against Tidrow and hit a home run, and had singled in another run off Lyle. Clay got him on a pop fly to Dent, and earned his salary for the season.

Billy Martin came into the clubhouse staggering like a man who had just crawled across a parched and open desert. "Out of my way before I pass out," he cried. "Beer . . . I need beer. Please, somebody. A beer."

The clubhouse was alive, there was a feeling that a turn had been made. And nobody was higher than Jackson. This is what he loves. A big team effort, a late charge and Reggie Jackson coming through in the clutch. "It was unbelievable," he was saying. A tremendous lift. A key victory. "I'm just glad I did my job and didn't let the team down."

You could argue whether that was the key victory of the season, or whether the key victory came in the opening game against Boston. Reggie Jax had the winning hit in that one, too. He wasn't up when that one was over, though. He was down. Way down.

The Red Sox had come to town flexing their muscles. They had followed the massacre of the Yankees by going to Baltimore and taking four straight from the Orioles. They had seven straight victories, and sixteen out of their last eighteen. Bill Campbell was unhittable. In his last ten appearances, he had two wins and eight saves, and an infinitesimal earned-run average of 0.94. The Red Sox were five games ahead of both New York and Baltimore. They had knocked Baltimore out of the race—everybody agreed about that—and by winning two out of the three games in New York, they could just about dispose of the Yankees.

Billy Martin's job was on the line, and everybody knew it. Just as in Detroit, a capacity crowd gave him a standing ovation when he brought the starting line-up to home plate. And as in Detroit, Billy came back suf-

162

fused in an unearthly light, contemplating the effect of his reception on George's digestive tract.

For the fourth straight time, the Red Sox were opening the series with their left-hander, Bill Lee. Otherwise known, to Billy Martin, as "that nut." At least Jim Piersall had the papers to show he was crazy, Martin liked to say; what was Lee's excuse? Never a man to let an ongoing feud get away from him, Billy had arranged to have a dead mackerel hung in Lee's locker. Either Billy had been informed by students of the occult that a dead mackerel is an Oriental bad-luck omen, or he just happened to have a dead mackerel lying around.

"Really romantic, huh?" Lee sniffed.

Lee was out of the game by the fifth inning. Clever people, these Orientals.

It had been Lee versus Hunter for the first game of the Boston Massacre. For the first game in New York it was . . . Hunter versus Lee. A surprise. After the bombardment in Boston, Hunter had been written off. For publication, Catfish maintained stoutly that there was nothing wrong with his arm. No matter how hard he was hit, he always said that. "I'm not discouraged," he would say. "My arm felt good." It hurt like hell. That's why he couldn't get the ball down. But Hunter had a special position on that ball club. He was the guy who had done it all in the past. For half a dozen years he had been the pitcher you wanted out there when you had to win a game. As a leader, Billy understood the power of symbols.

And as a leader, the need for a show of strength. Show—as in showdown. Showdown—as in Steinbrenner. An hour before the game, Billy erased Jackson's name from the line-up, and replaced him with Roy White. Instead of playing in the Mayor's Trophy Game, Reggie had gone for the eye examination Martin had suggested. Martin's story, which wasn't exactly corroborated in all its details, was that the trainer had told him that Jackson's eyes were still dilated. ("I've been worried about his eyes," Martin confided. "Both at bat and in the field.")

When Jackson saw the altered line-up, he slammed

his bat down and walked out to the outfield without bothering to take his glove along.

Whenever Billy benched Jackson, there happened to be a left-hander pitching against them. But in this case, that really didn't apply. In the nine times he had faced Lee during the season, Reggie had had five hits, including two home runs. Besides, Jackson was swinging the bat good. When Jackson is swinging the bat good, he hits anybody.

In the second inning, Gabe Paul sent the club physician to the clubhouse to examine Reggie's eyes. After the doctor had reported back on that modern miracle, a thirty-six-hour dilation, Gabe called the dugout to tell Martin that Jackson was "available."

Hunter went two outs into the ninth inning. The third out was a big one, one of those things that goes practically unnoticed, yet influences a game and, perhaps, the entire season. The scorecard on Hunter was that he pitched a better game than anyone had a right to expect, and though it was a spotty performance, he had gotten better as the game went along.

Although he allowed only five hits, three of them were home runs. A solo shot by Yastrzemski, picking up right where he left off as leadoff man in the second, and two-run shots by Butch Hobson (also in the second) and George Scott (in the fourth). Scott's home run was the difference. The Yankees had taken the lead briefly on Munson's single in the first inning, and Paul Blair's two-run home run had tied the game temporarily in the second. The home-park advantage. Yastrzemski, who always fields marvelously at Yankee Stadium, went up over the wall to make the catch, and came down empty-handed. Barehanded, you might say. The fans in the left-field bleachers had stripped the glove right off his hand. The glove came back, but the ball didn't.

Hunter actually retired the last two batters he faced. But he had walked Bernie Carbo to start off the inning, and with the top of the batting order coming up, Martin brought in Sparky Lyle.

Rick Burleson hit Lyle's first pitch into the gap in right center, and all the way to the fence. Carbo is slow, Rivers is fast, but with two outs, Carbo had been running. Rivers picked the ball up at the fence and made a casual, almost underhanded, flip to the cutoff man. But where was Carbo with the insurance run? Carbo is a poor base runner, Carbo might have stumbled a little rounding second, but still . . . Remember the Rivers throw that had cut off the tying run in the first trip to Boston? Eddie Yost, the third-base coach, had said that under the circumstances, he'd do the same thing every time. But maybe it was sitting there somewhere in the back of his head. Because here, with Rivers seemingly conceding the run, he had held Carbo up. (Ah, the little things that come back to haunt you.) Instead of trailing 6-3, the Yankees went into the bottom of the ninth trailing 5-3. Bill Campbell had come into the game in the sixth inning—early for him—with runners on second and third and nobody out and, as was his habit, got out of the inning without a run being scored. In his three innings, the Yankees had only one hit off him. He was breezing to his fifteenth save of the season, the eleventh straight appearance in which he had either saved the game or won it. Rivers grounds out. Martin sends Available Jackson to the plate to pinch hit for Bucky Dent. Jackson is greeted by boos, and grounds out. Two out, nobody on, and it's beginning to look as if the Yankees are never going to beat the Red Sox again.

Willie Randolph hits a routine fly ball into left center, something between a line drive and a fly. Yaz goes racing over . . . but wait, he has been playing Randolph in too far, and he has apparently misjudged the distance. Instead of slanting back, he has cut straight over. The ball sails over his frantic leap and rolls to the fence, and there goes Willie Randolph into third base. The Yankees are still two runs behind, but they are alive and the tying run, in the person of Roy White, is at bat. White, a switch hitter, originally had been inserted for Jackson, to bat right-handed against Lee. Against Campbell, he is batting left-handed. Carlton Fisk calls for a screwball, a pitch which Campbell uses sparingly, generally when he's going for the third strike. The pitch stays high, and *boom*—it's into the upper deck in right field like a cannon shot.

Two pitches, and the Yankees had climbed back

from the dead. The corpse had sat up. And, a not-in-considerable item, Bill Campbell had to keep pitching. Because even that early in the season, the question for the Red Sox was how often they were going to be able to go to Campbell before his arm fell off.

Zimmer allowed him to pitch the tenth inning, and that was it. Five innings, the Boston manager decided, were more than enough. With three left-handers due up for the Yankees in the eleventh, he brought in Ramon Hernandez, a left-handed relief pitcher Boston had just picked up to fill the obvious need. He didn't get a batter out. He walked Nettles, and immediately committed a balk to send him to second. Very important. Now they have to walk Rivers, and pitch to Reggie Jackson. If Rivers had sacrificed the runner to second, Jackson would have been walked. Reggie slashed the first pitch down the right-field line, and the ball game was over.

Roy White, the man who had started in his place, had tied it. Jackson himself had won it.

The hit that mattered was Roy White's. If it's possible to say that one swing of the bat could turn the season around, then Roy White had turned the season around. Instead of six games behind and fading, the Yankees were four behind and coming on. The wind had turned. You could feel it in the air.

Everybody could, that is, except Reggie. The Yankees had come pouring out of the dugout toward him and he had accepted their congratulations with considerable restraint. When the newspapermen gathered around him, he was flat and uncommunicative.

"Just lucky, I guess," he said.

"Lucky to be a Yankee?" someone asked, trying hard.

Jackson looked straight ahead. "Mmmmmm," he explained.

What were his emotions?

"I try to forget my emotions these days."

Did he feel good about the hit? "Yes, I feel good."

Was he excited about it? "Yes, I was excited."

Did it make him happy? "Oh, yes, I'm happy."

And what about his removal from the starting line-up? "I don't want to comment about that."

Were his eyes okay? "My eyes are okay."

How did he feel before the game? "I forget how I felt. I forget a lot of things lately. I can't say anything. If you were in my water for a week, you'd understand why."

For Saturday afternoon it was Torrez versus Tiant. Mike Torrez was finally getting his start, a full week after he had been riddled for thirteen hits and three home runs. "All I've got to say," he had said at the time, "is that they're going to be very uncomfortable the next time I pitch." And they were. Although not the way that Torrez had seemed to threaten. Torrez had his fast ball dipping low on the outside corner all day, and ended the Red Sox home-run jubilee that had grown to thirty-three over ten games. Fifteen outs on ground balls, helped by two tremendous plays by Nettles.

Luis Tiant had missed the Boston series, but he was coming off a three-hit shutout against the Baltimore Orioles. Luis was finally beginning to look like Luis. In his four previous starts, he had two shutouts and part of another one. But not today, Luis. The first batter to face him, Mickey Rivers, hit a home run, and there went that. Nettles, who hits his home runs in bunches, had another one with two men on.

If it's the Red Sox versus the Yankees on a Saturday, it's got to be Game of the Week. Nevertheless, Tiant had no trouble with Reggie Jax. Held him hitless, struck him out once, and had him flinging his bat and helmet around after he'd gotten him on a little pop-up. I don't know what the national television audience did about it. In Yankee Stadium, they booed.

The final score was 5-1. The Yankees were three games behind. The corpse was sitting up and taking nourishment.

The match-up for the final game was Gullett versus Cleveland. As the winning pitcher in the game featuring the dugout embroglio, Cleveland had run his record as a Yankee-killer to 7-1.

As for Gullett, if they weren't paying him $2 million to win this kind of game, what were they paying him for?

It was a World Series atmosphere. A crowd of 55,039—another "largest regular season attendance in reconstructed Yankee Stadium." If the Red Sox win it, they leave town four games ahead and can tell themselves that they had only expected to win one out of three in New York, anyway. If the Yankees win, they have cut the lead to two games and have wiped the Massacre off the books, come off the canvas, avenged their honor . . . and bounced back into the race.

Gullett loaded the bases in the first inning with nobody out. Transport that situation back a week, and the Red Sox would have been singing Hallelujah songs of power. This week, Gullett got out of it with one run. There is always a feeling that when you let that kind of pitcher off the hook, you're not going to get another chance. And, sure enough, the Yankees were holding a 4-1 lead going into the ninth. Roy White, who had done it with one swing of the bat in the opener, was doing it this time like an old pro. The Yankees, as a team, were doing it like the 1976 Yankees, with Rivers running, and White moving him along, and Munson and Chambliss, the contact men, driving them in. The running game of the pre-Jackson era, which Martin seemed to have abandoned. In the first inning, with Rivers running, White slapped the ball right through the position the shortstop had abandoned, and Chambliss singled Rivers home. With Rivers running again in the third inning, the second baseman covered, and White lined the ball into right. Munson slapped a single to left to score Rivers, and Chambliss brought White in with a sacrifice fly. It remained 3-1 into the seventh, and then Rivers led off with his third single. White fouled off a couple of three-and-two pitches, and drew a walk. Munson singled Rivers in again, and in the spirit of the Yankees of '76, White and Munson pulled off a double steal.

In this tale of two cities, there was still one piece of unfinished business. George Steinbrenner was going to make his presence felt. His team was beating the Boston team, and he wanted to spread the word that his fans were infinitely superior, too. Just coincidentally, Steinbrenner's picture had been flashed on the screen at Fenway Park on the night he was there, above the caption, "George Steinbrenner without his horse." Now, that's kind of funny. But not to George. His dignity as the principal owner of the New York Yankees had been affronted, and apologies from the Red Sox front office (who must have been laughing their heads off) did not avail.

Up in Boston, Mickey Rivers had been pelted with metal objects to the point of wearing a batting helmet in the field. A smoke bomb had been thrown onto the field, and there had been assorted acts of the hooliganism that afflicts American society. Few places, we may add, are worse than New York in this respect, and nowhere is it worse than in Yankee Stadium. Never mind. George wasn't out to lecture his own fans, he was out to praise them.

As the ninth inning was about to start, an announcement "from management" came over the public address system: "The Yankees want to take this opportunity to say, 'We're proud of you all . . . Not for the fact that 157,460 of you came to support us this weekend, but because, by the way you conducted yourself for this series, you have shown the nation, and particularly Boston, that New York fans know how to pack a ball park and conduct themselves in a manner our city can be proud of . . .' The Yankees are proud of you, the greatest fans in the world."

That's a twenty-five-way dead heat. Every city has "the greatest fans in the world," unless the owner's name is C. O. Finley. To answer the question that is undoubtedly on everyone's lips, a fan proves he is a "great fan" by not complaining when he's subjected to public-relations announcements over the public address system.

No sooner had the echo of the announcement died, than two kids wearing hard hats could be seen marching through the lower grandstand with a sheet banner reading, "Red Sox World Champions 1977." The fans arose and pelted them with anything that came to hand, and it took a couple of stadium cops to prevent the banner from being ripped from their hands. Maybe what Steinbrenner meant was that the New York police were more efficient.

His team came very close to disillusioning him even further. The Red Sox came up in the ninth, and all of a sudden it looked as if it were going to be a replay of the first game. In reverse. Gullett started it off all wrong by walking Carlton Fisk. Scott doubled down the left-field line, and Butch Hobson, whom Gullett had completely overpowered three straight times, hit a wicked line drive that went right back into Gullett's glove. Very fortunate for the Yankees, and also a tip-off that Gullett's fast ball was beginning to lengthen out. Though Steinbrenner was screaming at Martin to take Gullett out, Martin left him in to pitch to Tommy Helms and Steve Dillard. The Red Sox had picked up Helms at the beginning of the week, after their brilliant right-fielder, Dewey Evans, had injured his knee. Gullett had also handled Helms three times with ease. This time, Helms stroked a soft single to left to drive in two runs, and all of a sudden it was the Yankees against the Red Sox again.

Dillard singled, and continued on to second when Rivers' throw to third was way off line. Now the tying run is on third, the go-ahead run is on second, and Martin calls for Dick Tidrow. Tidrow's job is to get one batter, Rick Burleson. If it were a week ago, you know what would have happened. In many ways, Burleson is the leader of the Red Sox. He had come to the top of the dugout at the end of Steinbrenner's message to shake his fist at him. But this is this week. Burleson runs the count down, fouls off pitch after pitch, and finally hits a high chopper, wide of third base. Nettles has to make the play to first, the score is tied, and the winning run has moved over to third. But, you know, there is a rhythm to a ball game, and there was the sense that the rhythm had built to Burleson's time at bat.

In comes Sparky Lyle to pitch to Freddie Lynn. Lynn hits the ball deep to right, and for one second . . . But Paul Blair, who had gone in at the beginning of the inning for Jackson, goes back close to the fence, and the inning is over.

If you followed patterns, you'd say that the pattern of the first game was still holding. But not really. The Yankees had tied it, out of nowhere, with two out. The Red Sox rally had come early, and had petered out. And, of course, there was one other difference. The Yankees, as the home team, had another turn at bat.

Bill Campbell got the call again, and the five innings he had pitched on Friday night were showing. He was able to get Mickey Rivers on a ground ball, and that was the last good thing that was going to happen. Roy White, his nemesis, worked him for a walk and wheeled around to third on Munson's single. Chambliss was intentionally passed to set up a force play at home. It would have been Reggie Jax up there, with a chance to perform the heroics, if Reggie hadn't been taken out of the game. Instead, it was Paul Blair. With the infield drawn in, Blair hit a high chopper over the third-baseman's head, and the Yankees had swept the series.

It was a brand new season. "It isn't as easy as we were making it," Don Zimmer acknowledged. "Baseball's no different than life," said Billy Martin. "You have your ups and your downs. You just hope people stick with you in the lows, because the highs are going to come."

He had been saying that through the worst of times. "We're going to win, because we have the best team."

Billy Martin can't be discouraged. Or can he? As he was leaving to catch the bus that was waiting to take them to the airport, he reached into his pocket and took out a picture of St. Jude, the patron saint of hopeless causes. "St. Jude," he said, "you really came through for me."

He had been carrying it with him since Detroit, right? Wrong. He has been carrying it with him since he entered professional baseball in 1946. It tells something about Billy Martin that he can still see himself as a lost cause. Always the bad boy whom nobody will take the trouble to understand.

You can't say that Billy doesn't give them plenty of chances, can you?

The plane would be taking them to Toronto, where they would almost certainly extend their winning streak. All right, Toronto had beaten them the first two times they had faced each other. But that had been during the rotten beginning. The team that had just risen up to smite the Red Sox wasn't going to have any trouble with the Toronto Blue Jays, for crissake.

Toronto defeated them again, in the first two games

171

the New York Yankees had ever played on foreign soil. As good as the Yankees had been against the Red Sox, that's how bad they were in Toronto.

As a case in point, Ken Clay, in his first start, took a 4-3 lead into the seventh inning, despite miserable support, and became a loser because of the following revolting occurrences: A routine fly ball fell in front of Mickey Rivers; Reggie Jackson (who had complained bitterly before the game about having been removed from the Boston game for defensive purposes) dropped a fly ball hit right to him; Chris Chambliss picked up a ground ball and started to fire it home, but the ball rolled off the back of his hand; Graig Nettles overran the base runner on a misfired squeeze play, and Thurman Munson, trying to throw Nettles a lead pass in the race back to third, hit the base runner on the head.

It didn't cost them anything in the standings, because the Red Sox, who had never seemed to recover from the shock of Roy White's home run, were into a losing streak that was going to extend to nine games. Six days after the Red Sox left New York, and only ten days after the Yankees had hit rock bottom, the Yankees were back in first place. They held on to it exactly one week.

By then, the Red Sox had turned it around, and won six out of seven, and for the next three weeks, the Red Sox and Baltimore passed the lead back and forth, never separated by more than a single game.

Baltimore? *Baltimore?* Yeah, the Orioles had put together successive streaks of seven straight, and seven out of nine. Fourteen out of sixteen. The Orioles had come to stay. It was going to be a three-team race, down to the wire.

10

MUNSON IN JULY

"George doesn't want competition. He want a slaughter . . . He's destroyed Billy. He's made him into nothing.
Not a single guy on the club is happy. . . ."
                              —Who is that Masked Man?

July was not a good month for the New York Yankees.
On July 2, they were in first place. On July 31, they
were third.

July was not a good month for George Steinbrenner.
No month can be called good which begins with the
Justice Department announcing that they are investigating you, and ends with your $3 million Superstar
unable to throw.

It was not a good month for Billy Martin, since he
almost got fired two or three times, tying the all-time
record held by himself. He also threatened to fire the
press twice or, at least, to deny them access to himself, his ball club and his facilities.

For Reggie Jackson, it was a terrible month. At various times he was benched, insulted, isolated and sued.

As for Thurman Munson, I don't know what the hell
he thought he was doing.

After Steinbrenner's whirlwind descent upon the
Yankee clubhouse, and subsequent departure for

Tampa, Thurman let it be known that he was becoming mighty unhappy about the demands being made on him. "One day they stress one thing, and the next day something else. First Reggie and I get along; then Billy and I. If they just let us go out, and let us play, we'll get together. One thing ticks me off; I can't stand to be part of a circus every day. It's like the bleeping big top. I'd rather be on a last place club and enjoying myself."

For whatever reason, it was Thurman who got the big top spinning again.

Baseball is a funny game. The Yankees won three out of six, and took over first place from the reeling Red Sox. They then won six out of seven without gaining a thing, and went into Baltimore the next day and lost it. "Baltimore's been a hot team," the ever optimistic Billy Martin had said, as the Yankees prepared to open the series. "Maybe it's time for them to cool off."

The series having come to an end, he returned to the clubhouse, declaiming in tones both sonorous and dolorous: " 'Don't tell me how many storms you encountered,' the shipowner said to the captain, 'just tell me if you brought the ship home safely.' "

Who had written that? Martin was asked.

"Anonymous," grinned Mr. Anonymous.

The Yankees had cooled the Orioles off for exactly one game, and had then been iced three straight. The winning hit in the last two came off the bat of the no-longer-anonymous Eddie Murray, giving him a grand total of five winning hits in the Orioles' seven victories over the Yankees.

Storm warnings had been posted before that final game, when a "prominent player," also anonymous, accused Steinbrenner of dictating the line-up. "George doesn't want competition," he had added. "He wants a slaughter. To win, you need nine good players plus some capable utility players and a pitching staff. George wants twenty-five superstars. George doesn't care about anybody's feelings. To him, we're not professionals, we're all employees. He treats everybody like that. He's done something to everybody. He's destroyed

Billy. He's made him nothing. Not a single guy on the club is happy, except Willie Randolph." (Willie is always happy.)

"It's a lie!" said Steinbrenner over the phone from Tampa. "And any player who says it is a liar." The only suggestion he had made to Billy, he said, was to use Lou Piniella as the Designated Hitter against all pitching. "I put together some statistics on Carlos May recently, and they were horrendous. He's been hitting something like .130 with men on base. I wasn't ordering Billy to play Piniella; I was just suggesting it. I'm tired of these players saying I'm putting pressure on him. He hasn't had one iota of pressure from me about the line-up. Billy's doing everything expected of him. The people laying down on him are the pitchers, the catchers, the infielders and the outfielders. Especially the pitchers."

The "prominent player" hadn't really differed that much with Steinbrenner about the players' lack of effort. ("$20,000 and a World Series ring isn't bad. Maybe they found they didn't like winning so much.") He had been charging Steinbrenner with making a bad situation worse. "He expects us to run away with it," he said. "We'll run away with it when our pitching comes around."

His comment, when the not-unexpected denials came in from Martin and Steinbrenner, was short and pithy. "Do you believe that?" he asked. He then went on to question the use of Cliff Johnson as DH—especially in the fifth spot, where he had hit the previous day while Roy White was hitting eighth—and to decry both the frequent benching of Mickey Rivers and the failure to bat Rivers and White, the keys to the Yankee running game, at the top of the order.

And now you're beginning to wonder whether his criticism is being directed at Steinbrenner so much as at the "nothing" manager. And why he'd object to the use of Cliff Johnson, whose contribution already included three home runs in a single game in Toronto.

To put an end to the suspense, the "prominent player" was unmasked, eventually, as Thurman Munson. To try to understand what he was talking about, it's necessary to look into what was happening.

A week earlier, Munson had been hit with a foul tick which had necessitated seven stitches in his left pinky. He didn't miss a game. Stitches and all, he had led the Yankees to their opening-game victory in Baltimore by hitting a home run and single and knocking in four runs. In the second game, he had put the Yankees into a temporary two-run lead in the eighth inning with another home run. He was second in the league in runs batted in, and fifth in batting.

On the day before Munson spoke out, two things had happened:

1. The Yankees had fallen out of first place by losing, 6-0, to Ross Grimsley, who doesn't pitch shutouts. It was, in fact, his first shutout in two and a half years.

2. Thurman Munson had removed himself from the game with a "throbbing headache," after taking two fouls off his mask. Before the game, he had been cut over the eye by a pipe that had somehow been dislodged from the top of the batting cage. Add the sore finger, and you can draw a picture of a man who had spent an uncomfortable night thinking long thoughts about the meaning of it all.

A day earlier, Dell Alston had been used as the left-handed DH for the first time. Add to that the various references to Carlos May, Cliff Johnson, Lou Piniella and Roy White, and the persistent problem of the Designated Hitter seems to be weaving in and out of the picture, doesn't it? In point of fact, the whole DH situation was in the process of being overhauled. Jim Wynn had been taken off the roster, after going an almost unbelievable one for forty-four. Carlos May had been something less than a thrill a minute from the other side too; Steinbrenner was obviously right about that. In Steinbrenner's view, Carlos had come to camp overweight, and had then compounded the crime by resisting Steinbrenner's offer of a bonus if he could lose fifteen pounds. Steinbrenner had come to dislike Carlos so much that he was accusing him of being the "prominent player" well after everybody knew it was Munson. Steinbrenner was right about Lou Piniella, too—Piniella was outhitting everybody on the team, and was obviously going to have to be played with reasonable regularity. That wouldn't bother Munson.

Piniella was one of the inner group, and Munson is ferociously loyal to the Old Boys. Also the old ways. If you're DH-ing Johnson—or Alston—you've got to play Piniella in the outfield, and that knocks Roy White out of the line-up. Roy White is not only the oldest of the Old Boys, he is, along with Rivers, the heart of the running game that had been abandoned with the coming of Reggie Jax. So here we are again, back as always to the Living Presence. If you add Cliff Johnson and Lou Piniella to Jackson, you've got a power line-up.

So whom was Munson attacking? Well, why would Munson have to go off the record to attack Steinbrenner? He had been doing that at every opportunity. It was the only pleasure he seemed to get out of an otherwise unhappy season. But when you said that Steinbrenner was dictating the line-up, you were also saying that Martin allowed him to. Billy Martin's greatest boast is that nobody tells him how to manage. For Munson to have said that openly would have amounted to a formal break in diplomatic relations.

And that brings us to one final prospect for the Designated Hitter. The logical man for the job. Reggie Jackson. Tremendous hitter, rotten fielder. That's practically the job description. As recently as the trip to Toronto, Billy had announced his intention of making Reggie the DH. Do that and you could go back to the team that had won the pennant in '76. Until, of course, you were fired, which would be the day after tomorrow. When it came to Reggie Jackson, Steinbrenner was indeed dictating the line-up. If that's what Munson was talking about, then Munson was right.

Whatever his motives, Munson managed to pick the day after the Yankees had fallen out of first place to start his latest controversy, and when the reporters got George back on the phone for the second go-round George began to elaborate on his dissatisfaction with the pitching. The more he elaborated, the more he zeroed in on Billy Martin. "We should have the five best starters in the league," he said. "If this is the way they're pitching, the question is if they're handled right."

He was also convinced that he had the best starting line-up. He could prove it scientifically. "I took the line-ups of the Yankees, Boston and Baltimore, and wrote them side by side on a piece of paper. If I had to pick them player by player, you know how many Yankees I'd pick." Eight out of eight, presumably. Seven, anyway.

He didn't exactly say that Baltimore had the number three player in every position. What he did say was, "If Weaver can keep that team hanging in there, he should be Manager of the Year."

Where did that leave Billy Martin? "We got Billy everything he asked for, I shelled out a hell of a lot of dough. If we don't win, then I'm stupid for spending all the money, Gabe Paul for picking the players, and Billy for handling them."

For his part, Billy was willing enough to confirm that Steinbrenner was always sending him notes on statistics, *dit-de-dah-dit*. "I don't pay any attention to them," he said, very clearly. As to interference on the line-up, "I think what they are really thinking—they know George isn't making out the line-up—what they're thinking, I think, is that the whole club line-up has been changed since we got Reggie."

Bull's-eye. You will note that he said "they," not "he." The prominent Yankee had been voicing a general complaint by the players who had waltzed to a pennant without Reggie, and were stumbling all over the Re-Entry Ballroom with him. Everybody second-guesses the manager, and nobody second-guesses him more than his own players. If U. S. Grant had been leading an army of ballplayers, they'd have second-guessed him right up the steps of Appomattox Courthouse. And if George Steinbrenner had been Abraham Lincoln, he'd have told Grant how to dress, whom to take along, and which hand to use to open the door. While Martin was in his hotel room denying that there was interference from Steinbrenner, he received a telephone message telling him to call Steinbrenner in Tampa.

As soon as the team arrived in Milwaukee, Billy Martin called a press conference to state, for the record, that the stories about front-office interference were completely false. "Managing this team is tough enough without picking up the papers and seeing the manager against the owner, the owner against the players. I listen to the owners. I listen to the general manager. I still do my own managing. Would I have been fired three times if I was a company man?"

If the stories continued, he told the newspapermen, he was going to have to do something. What was he going to do? Unmask the "prominent player"? Hang up on Steinbrenner publicly? Well, no. "I'll keep the press off the bus and planes, and out of the clubhouse."

Sure, Billy, and maybe even off the sports pages. The old Billy Martin blame-it-on-the-press. Billy had a very good reason for wanting an end to that day's soap opera. George Steinbrenner was coming to Milwaukee, and Billy wanted no more talk out of his players. The official version, right from George's own lips, was that his visit had nothing to do with this latest controversy. Heavens, no. He had been scheduled to go to Duluth for the christening of one of his ships, anyway, and so he had set up this appointment with Billy more than a week ago to discuss what was wrong with the team. Gee, that's funny. The Yankees had been on a winning streak when they left New York. Catfish Hunter had just pitched his second straight complete game, the Yankees had become the first team in the majors to go over the million mark in attendance, and George had sat up in his box exuding happiness, good will and confidence. "We have no excuses going into the Baltimore series," he had said. "We are hitting. Our pitching is great."

Steinbrenner met with Martin and the coaches in his hotel suite, and went out to the ball park to watch a less-than-satisfactory ball game, the one game the Yankees lost in Milwaukee. Hunter had his home-run ball going again, and the Yankees fell behind, 9-3. Helped no end by Mickey Rivers' second home run in two innings, they scored five runs in the eighth inning, and had Nettles, Chambliss and Jackson coming up in the ninth. Reggie Jax, back in the line-up after resting a groin injury for two days, took three mighty swings to end the game, and there was no joy in Steinbrenner-ville.

179

Nor, it seemed, in Mickey Rivers. Although Mickey had probably never hit two home runs in a game before in his life, let alone in consecutive innings, he refused to talk to anybody. Maybe he wanted to find out whether a good sulk after a good game could be as profitable as a public sulk while the game was going on. With Mickey, who knows?

Late that night, there was a meeting in Steinbrenner's room with Piniella and Munson. And eventually, as an uninvited guest, Billy Martin. This is the meeting that remained secret until both Steinbrenner and Martin gave it to Bob Ajemian of *Time* for their World Series issue, and in certain ways it casts a light back across the entire season.

Steinbrenner's version is that Munson and Piniella came banging on his door at 12:30 A.M., just as he was going to bed. They wanted to tell him that the team was in chaos, and could not win with Martin as manager. "They urged me to become more involved with the team. They told me, 'You run your businesses, why don't you do the same with the team?'"

This is presumably happening, remember, two days after Munson had taken Steinbrenner to task, admittedly without attribution, for either causing or contributing mightily to the prevailing chaos, by constant interference.

The players' versions differed in some regards but not in certain essentials.

Munson said he had been called to the suite by Steinbrenner. "What I told Steinbrenner was, 'If you're going to fire the guy, fire him and get it over with. Nobody can live with the kind of pressure you're putting on him.'"

Piniella's story was that he had just happened to be with Munson when Steinbrenner summoned him, and had gone along for the ride. "It was understood that nothing of the meeting could come out. We were not entirely on Billy's side." The real issues, according to Piniella, were the restrictive clauses in Martin's contract. "We said, if we have a lame-duck manager worrying about his future, we're going to have a manager who can't do his job." According to Piniella, they had said, "Straighten out his contract and remove the clauses. If not, fire him."

Steinbrenner's rebuttal, which does seem to make more sense in this regard, is that nothing was said about Martin's contract until Martin brought it up himself. "When Billy came in the room, I asked him what his problems were, and he said one of them was the restrictions in the contract, that he didn't feel I was backing him, that the meetings with Gabe were driving him crazy. I said to him, 'You knew what the contract was when you signed it, but if it bothers you so much, I'll change it.'"

As to Munson and Piniella: "The reasons they came to me I won't discuss, because I don't want to put them on the spot."

Billy Martin's version went like this:

"It's one-thirty in the morning and I'm going back to my room. I heard Thurman's voice and Piniella's voice in George's suite. I say, 'What the hell's going on here?' and George said, 'Nothing, I'm going to sleep.' So I pushed the door open and there in the lavatory is Thurman and Piniella.

"George said, 'Calm down, Billy.' Right at the door, he lied to me. He doesn't know what the truth is.

"George said they were talking about personnel, and he said, 'C'mon, Billy, what's wrong with the club?' I said, 'You, you're what's wrong with the club.' He was shocked and surprised."

Well, there was obviously a great deal more going on than that, since they remained in the suite until five or six in the morning. When it was over, Martin had agreed that Jackson would bat cleanup, Piniella would become the Designated Hitter against all pitching, and certain pitchers would go on a four-day rotation. Steinbrenner had agreed to strike the offending clauses from the contract. Or, to be more precise, to remove the clause that put Billy in breach of contract if he violated any of the other clauses.

There's more to it. Steinbrenner had been telling other writers the Milwaukee story, off the record, during the final month of the season, to prove to them how bad things had become. That's one of Steinbrenner's favorite tricks. Just when he's got your blood pounding, he'll say, "That's off the record." A very vexing situation for writers. Steinbrenner would tell them things about Martin, off the record, that were almost beyond belief. Martin would tell them equally scarifying things about Steinbrenner, on the record. Since they were debarred from quoting Steinbrenner on Martin, they were often reluctant to quote Martin on Steinbrenner. "It was almost an unspoken agreement," one of them says. "If your pencil was out and writing, and Billy would crop up with something, you didn't stop writing, and that's when it would come out. When it came down to where he was on the verge of losing the job, and it was obvious that it was choking him, he was almost protected, I think, by us, to a degree. He said things I couldn't believe he would say."

Steinbrenner's off-the-record story about the Milwaukee meeting went something like this: George had just gotten into bed, preparatory to an early-morning flight to Duluth, when Munson and Piniella knocked on his door. "When are you going to run this place like you run your other companies, and step in and do something?" they had asked. "The locker room is a shambles." "Oh," said George, "I thought you were all in support of your manager. I'm really surprised to see you here." An hour and a half later, Martin came to the door. Realizing that a very bad scene could be in the making if he didn't handle it right, George invited Billy in and told him there were two ballplayers with him. "I ordered them to come up here," George told Billy, although the truth of the matter, according to what George told at least one writer, was that the players had asked to come up. "They had told me earlier that they wanted to see me."

Martin's version was pretty much the same as the one he gave when the *Time* story broke—with one notable addition. After he had pushed past Steinbrenner and found nobody there, he had gone to the bathroom, opened the door, and found the players hiding there, huddled together. "Billy, this isn't what it seems to be," they had said. "Don't jump to conclusions, now." Jumping to a conclusion, Billy had challenged Munson, and it had taken both Piniella and Steinbrenner to hold him off.

What really happened in there will probably never be completely revealed. What is known is that Piniella was in left field the next day, batting fourth for the first time all year (Martin's little joke, perhaps). Jackson was batting sixth, Roy White was batting second as DH (the first time he had DH-ed all year), and Ed Figueroa was the starting pitcher after three days' rest.

We'll get back to that. There are still a few questions about that meeting in Steinbrenner's suite.

Whether it was Steinbrenner or the ballplayers who initiated the meeting is, of course, crucial. Munson may have told George he would quit if Martin were fired over the Jackson brawl. That didn't mean he was crazy about Martin as a manager. Go back to Thurman's quote in Detroit: "One day they stress one thing, and the next day something else. First Reggie and I get along; then Billy and I." So they weren't getting along that well.

If you look at Munson's unattributed quote, and his version of what he said in the suite, his comments can be interpreted in very much the same way. In the first instance, he said, "He's destroyed Billy. He's made him nothing." In the second, "Nobody can live with the kind of pressure you're putting on him."

Martin's suite was right next to Steinbrenner's. I suppose he could have heard their voices as he was walking by. So what? What's so terrible about the owner talking to a couple of ballplayers, unless Martin had reason to suspect that they were talking about him?

With most managers, it wouldn't be so terrible. But Billy Martin is Billy Martin. In Detroit, the beginning of the end had come for him when he was called up to the front office and found Willie Horton, with whom he had been having some difficulties, with the Tigers' general manager, Jim Campbell. "What's he doing here?" Billy had demanded.

"We have a problem," Campbell said.

"Any problems I have with him," said Billy, "I settle downstairs, not up here. If you want to talk to him, you talk to him. I'll talk to him in the locker room."

There is a chain of command in baseball. Or, at

least, there used to be. No player is supposed to go to the front office without asking the manager's permission. There's a name for circumventing that code. It's called "walking up the back stairs."

But was this really the same thing? Steinbrenner does socialize with his players, in season and out. Lou Piniella is one of his favorites. Sweet Lou is everybody's favorite. Quick-tempered on the field, but warm and good-natured off. Handsome, witty and by far the most open and candid player on a team not noted for openness. Where the other players would give information on the condition that they weren't quoted, Piniella would come out of a Steinbrenner pep talk, or one of Martin's meetings, and tell the press, "Sure, you can quote me. This is a fuckin' circus."

When Steinbrenner would try to tell him to be more discreet, Lou would just laugh at him. "You're a bullshitter and I'm a bullshitter. We understand each other." He spent so much time in Steinbrenner's office that they had a regular routine. "Are you up here to bother me again?" George would growl.

"I got to talk to you."

"I don't want to talk to you, Piniella. I got nothing to say to you."

If Munson had wanted to talk to Steinbrenner, or Steinbrenner had wanted to send for Munson, Piniella would have been the natural choice to set it up. "I tried to do a favor," Piniella has said, "and I end up looking bad." I mean, they hid in the bathroom. Martin could hardly have made that up. When two men hide in the bathroom, they're doing something they're not overly proud of.

So now we are back to the question we asked at the beginning: Just what was Munson trying to do?

"Jackson and Munson are so much alike that it's laughable. They are two of the most insecure people I've ever met. They need the constant recognition, the constant approval, the assurance that 'you are the greatest, you're this, you're that.' A pat on the ass. And Billy would do it with Thurman. He would not do it with Jax, partly because he doesn't have a high regard for him as a ballplayer—as a hitter, yes, but as a ballplayer he doesn't like him very much. Partly because his recommendation was to get Rudi. And largely because Jackson was Steinbrenner's boy, and he was going to get back at Steinbrenner by his attitude toward Jackson."

—sportswriter's view

Martin didn't stroke Munson that much in 1976, but he sure did stroke him in 1977. There comes to mind a scene which took place during the press conference on the morning of the second World Series game. Martin, having made some comments and answered many questions, had turned away from the microphone. Then he came back to say, "Oh, yeah, I want to say a few words about what a magnificent catcher Thurman Munson is. He's brilliant." Nobody within Billy Martin's memory had been able to call a game as brilliantly as Thurman. Thurman was so brilliant that even when he wasn't hitting, he was invaluable to the team. Irreplaceable.

Something kind of forced about it, huh?

The dirty secret of the New York Yankees is that Billy Martin calls pitches for Thurman Munson.

At Texas, Billy called every pitch for Jim Sundberg, who had come to him as a rookie and immediately showed himself to be the best defensive catcher in the league. Sundberg let the world know that he didn't like it. Billy didn't care. When Billy came to the Yankees, Munson said, loud and clear, "If he thinks he's going to call pitches here, he's got another think coming."

Well, maybe he didn't call them in previous seasons, but when he found his job on the line he most certainly did. And wouldn't you have liked to have been in the room when Billy told Thurman he was going to have to look to the bench in certain situations? Munson has an ego. Munson takes pride in his baseball savvy. He is a genuine student of hitting. He is a smart base runner. But as far as Billy is concerned, he doesn't call a good game. As far as Billy is concerned, Munson has never been able to get it into his head that you don't give a good hitter a chance to beat you on the pitch he hits best.

But, then, you don't have to force the catcher to look to the bench. The easy way to do it is to give the signs to the pitcher. How many pitches Billy calls is open to question. He certainly calls all pitchouts. He almost certainly calls the key pitches in the crucial parts of the game. He may very well call the whole game.

And that was another of the internal conflicts that pulled at the 1977 Yankees. It remained submerged, I suppose, because Munson had an even stronger reason than Martin for keeping it submerged. Tacit or spoken, a formula for living with it was worked out. Billy called the pitches, and told the world how brilliantly Thurman called them.

It couldn't remain completely submerged, however. One writer who caught an undertone of hostility in something Munson said about Martin fairly early in the season blurted out, "Hey, I thought you and Billy were friends."

"Used to be," said Munson. "Used to be."

Billy has never been known to be the soul of discretion, either. When you're with friends, you get to talking, and Billy is a talker. "If we don't win the pennant this year," Billy told one of them, "nobody's going to blame Munson. I do it, and if I do it wrong, then it's my fault. And if I do it wrong, and someone says Munson didn't call the right pitch, I'm going to say it's *his* fault. What you going to do?"

How good a catcher is Thurman Munson? Let's put it this way: Munson is a hitter who catches, not a catcher who hits. At this stage of the game, he's a bat. Period. It wasn't always so. Munson is tough, remember. Munson plays hurt. Not just when he gets banged up or stitched up. Always. Munson has a damaged right shoulder. All you have to do is look at him. He throws sidearm because he can't throw overhand. Since you can't throw as hard sideways, he tries to compensate with a quick release. When he's throwing badly, it's the quick release he talks about; so does everybody else. A neat confusion of cause and effect. At one time, the Yankees also put out a story that under Martin's system, the second baseman and shortstop were not allowed to move toward the base until the pitch was by the batter, which would mean that Munson was always throwing to an open base. A neat confusion of fantasy and reality.

The statistics tell the story on Munson. In 1970, his first year, he had eight errors and ten passed balls. In 1971, he had only one error, and that came when he was knocked unconscious on a play at the plate. He also had nine passed balls. Generally speaking, a catcher will have a certain amount of trouble in his first two years and then settle into his natural groove. Munson appeared to be something extraordinary, and then all of a sudden he wasn't.

Except where it is indicated, the number of games played by the catchers in the following chart are reasonably equal:

	Passed Balls			Errors		
	Munson	Bench	Fisk	Munson	Bench	Fisk
1970	10	9		8	12	
1971	9	6		1	9	
1972	9	2	8	15	6	15
1973	10	3	3	12	4	14
1974	6	3	2*	22	6	6*
1975	9	0	0**	23	7	8**
1976	12	5	7	12	2	12
1977	10	5	4	12	5	11

* 50 games
** 71 games

Good catchers can make errors. They do not have that many passed balls unless there is some physical reason. When you play with an injury, you have to compensate somewhere.

When Munson's shoulder bunches up to the point where it becomes painful for him to raise his arm, he has to compensate by thinking high. Low pitches get away from him for passed balls, and even then his pitchers will get charged with wild pitches on high balls which Thurman would normally handle with ease.

One other thing. Thurman has streaks of atrocious throwing, followed by streaks of throwing very well. When he's throwing poorly, he also gets a lot of passed balls, and usually does not hit very well, either. And then all of a sudden, everything turns completely around. You look at that pattern, and it almost screams out, *cortisone!* Listen, you don't think the Yankees would continue to be so secretive about injuries if they were always found out, do you?

Before Steinbrenner left Milwaukee to keep his appointment with the hull of a ship, he promised to stop off in Kansas City on his way home, to tell the players personally that Billy Martin was managing the team without any interference from the owner. A very difficult decision for George to make. He hadn't done his Rockne routine for three whole weeks now.

If he had been able to stay in Milwaukee another day, he would have been able to see the Yankees win with the new line-up. Piniella, as we said, batting fourth; Rivers and White at the top of the batting order. Speaking of the running game, Roy White stole home. Speaking of Reggie Jax, Reggie hit two home runs and made a tumbling, juggling catch.

Billy continued to use the line-up that had been forged in the Milwaukee hotel suite until it lost, which happened to be the next day in Kansas City. For the second game of the series, it was Jackson batting fourth for the first time since mid-May, and Dell Alston, who had been hitting well, back as DH. In the third one, it was the pre-Milwaukee line-up: Randolph leading off, Cliff Johnson as the Designated Hitter and Chambliss back at cleanup.

That's how long Billy kept his agreement. But, it should be added, the Yankees were in the process of losing all three games. If Billy was going down the drain, he was going to go down his own way.

There was one other piece of unfinished business that carried over from Milwaukee. Catfish Hunter had gone on the radio before the final game, to be interviewed for the pre-game show, and when he was asked about the pitching rotation, he said, "I don't think we have one. I think you go from one day to the next not knowing who is going to pitch." At Oakland, the rotation had been made out three weeks in advance. "Over here, we know one day ahead. That's it. You can't prepare yourself to pitch."

The trouble with the Yankees, he said, was that they weren't pulling for each other. "If they put their minds on playing ball, instead of what the other guy is making—that's all they think about over here. I think it's criticism against the other guy. 'It's his fault, it ain't my fault.' You know that's a lot of baloney. When you get in between the lines, you play baseball. If you want to shoot the bull about so-and-so after the game, it's fine. But when you get between the lines, you've got to pull for each other. That's what this team is not doing. In Oakland, the players all helped each other. Over here, if you jump on a guy, he'll dog. He'll stop. He'll quit on you."

The curious part is that Martin had told Figueroa and Torrez that he was going to put them on a four-day rotation, and had asked Hunter whether he wanted to go on a four-day rotation, too. Hunter had said, "No."

Very odd. But, then, the Cat knew that he had become a once-a-week pitcher. He hadn't really been talking about himself, he had been talking about all of them. And he was right. It wasn't until mid-August, more than a month later, that Billy went to a four-day rotation for Torrez and Figueroa. Even Figueroa's start after the Milwaukee meeting had been an accident of timing. Billy had planned to start him the next day, anyway, for the very good reason that Don Gullett had been sent back to New York with a bad back, and Figueroa was the only pitcher he had.

"We had been told that George was going to be waiting at the hotel to give one of his famous pep talks, and everybody was maybe a little bit apprehensive about what he was going to say. Everybody knows he has that explosive temper. And yet, on the bus trip from the airport to the hotel, Mickey [Rivers] and Lou [Piniella] were getting on each other and everyone else, and made the team loose. You listen to these two guys go at it, and it's very funny. They really know how to get on you. They can get on anybody when they go at it, and it *is* funny. Ask some of the reporters, they can't believe some of the stuff that goes on. So they took us into

189

one of the banquet rooms, convention rooms or whatever, and we were all so loose nobody gave a shit any more."

—Yankee player's view

George's message was: "You guys better start playing ball, and stop all this bitching and alibiing, or I'll back up the truck and get rid of all of you." Quit blaming the owner and the manager, and start blaming yourselves! "You guys don't give a bleep. You only give a bleep about your salary. If you don't get it together, you're going to go down in history as the team that choked. Is that what you want?"

Having upbraided them and downgraded them, he told them they would all be getting $300 to take their wives to the All-Star game, or if they weren't going to the game, to take their wives out on the town. One thing you have to say for Steinbrenner, he sure does know the way to his players' hearts.

"Just a family affair," George told the writers afterwards. "Nothing earthshaking."

The players echoed him, almost to the word. Just a family affair. Nothing earthshaking had happened.

"Nothing that I heard, anyway," said Sparky Lyle.

Never was a more honest word spoken. Sparky hadn't been there. He had gone straight up to his room, and fallen asleep.

When the envelopes were handed out in the clubhouse the next day, Sparky only got $200. So did Ed Figueroa, who had arrived very late. Like the last two minutes. If you've got to be fined $100, there's no nicer way than to be given $200.

But Figueroa wasn't happy about it. He didn't see why he shouldn't be given credit for the two minutes he was there.

Mickey Rivers said, "I need more than $300, but I like anything I get free."

The press found out about the $300 only because Reggie Jackson, who was always interested in letting the world know about the nobility of George's character, couldn't wait to tell them about his magnificent gesture. "I mean, how nice can you be?" Nice, yes. But there was a question about whether it was legal to give players money, a basically nonsensical quibble that brought forth solemn *harrumphs* from the league office ("It is acceptable to award such bonuses if there is a clause added to the players' contracts"), official *ahemmms* and *ahaaaas* from the Commissioner's office ("The Commissioner was informed of the matter and he's having it investigated . . ."), and new heights of paternalism from George Steinbrenner ("I wanted to show the players I still care about them. Why would anyone worry about me giving three hundred bucks to my kids?").

You'd have thought at least one of his million dollar babies would have told him to take the $300 and send it to the starving kiddies overseas. Instead, they got mad at Reggie for blabbing about it. There were going to be repercussions.

We know by now that it had become a matter of principle for the Yankees to follow any inspirational and/or lacerating speech from their leader by racing out onto the field of play and blowing the ball game. In Kansas City, they outdid themselves, and managed to blow the whole series. For Reggie, it was one of the real horror series in his season of horrors.

They lost the first one, 7-4, with Reggie accounting for the last run for both teams. He gave the Royals their run by misjudging John Mayberry's fly ball, and got it back by doubling off Paul Splittorff (there he is again), and scoring on Cliff Johnson's pinch-hit single.

With a right-hander going in the second game, Martin kept his promise, and put Reggie in the cleanup spot for the first time since May. Now that he was back where he belonged, Reggie responded by going both hitless and fieldless. George Brett, the first batter for the Royals, hit a long line drive, and Jax cut across neatly, got there in time to see that the ball hadn't got there with him, backtracked hastily, plucked the ball out of the air—and dropped it. In Kansas City, they give Brett a triple on that kind of thing. Came the eighth inning, the Yankees were losing, 4-1, and Lyle was already in the game. Sparky hadn't allowed an earned run in nineteen innings over nine games, and had taken over the earned-run leadership in the league. He kept his streak going, although with the help of his right-fielder he did allow one unearned run. Hal McRae hit a line drive to the wall in right center, and while Reggie was picking up the ball four times, having dropped it the first three, McRae raced all around the bases. Back on the bench, Sparky came over to offer a few words of unsolicited advice about the most desirable approximate relationship of Reggie's head to his ass. It wasn't the first time a teammate had climbed over him on the bench, and Reggie had programmed himself to keep his mouth shut. He has his own system for turning away harsh words, which sounds as if it comes right off the psychiatrist's couch: "I hear it, slowed down."

Because of what had happened the first time the Yankees were in Kansas City, a team of special cops had been assigned to guard the Yankee bench. The cops heard it all quite clearly, and they couldn't wait for the New York writers to come onto the field the next day, so they could tell them about it. When Reggie was questioned, he answered truthfully. "He told me to get my head out of my butt. He accused me of loafing."

Lyle had probably forgotten all about it, and certainly would have preferred to keep it that way. "Whoever said it," he snapped, leaving no doubt who he thought the Big Mouth was, "the smartest thing of all would have been to keep his mouth shut."

Sparky wasn't the only Yankee superstar complaining about Reggie's Big Mouth on the last day of that disastrous Kansas City series. Communiqués about George's $300 gift were whipping back and forth at the same time, and when Munson was asked about it, he screamed, "What about it? Why is that shit going to be in the papers? Who the hell told everybody about that?"

"Who do you think?" asked Graig Nettles who, with that faultless timing of his, happened to be strolling by. They knew, of course. What Reggie says, he says openly, which was more than could be said for Thurman Munson. As so frequently happened with Munson, especially when Jackson became involved, Thurman was misunderstood. He wasn't angry because Jackson had given out information that was supposed to be confidential; what had him so furious was that Steinbrenner was getting away with looking like some kind of philanthropist, on the cheap, after he had cheated Thurman—in Thurman's view—of something like $120,000.

It had been a rough day for Reggie Jax all around, and after the Yankees had gone down to another listless, unresisting defeat, he sat by his locker with his head in his hands. Absolutely alone. Distraught. He hadn't done anything atrocious in the field, and he had even hit a home run, but the press could see that he wasn't talking, and his teammates clearly didn't want to go near him. At length, he got up and walked over to Lyle for a brief, quiet exchange.

Over in the manager's office, Billy Martin wasn't in a gay and gladsome mood, either. No sooner had the first pair of writers come to the door, than Billy was screaming at the guards to "get them bleepers out." Stand by the door, he ordered the keepers who were escorting the bleepers out. "We've got some eavesdropping bleeps."

Well, that's a pretty good description of one part of a newspaperman's job, even if it had no visible application to any of the current disputes. On the way to the airport, manager Martin and his no-longer-merrymen had to suffer the presence of the *bleeps* and *bleepers* on the team bus—Billy having been unwilling to carry out that earlier threat of banishment.

Eavesdropping can go both ways. After Jackson returned from his conversation with Lyle, he was asked what had transpired between them. Once again, Reggie answered an honest question honestly. "He said somebody had said something to him about it. I told him it didn't come from me."

Not exactly the most inflammatory words spoken that day, but as one of the writers was passing the quote on to another, the whole bus suddenly went silent. Bleeping eavesdroppers everywhere. Writers can't say a bleeping word without those bleeping ballplaying bleeps listening in.

"You're not going to quote me, are you?" Jackson asked, in rising panic.

Of course he was, the writer told him.

"I want everybody to know," Jackson announced,

193

"that I didn't volunteer anything. I was asked a question, and I answered."

That's what it had come to, as the Yankees returned to New York for the All-Star break. They were three games behind the Red Sox, and two behind Baltimore; they had lost seven out of nine games, and Reggie Jackson was issuing an official disclaimer about talking to the press.

The All-Star game is normally the best time of the season for the players. It is a time to relax, to meet old friends, and mingle with the players they most admire. The Yankees were represented by five players. Jackson and Randolph were in the starting line-up. Munson, Nettles and Lyle were on the squad. The Red Sox had six players on the squad: Scott, Burleson, Yastrzemski, Lynn, Rice and Fisk, with Yaz, Fisk and Burleson starting. The sports fans of the nation, having put the starting line-ups side by side, had disagreed markedly with George Steinbrenner. Baltimore was represented by Jim Palmer, the starting pitcher, and Ken Singleton.

After the game, as Reggie Jackson was going out to his car with his house guest, George Scott, he stopped, in his accommodating way, to sign autographs for the waiting kids. When he finally said he had to leave, one of the kids insulted him in what was apparently the vilest kind of way, something which is hardly new to the relationship between the autograph hunter and his prey. (It was one of the reasons Mickey Mantle refused to sign autographs over the latter part of his career. The other reason was that the little bastards flipped ink all over the back of his jacket.) Reggie started chasing the kid, who apparently tripped and fell down. George Scott, who had followed after him, said, "Hey, man. You can't win. Get out of here!" You can't win is right. Before the day was over, a complaint had been filed against Reggie.

It had been in a parking lot in Fort Lauderdale that Reggie Jackson told Steve Jacobson that he didn't think he was going to fit in with the Yankees. It was when Phil Pepe phoned to ask what had happened in the parking lot in Yankee Stadium that Reggie first gave voice to the tortured cry he was to repeat several times in the next few weeks: "I don't want to play in New York. I don't want to be here any more."

11

THE SEVEN COMMANDMENTS

"It's like being on death row. You never get used to it. You never know when they're coming to get you."
—Billy Martin

"What we need is a whole new everything."
—Mickey Rivers

After the three straight losses in Kansas City, Martin had retreated to the long philosophical view. "I'm not going to blast the players, anyone knows they have been blasted enough. We just have to battle back. Start right off the bat Thursday, put it right to them, and get off to a big winning streak."

They were going to open the second season against a Milwaukee club which had just lost half its offense and most of its defense through injuries to their short-stop, Robin Yount, and second baseman, Don Money.

It started with Catfish Hunter and Ed Figueroa pitching seventeen innings of shutout ball. Unfortunately, a doubleheader goes eighteen innings. The second season started, you might say, as the season itself had started, with Catfish Hunter shutting out Milwaukee. The score this time was 7-0. In the second game, the Yankees scored four runs in the first inning off Jerry Augustine, who had given them all the trouble earlier, and took the 4-0 lead into the ninth. Taking all things into account, the ninth inning of the second game was the worst single inning of the year.

Cecil Cooper started it with a home run, and Milwaukee was off the schneid. Fred Stanley failed to hold on to a pop fly in short left center, a play on which he is usually deadly. With one out, a centerfielder named Dick Davis, who had just come up from the minors, lined a single to center, and Martin brought in Sparky Lyle. Sparky threw three ground balls. He got no outs. Ken McMullen, a thirty-five-year-old itinerant who was playing third base because the regular third-baseman, Sal Bando, was playing second, hit a ground ball under Nettles' glove in the hole, a ball which Nettles usually eats up. The dreaded Ed Romero, a nineteen-year-old shortstop who had been brought up from Class AA because of the injury to Yount, hit a soft ground ball to Fred Stanley, and Stanley, making sure of the throw to second, threw it into the wild blue yonder. The third run was in, there were runners on first and second and there was still only one out. Catcher Charley Moore hit a ground ball that went off Chambliss' glove into short right field. With a good chance to cut the tying run down at the plate, Blair, whose arm is usually strong and accurate, threw the ball halfway up the third-base line. The Brewers had men on second and third, there was still only one out, and Tidrow came in and kept the go-ahead run from scoring.

In the tenth, Cooper, leading off again, singled. After two outs, he tried to steal. Fran Healy, who was catching the second game, called for a pitchout, stepped forward to gun the runner out, and dropped the ball. Young Dick Davis lined another hit into right. This time Blair went racing over, trapped the ball on the dead run, and made a remarkable throw to the plate. Cooper barely slid under it.

The Yankees weren't through. Having befouled themselves in the field, they would now bemire themselves on the base paths. Munson, the DH, led off the Yankee tenth with an infield single. Martin put the hit-and-run on, Chambliss drove the ball toward the hole at second, and Sal Bando, no second baseman, just managed to get his glove on the ball. Munson, seeing the ball bounce off the glove, started toward third. The ball, however, had gone off Bando's glove and ricocheted off his knee straight up into the air. Bando grabbed it with his bare hand. Munson tried to scramble back, but Bando fired the ball to Romero, and Munson was tagged out. Piniella hit into a double play, went back to the clubhouse and smashed a chair against his locker.

Steinbrenner had admonished his players to stop alibiing, and his players were certainly taking his words to heart:

Stanley: "Fundamentally, I did everything right. Mainly, I was trying to get the force at second, but the ball rolled off the palm of my hand as I released it. As I let the ball go, I said, 'Aw, shit, I blew it.' When it goes, it goes."

Blair: "I just had to straighten up on my throw. If it didn't hit Chris's glove, it would have rolled to me faster, and McMullen wouldn't have thought of scoring."

Healy: "I tried to get rid of the ball too quick. A catcher is supposed to throw out base runners, and get the ball away quick. It's a fine line."

Munson: "I'm not sure it's a mistake rather than an aggressive move. I saw the ball hit Bando's glove, and all I was going to do was round the base to see how far it rolled. If the ball gets by and I don't get to third, there's a better possibility of a double play, and I'm an ass."

As torturous as the loss had been, Martin could tell you that there would be no carry-over effect. "When you're a professional, you come back, no matter what happened the day before." They came back and got beaten, 6-3, by Mike Caldwell, a twenty-eight-year-old sinkerball pitcher who came into the game with a 1-3 record and a 4.65 ERA. Caldwell had been a good pitcher with San Francisco, once upon a time, but an operation on his pitching elbow had almost ended his career. He actually had them shut out, 6-0, on three hits going into the eighth, when Piniella walked, Reggie knocked him in with a double (his third hit), and Nettles followed with a home run. "I

198

couldn't believe I was getting them out with the same pitch I've been throwing to everybody else," Caldwell said. It was the first complete game he had pitched in two years. It was also the last win he would have all year.

Statistically, the Yankees were only seven games above .500, the low point of the year. They had lost nine out of twelve, and were very lucky to be only three and a half games behind first place.

It was one of those games where everything comes out in reverse. Milwaukee had lost yet another of its key players in the very first inning, when a Mike Torrez fast ball broke a bone in Sixto Lescano's wrist. Lescano's replacement, Steve Brye—coming off the bench with a .226 average—singled in the first run, singled in the second run, drew a base on balls to keep the big four-run inning going, and singled again the next inning.

Two of the runs came in when Mickey Rivers turned the wrong way on a Sal Bando drive. Sparky Lyle came in and celebrated his thirty-third birthday by throwing a wild pitch and giving up a home run to bring that long stretch of giving up no earned runs to an end.

After the game, Martin told the reporters he was going to start Blair in place of Rivers the next day. "It don't bother me," said Rivers. "I don't care if I don't play. I just don't. I don't see nobody doing so much greater than anyone else. What we need is a whole new everything."

George Steinbrenner had a slight cavil. George was sure he had a great everything. What he needed, he thought for about the twentieth time that season, was a whole new manager.

Before the Caldwell game, there had been talk around the park that Billy was through. Why wouldn't there be? George had called at least two newspapermen from North Carolina to ask them, in confidence, whom they would recommend if the Yankees hired a new manager, and how they felt about Walter Alston. With Alston you don't get a thrill a day, but you do get law and order.

By the time Billy came to the Stadium on Saturday morning, the rumors of his demise were everywhere. Every news medium imaginable was alerting its people.

This was right after the All-Star game, the traditional vacation time for writers who have been covering the team. Traditional vacation times were being pushed back all over town.

On Saturday morning, Dick Howser was called to Gabe Paul's apartment to be interviewed for the job. Note the distinction. He wasn't being offered the job, he was being interviewed for the job. That means you have to talk a little before you're hired. Putting all distinctions aside, as of the moment Gabe called Howser, Billy Martin was fired.

Obviously, Howser didn't give the answers Gabe wanted to hear. If you're Dick Howser and you want the job, what do you say when the questions turn to the relationship between the front office and the manager? There are ways to get across the message that you're always willing to give the owner's views the utmost weight and consideration. There are ways of saying that you won't stand for interference. One of the ways of saying it is to say it. And that is apparently what Howser said to Paul and Tallis on that Saturday morning.

It can be stated with some degree of certitude that not standing for interference from the owner was not one of the prime requisites for the job.

Billy knew, all right. "It was all over the park when I came in." He was near to tears. Where had the rumors started? "I don't know. Probably the people that are trying to fire me." Where were they? "I don't know."

Steinbrenner wasn't returning calls. (The calls had been made to Tampa, and Steinbrenner was, of course, in North Carolina.) When Gabe Paul was finally roused, he declined to comment, and did not disagree when it was pointed out to him that his refusal to quash the rumors could only give them a certain amount of validity.

"The only real way to know you've been fired," said Martin, "is when you arrive at the ball park and find your name has been scratched from the parking list."

Before the game, there was a meeting in which first Martin, and then Lou Piniella, addressed the players.

The topic was the pride of the Yankees. He knew they had all heard the rumors, Martin told them, and he implored them to have pride in themselves and the Yankees, because they were part of a proud organization. He had a few things to say about individual players and their lack of hustle, and ended, as always, by telling them not to talk to the writers. "The writers are trying to pull this team apart. Let's keep our problems in the clubhouse."

The players were beginning to talk openly, as if they sensed the end was near for Billy. Piniella, always unafraid to talk, gave the writers a pretty good idea of what he himself had talked about in the pre-game meeting. The lack of discipline. Kids running around the clubhouse. Players coming and going as they chose. "You keep seeing certain things," he said, without getting into specifics. "They happen, and other people see them, and it spreads. It's disgusting. That's what's happening now. Guys come to the ball park wondering why they should bust their butt when some things are going on. No one is blaming Billy. He led us to a championship last year. It's not his fault we don't win. But deplorable things are happening around here."

Jackson was very careful. "The manager, he's a fine man. He doesn't try to discipline anybody. He tries to let everyone be their own man. We don't have to like the guy. You don't have to be his friend, or wash his car, but we should stand by him for nine innings a day. The manager doesn't strike out. He don't make errors, and he don't throw up on the mound. You can't ask for a better owner . . ." Owner? How did the owner get in there, Reggie?

In what was clearly an act of defiance, a message to the front office, Billy had Dick Howser bring the starting line-up to home plate for the first time all year.

Piniella went out and got three hits, knocking in a run in the first. Blair, who was rapidly becoming invaluable, hit a two-run homer to make it 3-0. Guidry, his ankle completely recovered, allowed only one run, struck out nine, and was so overpowering that only one ball was caught in the outfield.

After the game, Billy turned the first questions away by calling the writers "pallbearers." But then his voice choked up, that look of hurt came over him and he was saying, "I never thought I'd get to manage this team. It was like a dream for me when it happened . . ." It was just too much for him. The tears had begun to come and he strode off to the sanctuary of his bathroom.

In point of fact, Billy Martin's job was hanging on Gabe Paul's belief that it would be sheer disaster to bring an outsider into this mess. Although nobody seemed to believe that Billy's fate was in Gabe's hands —least of all Billy himself—we know that it was. Sure, Steinbrenner could take it out of his hands any time he wanted to. But he couldn't take it out of his hands without Gabe getting back on that plane to Tampa. That's why the job wasn't offered to Walter Alston.

The combination of the Saturday win and Howser's unwillingness to take on a job which could so easily destroy him (how smart did Howser have to be to know that he was giving the wrong answer?) had brought this particular crisis to an end. Unfortunately, Billy didn't know it. He came to the park on Sunday after a sleepless night, so sure the end was near that writers found him at his desk in civilian clothes, drinking coffee and puffing a cigar. "I feel like those guys on death row," he told them. "I need a reprieve from the Governor."

The win on Saturday, as far as he was concerned, had given him a reprieve for exactly one day. "If they're going to make a change, you usually get a call in the morning, so you won't come to the park."

Whatever he had heard overnight, he talked like a man who was about to manage his last game. "I heard the same rumor when I was manager of the Texas Rangers. Only that time, I made the mistake of picking up the phone and calling Brad Corbett, and asking him about it. 'It's true,' Corbett told me. 'You're fired.'"

They could ask George Steinbrenner about it, if they could find him. Billy wasn't going to. "I'm going to continue to manage my way, no matter what happens. I'll live or die on my own convictions. My mother didn't raise me to be scared. I've got an obligation to the

Yankees to go out and do my job. I don't want this feeling to spill over to the players in the clubhouse."

While he was talking, the phone rang. "That was Gabe," he said. "I better keep my street clothes on."

Gabe had come to the park, finally, after two days, and Billy was so certain that the ax was about to fall that he sat back down and said, "I'm not rushing up there. The first time you get fired, you think nothing can be that bad again. But each time it gets worse. It was bad when I got fired in Minnesota, but it was worse in Detroit and even worse in Texas, and each time I cry. I guess that shows how weak I am."

He was more than willing to go along with one writer's theory that it had taken twenty-four hours to find his successor. Like maybe Dick Williams, whom Steinbrenner had tried to hire once before.

As always, he set forth his own version of why he was being fired. The old familiar litany. It had all started, according to Billy, on the day Steinbrenner came raging into the clubhouse in St. Petersburg after the loss to the Mets. "He tried to show me up in front of my players. He yelled, 'You lied to me.' That's one thing I can't stand." Billy gave a somewhat fanciful account of how he had accidentally splattered George with water, and had thrown him out of the clubhouse. "Ever since then," said Billy, "I knew I was gone."

"You wait and see," he said. "When I'm gone, some of these players will be at each other's throats. I been keeping them apart."

As he was getting ready to leave, almost half an hour after Gabe had called, a club official came to the door to ask if it would be all right to have some of the players sign autographs alongside the dugout before the game. Billy nodded, turned back to the writers and, almost in tears again, said, "My last act of authority."

Twenty minutes later, he came back smiling. "Everything is all right," he said. "Nothing's changed."

Naw, he said, none too convincingly, he hadn't thought he was going to be fired when he went up there. "I think they would have done it another way. Gabe's a classy guy."

The phone rang, and Billy said, "But wait."

It was Gabe calling, he said, as he hung up. But only to pass on a message. He saw the dubious looks. He smiled. "Honest."

They speak the same language, Billy and Gabe. They come from the old days when the grass was green, and the roads were dusty, and the guy sitting behind the desk held your fate in his hands.

Billy ridiculed Gabe to his friends at times. He would tell them how shaky Gabe had become since his cerebral spasm. He would describe how Gabe would sit there shaking, while George and Billy screamed at each other. But there was a relationship there. They were both tough, and if it came down to it, Gabe Paul, the quiet, smiling man, was the tougher. Not for nothing is Gabe Paul known as "The Smiling Cobra" to his colleagues.

Knowing Gabe, knowing Billy, knowing the situation, the conversation between the two men, in that crucial Sunday meeting, would have gone something like this. Gabe would have talked about some problem on the team, the same kind of problem he talked about in the constant meetings to which Billy objected. Sooner or later, not at all to Gabe's surprise, Billy would begin to rail about the rumors that were all over town, and he would be very explicit about who was spreading them. Gabe has an old Branch Rickey quote he pulls out for these occasions. (It wasn't, after all, the first time they had been through this.) "Thinking of the Devil is worse than seeing the Devil," Gabe would tell him. That was one of Rickey's favorites, and it is also one of Paul's. Billy was here, wasn't he? That meant he was still the manager. Gabe had told him that the win-loss column was not going to be the determining factor and, barring a complete collapse, he would still be here at the end of the year. Just so long as he kept these appointments.

Billy didn't believe it? "Time proves all things." That's another Gabe Paul axiom, out of Branch Rickey.

Gabe has an axiom or two of his own, some of which would never have befouled the old Mahatma's lips. There is one in particular he had frequently cited to Billy, trying to convince him that he could only hurt himself by taking on the front office in the newspapers. "If you stir shit, it stinks."

What Billy knew, and Gabe did not yet know, was that while Gabe had been sitting up here waiting for him, Billy had been down there stirring it up good.

And, oh yeah, Gabe had told him one other thing. He had told him that Steinbrenner was on his way up from North Carolina.

And so, after Billy had returned to his office to tell the waiting newspapermen that nothing had changed, he turned to Phil Pepe and said, "You can take your vacation now. But if I were you, I'd stay by the phone."

Kansas City was in town for a two-game series, and the largest walk-in crowd of the year came to the park. What had brought all of those people there became evident by the mighty cheer that rose when Billy took the line-up card to home plate, and the even mightier cheer that rose as he traipsed back. He couldn't pop his head onto the field all day without getting cheered. "The fans are great," Billy agreed, after the game. "Now, if I can only get George to be a fan."

They had won another 3-1 game, a game remarkably similar to the Kansas City one. In both games, Munson reached base on an error with two out in the first inning, and was driven in by Piniella. In the Milwaukee game, Chambliss had walked after the error and Piniella had singled Munson in. In the Kansas City game, Chambliss followed the error with a double and Piniella singled them both in. Reggie Jackson had very similar games, too. In both games, he was used as DH against a left-handed pitcher. He had done nothing against Billy Travers, and he did nothing against Andy Hassler. Don Gullett, pitching again after a 12-day rest, didn't really look that good. He allowed eight hits, gave up five walks, and had to pitch out of trouble every inning. The guy just had a way of winning, that's all. Since those losses on his first two starts, his record was nine and one. He still wasn't being awfully communicative. "I have only two things to say. One, I was very happy to win. And I'm not going to answer any questions."

What that really meant was that he was hurting

again. I don't know where Billy's mind was, but he had allowed a man coming off a sore back to throw 146 pitches, before sending Dick Tidrow in to get the last out.

On Monday, George Steinbrenner came in to impose a little law and order upon his messy little domain and, in his honor, it rained. Well, it didn't exactly rain. Gabe Paul called the game off early in the afternoon, on the weather bureau's prediction of possible rain. Listen, if you can't believe the weather bureau, who can . . . no, that's not right.

By calling the game off that early, he was able to accomplish at least three things. He enraged the Kansas City Royals, who were now going to have to come back to New York from Baltimore in late August instead of going home for a day of rest, he gave his own pitching staff an extra day of rest for the important three-game series coming up against Baltimore and, last but hardly least, he gave George Steinbrenner a chance to hold his press conference a couple of hours earlier than originally scheduled.

George could hardly wait. He had read all those nasty things Martin said when he thought he was about to be fired, and he was constitutionally incapable of not answering back. George was going to stir it up again, and it was he who was going to come out smelling. Poor George, he never could get it through his head that when it was big, bad George against Billy the Kid, the entire population of Greater New York (minus Reggie Jackson) was going to rally behind Billy. Billy was looked upon as a native son, the bad boy of the family to whom everything is forgiven because he is essentially good and can always be counted upon when he is needed. George was looked upon as . . . well, a convicted felon from Cleveland. He may be able to shed that identification some time around 1985, and be considered nothing worse than a ravenous industrialist, but until then . . . Sorry, George, but that's the way it is.

And he knows it, just as Jackson knows that his big mouth is always going to get him into trouble. But people do what they do, as Gabe Paul says. And that's

want to make it perfectly clear we're not out to get Billy Martin. I'm not totally down on Billy. We're not thinking of making a change."

Was he in a precarious position? Paul was asked.

"Sure, he's in a precarious position, but every manager in baseball is in a precarious position. Especially in New York. But Billy is the manager of the club, and we're not thinking of making a change. We're thinking of winning, and winning with Billy Martin."

Steinbrenner, who could see the thing wasn't going the way it was supposed to, jumped in to echo that. "There's nothing imminent, and this session is not to be construed as just another vote of confidence for a manager." In the world of baseball, for the uninitiated, a vote of confidence is tantamount to a 48-hour notice of termination of services.

Was there a sword hanging over Billy Martin's head? Steinbrenner was asked.

"There's no more sword hanging over Billy's head than there is over yours," George said. "If you want to say sword, there's a sword hanging over every man's head working in the world."

So much for the international union movement.

An unmitigated disaster.

In attempting to de-mythologize Billy the Kid, George had turned him into the greatest martyr since the British did that shitty thing to Joan of Arc. And, in the process, made himself look like a tin-hat, banana-country dictator.

Having defended himself against some rather mild slings from Martin, George now had to suffer the slings and arrows of the entire press. How dare this convicted felon set himself up as the arbiter of another man's honor? Poor George, he hasn't won a press conference yet.

Billy had been up to talk to George earlier in the day, and as soon as the game was called off he went home. His only comment before he left was, "Loyalty is a one-way street to him."

For the first time since he had taken his promptness pledge in Detroit, Billy came to the park late the next day. Through the three remaining games at home, he was so silent that an unconfirmed rumor went racing through the park that he was taking a crash course in sign language.

Baltimore, having won three straight games while the Red Sox were losing three straight, was coming to town in first place, three full games ahead of the Yankees. It seemed a very good idea, as far as Billy was concerned, for their lead to be something less than that when they left.

"A Yankee regular," whose sentiments seem remarkably indistinguishable from, if just as anonymous as, those of the "prominent player," was quoted as saying, "Every day is critical for Billy. You know how impulsive George is. He's continued to make a mockery of this. I can't have the same respect I had for Billy last season, but George has less than he had ever had before. The whole league is laughing at us. Every time we start to come together, something like this happens."

The first game became one of the big ones of the season. Baltimore got off to a 4-0 lead, and the Yankees were still behind, 4-2, in the ninth. Ross Grimsley was doing it to them again. With Roy White on first base and one man out, Martin sent Cliff Johnson up for Bucky Dent, who had hit a home run his last time up. Johnson tied the game with a line shot into the right-field seats, and Reggie Jackson, DH-ing for the third straight game, won it with a home run leading off the tenth.

Was the pressure off him? Billy was asked.

"What pressure off me?" said Martin. "You mean, I can sleep tomorrow?"

Having won three games in a row from left-handers, the Yankees were beaten in the next night game by a right-hander. Since the right-hander was Jim Palmer, they were entitled. No, Eddie Murray didn't knock in the winning run. All Murray did was hit a long home run off Catfish Hunter in the eighth inning to tie it. The winning runs were knocked in by Elliott Maddox, who had a five-year hate-on with Billy, going back to when Martin had him in Texas.

Was it a sweet moment for him? Maddox was asked. "I won't say it," Maddox answered. "But I'll think it. Just say it was very, very nice."

Over in the Yankee locker room, the mood was

gloom. Tomorrow they would be playing Baltimore for the last time all year. If Baltimore kept winning—impossible thought—the Yankees would never again be able to cut into their lead through their own efforts.

For the final game, Reggie Jax was on the bench. Against Palmer, he had been out in right field, and an announcement was made that he had "a slight hyperextension of the left elbow," due to a collision with Mickey Rivers. The contact had been so slight that it had gone unnoticed. And, anyway, when a right fielder runs into a center fielder, it's the right elbow that gets jarred. Well, the last time Rudy May had pitched against them, Jackson had been on the bench, too. "Sure," Jackson said, as if to confirm that there was nothing wrong with him, "everybody knows that when you get hit on the right elbow, it's the left elbow that gets hurt."

Reggie was going along with the tell-them-nothing policy. In addition to his other problems, his elbow had been hurting for days. That was why Martin had been using him as DH.

Without Reggie Jax, the Yankees scored the most runs they had accumulated in a game all season, and beat the Orioles, 14-2. Mike Torrez pitched his first complete game in over a month, a four-hitter. Always a late-season pitcher, Mike was off on a winning streak that was going to make him the solid man of the pitching staff.

Munson had three hits, including a home run, before he had to leave the game with an injured knee. Which seemed to sum up his entire season against the Baltimore Orioles. To sum it up statistically, it was 24 hits in 56 times at bat for a .429 average, with five home runs and seventeen runs batted in.

Graig Nettles had two hits, including a three-run homer, to bring his figures against the Orioles to .333, including six home runs and sixteen runs batted in. As a team, the Yankees hit .296 against Baltimore, and lost the season series, 8-7.

Eddie Murray had hit only .259 against them, but ooooh, the damage that was done.

The feeling in the Yankee locker room was relaxed, but not really happy. Munson was unusually talkative, injured knee and all. His home run had been the 100th of his career, a landmark achievement which permitted him to snub the magnum of champagne Steinbrenner had sent down for him, in favor of good old beer. (Don Gullett had been sent a magnum of Steinbrenner champagne on his 100th career victory a few days earlier, and Don doesn't drink at all.)

Reggie, trying to get into the spirit of whatever-it-was, asked Graig Nettles how many career homers he had. Nettles ignored him.

A few minutes later, Nettles was telling one of the writers, "They keep you down on this team if you don't pop off. The only way to make money on the team is to complain. Roy White and I are not controversial enough to get money from the owner."

For the second time in the season, White had been dropped to the eighth spot in the batting order. The first time had been followed by the Munson flap. When Roy White, a non-wave-maker, was asked whether he thought batting eighth cut down his effectiveness, he answered, "You say that. I won't. If something seems obvious, go ahead and say it."

You wouldn't have thought that White had just had three hits including a home run, two singles and three runs batted in. You wouldn't have thought the Yankees had just scored 14 runs on 15 hits, either.

Asked whether winning the Baltimore series was important to the ball club, Thurman Munson said, "I don't know. I don't know whether it's more important to Steinbrenner, Martin or the ball club. Momentum is the most important thing to me in sports. Baseball is 50 percent psychological. If you believe you can do it, you will. But all that mess with the manager and owner can take the players away from their main business, which is baseball."

Did he think that winning the series had saved Martin's job? "I don't know. Whatever they do, they ought to do it. They've got to go one way or the other." But maybe winning would shut everybody up. "Winning leads to money. When baseball players make money, they don't care what's happening in the manager's office."

Nor did he overlook the opportunity to take a final rip at Steinbrenner, whose champagne sat unopened in a bucket of ice in front of his locker. "But there's another thing. I don't like being laughed at. When a manager gets seven rules thrown at him, people laugh. The Yankee uniform stands for more than that."

He sure does know how to hurt a guy.

They were only two games behind as they headed out on their second western trip. Oakland, California and Seattle. Oakland and Seattle were patsies. California, having lost Bobbie Grich, Joe Rudi and Frank Tanana, wasn't much better. The first western trip had started in Seattle, and Martin had almost gotten fired as a result of the Hendricks flap the first day. This trip was ending in Seattle, and Martin barely survived his last day there.

If Horace Greeley ever shows up in Yankee Stadium, he's going to be tossed out on his ear.

12

MUNSON'S BEARD

"They're like a bunch of hens getting together . . . All
players bitch and moan but on the field, show me
some heart."

—Bill North, Oakland A's

The Yankees had played exactly one hundred games,
and their record was 55-45. The ragamuffin, one-legged
Chicago White Sox, who had sold Bucky Dent to the
Yankees for the money needed to start the season, and
then sold Ken Brett to California for operating money,
were leading the league with 62-38.

The western trip started on the last three days of
July, with three straight wins over Oakland, 4-0, 9-3
and 9-2. Guidry, Gullett and Figueroa. What could be
easier.

Not so easy. In an echo from the past, Guidry
pitched eight and two-thirds innings of shutout ball,
and then Sparky had to come in with the bases loaded
to strike the last man out.

Gullett left his game after six innings with his shoulder aching, and he refused to come out of the trainer's
room to talk to reporters. Martin said it wasn't serious.
It was very serious.

At the same time Gullett was refusing to say anything, Reggie Jax, having hit his 19th home run of the season, was talking up a storm on the A's post-game radio show. "Ninety percent of what the New York press has written about this team isn't true," Reggie assured his old fans in Oakland. The press had "used human beings for their own purposes," Reggie said (a favorite plaint of his), and had thereby put such pressure on the team that it wasn't living up to its potential.

Although most of the regular Yankee writers were on vacation, a couple were still there, and when Reggie returned to the locker room they confronted him. When had they been unfair to him, personally? And what were the specific untruths that had been written about him or anyone else? "You guys heard that?" Jax said. "Jeez, I wouldn't have said it if I knew you were listening."

Which seemed to say it all for integrity. Reggie did know the show was piped into both clubhouses; what he really meant was that it had slipped his mind. Things have a way of doing that when Reggie's talking. He didn't deny that he had taken a cheap shot. "I'm embarrassed," said Reggie.

Despite the Yankee sweep, Reggie's old friend and sparring partner, Bill North—they once had a fist fight in the Oakland dressing room—had some unkind things to say about the Yankees. "You see all the talents they have, and they're caught up in all that bull. They're like a bunch of hens getting together. I said even if they didn't get along they should win by ten games. I was mistaken." The old A's had fought and bickered, too, but once the game started, they had gone about their business. "Players bitch and moan; we all do it over a drink after a game, cut up the whole team. But on the field, show me some heart."

North has a way with words, too. "For that money," he said, waving their excuses away, "they *conscripted* to every bit of scrutiny."

Reggie knew what the other teams were saying about them. "Right now," he said, "they all think of us as a zoo."

Through the first week of August, the Yankees

215

seemed intent upon recapitulating the madness of the entire season. Like a patient coming to a high fever in order to recapture his health.

THE FEVER CHART

AUGUST 1:

Kentucky state police report that Marijuana has been found on Don Gullett's farm.

In strict defiance of Steinbrenner's dress code, Munson is growing a beard.

Jackson, unhappy at being benched, hints that he will be leaving the Yankees before his five-year contract expires.

AUGUST 2:

Criminal harassment charge filed against Jackson in New York.

Hunter and Gullett sent to Los Angeles orthopedic surgeon, Dr. Frank Jobe, to have their pitching arms examined.

Reggie Jackson is hit from the rear on the freeway while also on his way to Dr. Frank Jobe to have his troublesome left elbow examined. Upon finding out who he is, the woman who hit him asks for an autograph for her son.

AUGUST 3:

California runs wild on Yankee outfielders' arms.

Bobby Bonds hits ground-ball home run.

Mickey Rivers, red-hot at bat, asks to be traded.

AUGUST 4 (off day):

Reggie Jackson comes right out and says there is an escape clause in his contract that will permit him to leave at the end of two years.

Ken Holtzman calls Steinbrenner "a fool" for paying him all that money for doing nothing.

Don Gullett doesn't shave for a day, and story goes out that he is growing a beard.

Asked to comment on rumor that Frank Robinson is going to replace Martin as Yankee manager, Reggie Jackson says, "Just say that Jackson smiled for the first time all year."

AUGUST 5:

Gabe Paul issues statement that there is no escape clause in Reggie's contract. Tells players to shut up already.

Martin castigates reporters, then apologizes with tears in his eyes.

Munson is thrown out of game. Stops talking to the press.

Jackson hits 300th home run of career. Torrez congratulates him. Hunter congratulates him. End of congratulations.

AUGUST 6:

Yankees lose second in a row to Seattle. Drop five games behind Boston.

Catfish Hunter gives up three home runs.

Piniella excoriates his teammates in the clubhouse.

Steinbrenner apologizes to New York City.

AUGUST 7:

Yankees defeat Seattle. Wow!

Jackson not happy about having to play exhibition game in Syracuse instead of keeping appointments to have elbow examined and to close private real estate deal.

Lyle not happy about going to Syracuse.

Nobody happy about going to Syracuse.

AUGUST 8:

Lyle does not go to Syracuse.

Syracuse beats Yankees, 14-5.

Rivers sulks in clubhouse when he's supposed to come to bat.

Lyle and Rivers fined $500. Wanna bet that Rivers' fine is purely ceremonial?

Gullett's marijuana crop started things off on an appropriately hilarous note, because if you had lined up every ball player in the country and pointed to the one guy who would be least likely to know what marijuana was, the pointee would have been Don Gullett.

For connoisseurs of this kind of thing, there were 882 plants lined up neatly in seven rows, alternating with seven rows of corn. The plants had been so infinitely cultivated that the police thought they must have been initially grown in a hot house. The street value of the impounded 2800 pounds of marijuana was put at $112,000, which obviously didn't make it worth the effort for a big-league baseball player.

Or maybe it did. After the story had broken, Piniella stationed himself at the front of the team bus. "I'm quitting," he announced. "I'm retiring from baseball. What the bleep do I need baseball for when all I got to do is go to Kentucky, stick a few plants in the ground and make a couple of hundred thousand. I quit!"

Piniella and Gullett were members of the race-track contingent which also included Mickey Rivers, Ken Holtzman and Roy White, five as disparate personalities as you could possibly find. During their last trip to Cleveland, they had decided that if they won the World Series, they would fly immediately to Thistletown and buy a couple of race horses. The horses would be shipped to Gullett's farm, and he would race them at nearby Keeneland. In other words, a horse player's pipe dream.

"Hey," Rivers piped up, "we can't keep our horses on Gullett's farm because if that sucker takes a bite of one of those funny plants of his, it'll start to fly, or it'll start to wobble, and either way, they'll lock us up."

It took the state police exactly one day to clear Gullett. That wasn't good enough for George Steinbrenner. The official seal of purity was stamped upon him by George himself, in a statement which surpasses all known records for silliness: "In 25 years of dealing with athletes as a coach and an owner, I have never met a finer young man than Don Gullett. If there is a modern-day Jack Armstrong, Gullett is it . . . Two years ago, they found marijuana growing in the outfield at Anaheim Stadium, and nobody ever mentioned that Gene Autry was involved in that."

Nobody ever accused Autry of riding to the rescue of a fair damsel who wasn't in any particular need of rescuing, either. There's poor Gullett 3000 miles away, and unable to defend himself against Steinbrenner's defense.

There was nothing else funny about the expedition into the fever swamps of Anaheim and Seattle. Not to the Yankees, anyway.

In the opening game in Anaheim, they were beaten, 4-1, by Ken Brett, who had belonged to them for about a minute-and-a-half, and was not looked upon as one of the premier pitchers in the league. How he was able to handle them so easily with the stuff he had was explained rather vividly by Roy White. "It's the mystery of the year," Roy explained.

Reggie Jackson was on the bench against a left-hander for the fourth straight time. "He said he wanted to play," Billy announced. "But his elbow still isn't 100 percent."

"They told me I was hurt," said Jackson. The one time he had faced Brett during the season, while Brett was still with the White Sox, he had hit a monster home run. He had hit a grand-slam home run off him the previous year for Baltimore. After the game was over, Reggie fingered the lettering on his Yankee jersey unhappily, and said to the reporters, "I'm going to remember this uniform. It's going to be a collector's item."

By the next day he was asking them, "If I played only two years on a five-year contract, how much could they take back?" It was a trick question. By the end of two years he'd have been paid most of the money.

The club was in Seattle when Gabe felt called upon to dictate another statement:

"I believe the loose talk about contracts and agreements between players and the Yankees has reached the ridiculous stage. To set the record straight, the Yankees do not have any agreement with any player that is not on file with the American League office, and approved by the league president. That includes the much-discussed Reggie Jackson contract, which does not include the so-called 'release provision' alluded to by many writers. . . .

One thing I do know is that we are leading the league in loose talking. If we are to win the pennant, we've got to stop talking and start playing like we can. All I can say to our players is to stop the B.S., and start concentrating on the game.

An intriguing statement.

1. There had better not be any agreement that was not on file with the American League office. That's against the rules, and would subject the team to a stiff fine and—if it were Charlie Finley instead of George Steinbrenner—perhaps even the loss of the player.

2. The statement was delivered by Gabe Paul, not George Steinbrenner. All it means is that as far as Gabe Paul knew, or wanted to know, there was no side agreement.

3. Reggie Jackson never could be brought to make a flat retraction. His Oakland lawyer, Steve Kaye, said, in faultless lawyerese: "That is privileged information. Actually, I don't remember just what all the agreements were. I know that Reggie is an honorable person, and intends to honor a five-year contract."

There's an agreement, buddy. Reggie had begun to talk about it as far back as spring training. Can anybody really believe it's a figment of his imagination?

Thurman Munson had just come back from Disneyland, and was in an uncharacteristically playful mood when the first sproutings of a beard were observed beneath his handsome walrus mustache. "I like a beard," he said. "Billy doesn't mind. If he doesn't mind, it probably means that George does." He reminded his audience that he had grown a beard in 1975, the year before Steinbrenner laid down his dress code. That was the year Steinbrenner wasn't there, Munson said, blowing out a puff of smoke. "He was expelled for a while."

Who knows what he was trying to do this time? He had been used as DH through the entire Oakland series, and, as wise men have been telling us through the centuries, an idle mind is the devil's tool.

Munson's beard was supposed to get Steinbrenner's goat, there's no doubt about that. "Isn't it against the Constitution to say I can't grow a beard?" he asked, with exaggerated innocence. "Or the Fair Employment Act or something? Did you notice how short my hair is? I got a haircut yesterday. Other guys are running around here with long hair. I try to keep up with the team code. I'm a *team* man, a *team* player."

The front office's attitude toward Thurman's beard was that anything they didn't have to know, they didn't want to know. Knowledge was thrust upon Gabe Paul in the same phone call in which he was asked about Reggie's escape clause.

Now that he knew, he had to call Billy Martin and ask him what was going on. Martin told Gabe that Thurman had told him, in advance, what he was going to do. Thurman had also told him that he hoped it wouldn't get Billy in trouble. (Which was also pretty much what Thurman had been saying, off the record, when he was saying anything.)

Gabe made it explicit that one of the functions of the manager is to enforce the rules. As far as Gabe was concerned, he didn't have to act upon anything he didn't see with his own eyes. The Yankees were going to be in Syracuse in three days. Gabe would be there. If Munson's beard was there also, Billy was going to be held responsible.

After his talk with Paul, Billy gave the writers the same story about having been notified by Munson ahead of time. But when the writers brought it up again at the ball park, he'd had enough. "Petty shit," he snarled. "Worried about beards like babies." And launched a personal attack on the writer he believed to be responsible for Gabe's call. A few moments later he came out to the clubhouse, with his eyes full, and apologized to him.

The Yankees had lost the first two games in Seattle by then, while the Red Sox, playing the same western teams, were in the process of winning nine straight. The Yankees had lost the first game, 5-3, with the two decisive runs both coming in on wild pitches. On one of them, the runner scored all the way from second base. Munson was called out on a checked swing during a last-ditch Yankee rally, and then thrown out of the game because he didn't check his gesture of disbelief and disgust, either.

The second game was great—if you lived in Seattle and were among the 42,000 fans in the park. Catfish Hunter had gone the distance in the 4-1 loss to Brett. This time he had another of his first innings. The first three batters singled, then there was a double play, a walk and two home runs. Martin stayed with him, and the Cat shut the Mariners out until Lee Stanton hit a three-run home run in the seventh. Sparky Lyle came in, and Rupert Jones immediately hit an inside-the-park home run, something which was thought to be impossible in the small Kingdome Stadium. The way to do it is to have the ball hit the center-field fence, carom past Rivers, and have nobody coming over to back him up.

"In brutal frankness," wrote Seattle veteran sportswriter Hy Zimmerman, "the Yankees looked terrible in both games. They pretty well proved the discrepancy between talent and teamwork."

Piniella was even blunter. "Let everyone speak up now, after getting beat by a horseshit ball club like that," he raged, after the game. "All that shit in the papers. I want to go here, I want to go there. Everybody should speak up when you get your ass beat by a horseshit ball club."

George Steinbrenner wasn't going to take it lying down, either. "The thing that disappoints me most," he said, "is the lack of pride the players have. They don't seem to care if they're known as the team that choked. I'm embarrassed. I apologize to the City of New York."

The last true believer was Billy Martin. The Yankees were going to win, as far as he was concerned, and that was all there was to it. "I'm an optimistic-type guy," he could still say. "I've got a little more patience in me than most guys."

Ah, but was Billy going to be around to see it. "I don't want to comment on that," he said, softly.

Before the final game, he called a team meeting. Visibly upset, he told the players they still had 92 games left, and that if they were the professionals he thought they were, they could still get together, forget their difficulties and win this thing. He then asked Munson, in front of all of them, if he'd shave the beard off, as a favor to him.

To the press, Billy could only say, "I can't force him, I can ask. He's too hard of a player, too good a player, to force him. If it's a reflection on me, it's a reflection on me."

Munson wasn't committing himself. "He kind of mentioned it to me," he said. Nor was he explaining what he was trying to do. "No comment, because it's none of your business."

What if Steinbrenner made the request himself? "Isn't there supposed to be a rule against long hair?" Munson asked. "Well, look around. I'm tired of being called a troublemaker. I've been here seven years before this. Doesn't anybody remember? I get blamed for not getting along with Reggie, then it's my fault that George and Billy don't get along, my fault that Billy and Reggie don't get along. Doesn't anybody have any respect for me? . . . Why doesn't anyone stick up for me?"

Yeah, but couldn't he have avoided all that by simply following the rule?

"What's a rule?" Munson asked.

There you had it. There were no rules.

As if to demonstrate the thesis, Mickey Rivers' tape deck was blasting from the front of his locker while Rivers was toweling himself off. There's a rule against loud music. Reggie Jackson went over and turned the volume down. Rivers came back and turned it up. Precisely what the veterans like Munson and Piniella and White had been complaining about all along. Martin had few enough rules, and he didn't enforce even those.

Behind Munson, a player who didn't want to be identified said, "This is the most disorganized effort I've ever seen. People here are making a lot of money. They're told to get to the ball park at a specific time; they come whenever they feel like it. We're told no loud music in the clubhouse, in the shower, in the latrine, in the bus. Maybe it all gets back to the manager. A lot of problems may come from the manager."

223

You keep getting back to it. Martin wasn't loved by his players. He was disliked by many of them, for many reasons. It was only when it came to Steinbrenner interfering in the clubhouse that they closed ranks behind the manager.

To the writers who covered the team, the guys who were there, there was always the perception of a battle being fought by Martin and Munson on one side, and Steinbrenner and Jackson on the other. And it was a remarkable group of writers covering that team; they covered that clubhouse so thoroughly that they became as much a part of the story of the 1977 Yankees as the players themselves. Wasn't he hurting Billy with his Beard of Defiance, they would ask Thurman. And wasn't Billy his friend? "If the owner is looking for an alibi to fire him," Thurman would say, "he doesn't need me as an excuse."

A puzzlement.

Gabe Paul was going to meet the club in Syracuse, which sounded more ominous than it was. The Yankees play an exhibition game against Syracuse every year, and Gabe Paul always goes there at that time.

August 8, Syracuse, N.Y. Where was Thurman? Was Thurman going to come to the park with his half-a-beard, or was Thurman going to be a good boy and shave it off? That was the cosmic question agitating the best minds on the sports beat. Thurman was not on the players' bus. What did that mean? Had he gone to the barber? Had he rendezvoused wih George Steinbrenner? Had he flown the coop? An hour later, into the Syracuse clubhouse walked a surly Thurman Munson, mustache a-twitch but the half-a-beard gone. Clean-shaven beneath the tightened lips. George or Billy had won. What had they won? I don't know.

His comments were just as barren as his chin. "It's shaved," he said. "That's enough. Let's just let it go at that, okay?"

There's always a guy who won't let it go at that. "I'm not talking to writers," Munson told him, very distinctly. "Didn't you hear what I just said? Don't even bother coming to my locker for the rest of the year."

When the tenacious reporter wanted to know what was eating him, Thurman called over to Billy Martin, asking him to get the writers out of his face. Seemed the least Billy could do, after the sacrifice Thurman had just made. "Gentlemen," said Martin, "would you leave Thurman alone, please?"

Beyond that, Billy didn't want to say a thing. "He shaved, that's enough. Now the beard issue is dead. Tune in tomorrow for Chapter 13 of *As the World Turns.*"

Gabe Paul waited until Thurman came out onto the field. "A good-looking fellow like you shouldn't hide his face," Gabe told him.

Billy had met with Paul earlier in the day. "Reggie's swinging the bat good," he had said at one point. "I'm thinking of batting him cleanup." Reggie wasn't swinging the bat *that* good, but Chambliss was in a terrible slump.

On August 9, an off day, there was a meeting between Steinbrenner and Martin at Yankee Stadium. Steinbrenner pressured him once again to bat Jax fourth and play Piniella every day, and once again Billy agreed. It was an easy promise for Billy to make. He had already decided to bat Jackson fourth, and had done it in Syracuse. He had already shown every willingness to break that kind of promise, and he had done it after Milwaukee.

And do you know something? The Coach was right. Never turn a deaf ear on a Superfan just because he happens to own a baseball club.

Martin had a request of his own to press upon Steinbrenner. You might even call it a deal. From the time he took over, Billy had been after him to let him have Art Fowler as his pitching coach. Fowler was his drinking buddy. His pal. Fowler is a remarkable man in many ways, and Billy worships him. After a long career in the minors, Fowler had become a successful major-league relief pitcher at the age of thirty-one. As the pitching coach at Denver, in 1970, his staff became so deunited that he was forced to reactivate himself, and at the age of forty-eight, won nine, saved fifteen, and probably would have been voted MVP of the league if he hadn't asked that his name be withdrawn from consideration so that it could go to a younger player.

Art Fowler had been Martin's pitching coach in all

his previous managerial jobs. He had also been standing at Billy's elbow when Billy either got into a fight with a Tiger outfielder named Ike Blessitt, or tried to break up a fight, and got belted by Blessitt.

It had been Gabe Paul, far more than George Steinbrenner, who had felt that Martin had a better chance of staying out of trouble without Fowler at his side. With the pressure building up so visibly on Billy, they decided to let him have Fowler. Sure. Steinbrenner got what he wanted, when Billy got what Billy wanted. Just a coincidence, of course.

From the day Fowler came, it was as if a weight had been lifted from Billy's shoulders. Ask Art Fowler about the turbulent season of 1977 and he'll tell you, "What turbulent season? It was great for me."

In the Almanac of New York City, August 10, 1977, is notable for two historic entries: Son of Sam, a psychopathic killer who had been terrorizing the young women of the city, was captured, and the Yankees began their wild run for the pennant.

13

FIFTY-THREE GAMES
FROM AUGUST

"I've got something inside of me that nobody can deny. You can fire me, but I'll haunt you."
— Billy Martin

There were fifty-three games to play. In those fifty-three games, the Yankees were not only the Best Team Money Could Buy, they may very well have been the best team anybody had ever seen.

Batting cleanup for the first time since July 16, Reggie came to the plate against Vida Blue with two men on, and singled in a run. Piniella doubled in another, Chambliss walked, and Cliff Johnson brought them both home with a double. The next day, Reggie singled in the first run in a 3-0 victory behind Torrez. And then, in a doubleheader against California, he hit a double and a triple in the first game to knock in three runs, and two monster home runs in the second. The fans were cheering him again, and he was responding by doffing his cap.

His hitting was better than his prognosticating. Having apparently figured out what the Yankees had to do to win 100 games, he said, "Asking this team to win 75 percent of the time, is asking too much." Wrong. If you count the last game the Yankees won in Seattle,

227

that's exactly what they did. They won forty of their next fifty games.

Left-handers? They laughed at them. They ate them up. During that fifty-game period, they defeated the first fourteen left-handers they faced. Overall, they beat nineteen out of twenty-two.

Piniella was hot, and he stayed hot. Johnson hit with power. But the left-handed hitters were hitting, too, and they were hitting everybody. During the month of August, the team average against left-handers was .320.

In his first 16 games in the cleanup position, Reggie hit .310 and knocked in 29 runs. From August 10 to the end of the season, he hit 13 home runs, and drove in 49 runs.

Mickey Rivers batted .405, and drove in 21 runs in August, and he wasn't even voted the American League Player of the Month. Graig Nettles was. Nettles had hit ten home runs, driven in twenty-five and batted .340. In one 14-game stretch, Chambliss hit .386, with five home runs and 20 runs batted in. During that stretch, Chris was at bat 17 times with men on base, and came through with hits 11 times.

Rivers had a string of eight consecutive hits—13 out of 17—and seemed to be knocking in the winning or tying run every other day. After Mickey had singled in the tying runs in the ninth inning against Cleveland in mid-September, Steinbrenner's computer showed that in the 115 times he had come to bat with runners in scoring position, he had come through with base hits fifty-two times, an incredible clutch batting average of .452. The print-out didn't tell his teammates anything they didn't already know. For two years, they had been saying that when a hit was needed to win the ball game, the man they most wanted to see at the plate was Mickey Rivers.

A day later, he beat out a drag-but to set off a winning rally. Why had he finally decided to change his habits? "I'm not giving my secrets away," Mickey said.

They won eight out of nine and gained only half a game on the Red Sox, who were in the process of winning sixteen out of seventeen. A pessimist would have seen the empty half of the glass. Billy Martin, the eternal optimist, saw the half that was filled. "The Red Sox have got to be conscious of us," he exulted. "They're winning all those games and they're not gaining any ground."

The key game, one of the key games of the season for both clubs, came against the Chicago White Sox, who were beginning to wither in August, as the Yankees bloomed. In the opening game of the two-game series, the Yankees had knocked them out of first place in the Western Division. In the second game, the Red Sox win was already posted. A loss would have dropped the Yankees five and one half games behind, and put a brake on their momentum. Especially the way they would have lost.

The Yankees were leading, 5-4, behind Guidry, in a seesawing game in which the White Sox, as was their custom, had thrown away about as many runs on their atrocious base running as they had handed the Yankees through their miserable fielding. In the last of the eighth, Cliff Johnson, up as a pinch hitter, hit one of his towering fly balls into short left field for an easy out—and then, all of a sudden, you could see the ball wasn't going to be caught. Ralph Garr, in left field, had come in slowly; Alan Bannister, the shortstop, assuming it would be easy for Garr, had started back too late. The highest Texas leaguer in the history of baseball. Before the inning was over, the Yankees had scored four runs.

The White Sox came back in the top of the ninth and scored six.

Ron Guidry didn't achieve his eight and one-third innings this time. He never did get anybody out. After three straight hits, Lyle came in to put a stop to it, and Sparky got hit even harder. Lyle managed to get two men out. One of them was Richie Zisk, who was up at bat with two on and the score up to 9-6. Richie hit two balls that barely went foul, into the upper deck in right field, and then hit a booming drive into that right-field alley of his at the deepest part of the park. Lou Piniella had just gone out to right field because Reggie had jammed his knee stealing second base.

Piniella went back, leaped high, and took a home run away from him. The White Sox kept hitting and scoring, Lyle departed in favor of Clay, and Oscar Gamble, who had been destroying Yankee pitching every time he saw it, came in to pinch hit with the bases loaded, and knocked in the two runs that put the White Sox ahead, 10-9. (It should have put them two runs ahead. Rivers' throw to third base was far off the mark, but instead of bouncing into the dugout or the stands, it hit the railing in front of the box seats and bounced back into play.)

The White Sox had brought in Randy Wiles, a rookie left-hander just up from the minors, to finish out the eighth. Wiles walked Munson, Piniella sacrificed, and Chambliss hit the ball into the second deck.

Something was going to have to give, and it was the Boston Red Sox. The Sox lost eight of their next nine. The Yankees went into first place in Chicago, exactly one week after the 11-10 win in New York. Another interesting game. In the opener of the Chicago series, the White Sox had broken the Yankee streak that had reached eight games, by permitting the Yankees to imitate the White Sox. Figueroa was breezing along with a 3-0 lead in the seventh inning, on home runs by Rivers, Piniella and Chambliss. The Yankees gave two of the runs back when Reggie Jax, whose knee was still sore, played a line drive into his area as if it were a thing contaminated.

Maybe it was. With Bannister on first base in the eighth, Rivers came charging in for Richie Zisk's line single, reached down for the ball and never touched it. Bannister was waved around third, the relay from Randolph had him, Munson blocked the plate, the ball came in on a short hop, skidded away from him, and in the ensuing scramble, Bannister was ruled safe. Zisk had gone to second. Gamble, who was hitting .500 against the Yanks, got another hit. Rivers threw it home again, they had the runner again, the ball bounced high, went off Munson's glove again, and this time the error was charged to Rivers. With Gamble all the way around to third, the next batter was purposely walked to set up a double play. Jim Spencer hit an obliging ground ball to Chambliss. Chris looked to the plate, looked to second, looked back to the plate, and by then it was too late to throw anywhere.

On August 23, in the 124th game of the season, the Yankees took over first place behind Torrez. Mickey Rivers went five-for-five, including the two-out single in the seventh that put the Yankees ahead. Nettles, who doesn't seem to hit anything except three-run homers, hit another three-run homer the next inning, to put the game out of sight. For Nettles, it was his 30th home run, and put him in a tie, with Jim Rice and Bobby Bonds, in his defense of the home-run championship.

The Yankees were in first place, and Steinbrenner celebrated the occasion by sending an angry letter of protest to the league office. Why is that man unhappy? Well, George had sent his assistant, the ex-Yankee shortstop Gene Michael, around with the team, to sit up in the press box with a walkie-talkie, chart every pitch, and make sure that the Yankee fielders were positioned correctly. Just like football. Elston Howard was on the other side of the walkie-talkie in the dugout. They had finally found something for Elston to do when he wasn't breaking up fights.

Bill Veeck decided to have some fun with it. Since Michael had no press credentials, he was removed from the press box, and harrassed so much, when he repaired to the radio booth, that Bill White, who was doing the play-by-play, kicked everybody out. In the grandstand, Michael was completely brutalized, to the extent that Harry Caray, the White Sox announcer, decided to conduct a man-in-the-grandstand interview show, in mid game, in the general vicinity of Michael's left nostril while the White Sox's wandering Drummer Boy beat away in his left ear. While all this was going on, earphones and antennae had been rigged up for the White Sox coaches to wear, as if they were getting messages from someone out there in the Great Beyond.

All George had to do was go along with the gag. Send Veeck a telegram that said something like, "I agree with you completely that using electronic aids against your pitiful ball club is unfair. We will hereafter use them only against everybody else." Instead, George huffed and puffed to the league office, and made himself look like a stuffed shirt.

The Yankees were in first place to stay, though. Once there, they ran the new streak to 11 out of 12 and, with 27 games left, they had taken a 4½-game lead.

Jackson had nothing but words of praise for his teammates. They were playing "connoisseur's baseball," he declared. "We said, the hell with the bull, let's play baseball to get the heat off. So we don't have to go home at night, turn on the TV, and see what happened in the soap opera on 161st Street."

"The same problems are always going to be there," Martin said. "They're there now. They'll be there at the end of the season, and the next spring, too. They'll still be there next fall. But they realized they still have to do a job."

Billy was not willing to admit that moving Reggie to cleanup made the difference, let alone that the move had been prompted by Steinbrenner. "I can bat Chris any spot in the line-up, and he won't complain," Martin said, succinctly. "I wasn't getting the best out of Reggie."

It reminded you of the time, during the dark days, when Billy had been asked to evaluate the effect of the free agents on the pennant race. "I don't think I could do that," Billy had said. "There could be somebody who hasn't helped to improve the team even though his statistics are good."

Reggie wasn't going to let his joy run unrestrained either. No, it wasn't more "fun" coming to the park these days, he said. It was more like a relief.

With the kind of hitting they were getting, you wouldn't think they'd need much pitching. Except that you never win without pitching. Guidry got them started on August 10, in the rematch with Vida Blue, leaving the game after seven innings with a 6-1 lead. Before he was done, Guidry had run off eight straight victories. The scores were 2-1, 1-0, 4-0, 4-3, 4-2, 6-5 and 5-0.

The 6-5 game was a shutout against Detroit going into the ninth inning, and should have been a shutout going out. The first three batters hit easy ground balls, which were booted. Guidry left the game, after two were out, when a catchable line drive went under the glove of rookie Dave Bergman, who had been sent to right field to give Reggie Jackson a rest.

The 1-0 game was pitched most fittingly on Guidry's 27th birthday. A two-hitter against Texas, with eight strike-outs and no bases on balls. "There were some people who wanted to get rid of Guidry in the spring," Billy Martin announced. "I wasn't one of them. Gabe Paul wasn't. Maybe it was the trainer."

Ahhh, how quickly they forget. Maybe Billy hadn't given up on Guidry as quickly as Steinbrenner had, but he had given up. He had given up so completely that he would say to Ron, in one of those cruel baseball lines that would be even more cruel if it weren't so common, "Tell me somebody you can get out, and I'll let you pitch to him."

The run was knocked by Reggie Jackson, when Martin let him swing at a 3-0 pitch. Martin said he had let Reggie hit because he had been swinging the bat good. "I would have let Munson, Chambliss or Nettles hit in the same situation."

"First time all year for *me*," said Reggie.

The Texas pitcher was our old friend, Dock Ellis, pitching for his third team of the season. Don't feel too sorry for Dock. He was not only getting more from Texas than Steinbrenner had offered him, he was getting more than he himself had been asking Steinbrenner for. I don't know how Dock does it, but these days the answer seems to be to keep moving.

Mike Torrez had pitched three straight complete game victories before he went on the four-day rotation. He ran the streak to seven straight, and became the anchor of the staff, the late-season pitcher he had always been.

And they did it without Don Gullett, who was on the disabled list through the entire month. The replacement Billy Martin found for him was either a stroke of genius or an act of desperation. With Torrez and Figueroa on a four-day rotation, and Guidry and Hunter on a six-day rotation, he needed a swing man who could be dropped into the empty slots as they came up. The man he chose was Dick Tidrow, who had been a total loss in relief since the shelling he had undergone in Boston. All Billy was asking him to do, was hold the fort long enough so that he could bring in Sparky.

Tidrow started seven times. Here is his record:

August 14. Pitched six innings against California, allowed two hits, and was leading 12-0 when he was removed from the game. Yankees won, 15-3.

August 20. Pitched seven innings against Texas, was leading, 6-1. Yankees won, 6-2.

August 25. Pitched seven innings against Minnesota, was removed after the first batter got on in the eighth, leading 4-2. The Yankees won, 6-4. Lyle got the win.

September 6. Removed in sixth inning with 4-2 lead after walking first two men. Yankees won, 8-3.

September 11. Pitched seven innings against Toronto, was leading 4-2. Yankees won, 4-3.

With Gullett back, Tidrow's starting assignments were over. For one day. And then Hunter's arm went bad, and he was dropped right back in.

September 17. Pitched seven innings against Detroit, was leading 6-2. Yankees won, 9-4.

September 27. Leading 1-0 after seven, removed with one man out in the eighth, with a man on first and two balls on the batter. Cleveland tied it off Lyle, Yankees won, 2-1, in ninth. Lyle got the win.

In his seven starts, Tidrow had five wins, and Lyle got the other two in relief. The Yankees won the pennant by two and one half games. After the season was over, Tidrow revealed that he had been pitching with chips in his elbow. That hurts.

By the time the Yankees had run off their streak of 24 wins in 27 games, they were 4½ games ahead of the Red Sox, and those final five games didn't seem so important. And then the Yankees went into Cleveland, and lost both games of a doubleheader to the Indians on "Yankee Hankees" day, a promotion dreamed up by a Cleveland radio personality to permit all Yankee-haters to vent their spleen—for no more than the price of admission—by waving hankies, bearing the terrible device, "I hate the Yankees."

To show how foolish the whole thing was, the Indians started two left-handers named Don Hood and Rick Waits. Opposing managers were still doing that, despite the fact that the Yankees were knocking them over like tenpins.

You want to know something? It worked. The Indians beat the Yankees twice, with late-inning, hankie-waving rallies. Fortunately for the Yankees, the schedule makers had been kind again, and they had four games against Toronto before the Red Sox came in. The Blue Jays had lost 11 out of 12, scored only 14 runs in their 9 previous games, and were 38½ games out of first place. In the first game, all those figures went up a notch except the number of runs they had scored. The Yankees shut them out. In the second game, the Blue Jays beat them, 19-3, the most runs scored by an opposing team in Yankee Stadium since June 17, 1925, when Ty Cobb, we can assume, had himself a great day for the Tigers. Although hardly as great as the immortal Roy Howell's five hits (including two home runs and two doubles), and nine runs batted in, on September 10, 1977. (In his previous 86 games, Howell had knocked in a total of 27 runs.)

The Blue Jays got themselves another series split by winning the second game of the Sunday doubleheader. In another joust with the record book, they pitched Tom Murphy, who hadn't started a game since 1973. Howell had increased his RBI output by 25 percent; Murphy increased his victory total by 100 percent.

The pennant race was on again. The Red Sox, having won ten out of eleven, were coming into Yankee Stadium only one and a half games behind. Baltimore, hanging in there, had won eight out of nine. The Orioles were only two and a half behind.

Although Guidry had established himself as the ace of the staff, it had not been Martin's intention to start him against the Red Sox. Nobody started left-handers against the Red Sox on purpose. Billy Martin's original plans had been to start Guidry against Toronto with three days' rest, and duck the test against the Red Sox. A ten-inning game against Cleveland, in which Guidry threw one hundred and fifty-four pitches, eliminated that. Guidry was going to be the first left-hander to start against the Sox in more than three weeks. If he beat them, he would become the first left-hander to have done it in a month and a half.

The Red Sox were starting Mike Paxton, the very opposite kind of a pitcher. A bulldog of a pitcher, who had been unbeatable at their minor-league club in Pawtucket, and had been brought up when Jim Willoughby stepped in a hole and broke his ankle.

It wasn't a weekend series this time, it was a midweek series, starting on Tuesday. They not only sold out the Stadium for all three games, they surpassed the weekend total that had been set in June.

In the first inning, Guidry threw ten strikes in a row, and that was that. In the second, Yastrzemski barely missed a home run into center field, and had to settle for a triple. A walk to Fisk, a wild pitch and a single by Butch Hobson (his 100th RBI of the year), and the Red Sox had a 2-0 lead. Guidry was never really in trouble again. The Yankees got one of the runs back in the fourth on singles by Chambliss, Nettles and Piniella, and put Paxton away the next inning on the first two pitches he threw. Bucky Dent dropped the first one into center for a single, and Mickey Rivers deposited the second one—another gamer for Mickey—in the right-field bleachers. Before the inning was over, a single by Munson and a double by Chambliss had made it 4-2.

Rice singled to open the ninth, and Fisk sent Rivers back to the wall in left center. With Lyle warming up in the bull pen, you had to wonder whether Guidry was one batter away from another eight-and-one-third inning effort. He threw nothing but fast balls, and struck out Scott and Hobson, his eighth and ninth strike-outs of the game.

For Guidry, it was an example of what Martin had been screaming at him all year. When you get to the ninth inning, don't take a chance on hanging a slider, just rear back and throw that heavy fast ball by them. It was also a marvelous example of the difference between pitching in Yankee Stadium and Fenway Park. Carlton Fisk had hit three hard shots, two of them home runs in Fenway Park or, for that matter, any place except Yankee Stadium.

"This is a park for giants and rabbits," Fisk said, afterward. "You've got to be a giant to hit it out and a rabbit to catch it."

In any other park . . . That's the way the losers talk.

"I've been playing here for nine years," Thurman Munson said, in parched tones. He didn't have to say another word. At the time he hit his one hundredth home run, he had nodded in the direction of Steinbrenner's unopened magnum of champagne, and said, "That isn't for the hundred I hit, it's for the hundred I didn't get because I lived in this ball park."

It's easy to forget what a tremendous hitter this guy is. Playing in the toughest park, in the toughest position, and playing hurt, Thurman Munson was going for the third straight season of batting .300 and knocking in 100 runs. If he succeeded, he'd become the first catcher ever to have done it. The first hitter of any kind—speaking of unappreciated hitters—since Bill White did it with St. Louis (1962-64), and the first American League batter since Al Rosen (1952-54). He was coming out of a slump, his figures were .291 and 87 RBI, and he had only 17 games to make it up.

"Do you think I can do it?" Munson began to ask the writers.

They didn't see how he could. "I'll do it," Munson told them.

The second game goes into the book of Yankee-Red Sox thrillers, and into the golden book of memories being compiled by Reggie Jackson, one of the few good memories he could take out of the 1977 season. "The only pleasure I got all year was in the batter's box," Reggie would say.

Ed Figueroa pitched a shutout, the first really good game he had pitched in a month. On paper, anyway. What was really happening was that the Red Sox were belting everything he threw up, and going back on the field, inning after inning, with nothing. In the fifth, for instance, they loaded the bases with nobody out. Fred Lynn, playing on two sore ankles, hit the ball right back to Figueroa for an easy home-to-first double play. That left runners on second and third, with Yaz at bat. Given the green light on a 3-0 pitch, Yaz hit a shot up the middle for what looked like two runs. The ball hit Figueroa's trailing foot squarely on the instep, dropped dead at his feet, and he was able to throw Yaz out.

There were Boston runners on base in every inning. Mickey Rivers was running down balls in deep left center, deep right center, and short everything. It was Reggie Jackson's day, though. Reggie had come in early to have his bruised knee worked on, and, defensively, he was having his best game of the year. In the fourth inning, with Rice on first, George Scott boomed a line drive deep into his power alley in right center. Reggie raced back to the fence, timed his leap perfectly, and plucked the ball out of the stands. In the seventh, with one out and Denny Doyle on second base, Bernie Carbo hit a soft line drive into short right center. Reggie hesitated for the merest fraction of a second, then raced in and made a brilliant diving catch, just barely getting his glove under the ball before it landed.

And all the time that the Red Sox were leaving runners on base, Reggie Cleveland, the certified Yankee killer, was doing his thing. Not that he didn't have a little help from his friends, too. This was the Yankees vs. the Red Sox. Yaz had gotten him out of trouble with two on in the third, by making a tumbling catch off a Munson drive down the line. In the eighth, Hobson dove through the air, flat out, like a horizontal bird, to catch Willie Randolph's screaming line drive.

Munson, who was beginning to come alive, singled to start the ninth. Martin wanted Jackson to sacrifice him to second. (What's percentage? the master, Stengel, used to ask. Is percentage what the book says you're supposed to do, or is it what the guy at the plate can execute? In other words, what's the sense of telling a man to bunt if he can't bunt?) They didn't even have a bunt sign for Jackson. Dick Howser, the third-base coach, had to call time, and tell him, "The bunt is on, but keep your eyes on me." When Howser asked him where he bunted best, Jax just looked at him. "Down third, I guess."

The first pitch was a ball. To no one's great surprise, Jax hit away on the next pitch and fouled off a fast ball.

The bunt was put back on. Howser didn't come down to tell him again. He went through the usual wiping motions and, as Jax looked down at him, said, "Bunt," silently, with his lips. The Mickey Rivers sign. Another ball. A mistake. When Jax wants to bunt, you ought to let him. The bunt was off. A called strike, the count is two and two. Another ball, and the count is down to three and two. Cleveland threw a hard sinker that dipped below the strike zone; if Reggie had taken the pitch, it would have been a walk. But Jackson is a low-ball hitter. The ball was gone from the moment it left his bat.

Jackson went dancing around the bases. He was mobbed at home plate, and Billy Martin was right in the middle of it, pounding him on the back. When they got into the clubhouse, Billy said, "I'm sorry I gave you the bunt sign."

"I understood the situation well," Jax said.

Outside, the people didn't want to go home. They remained there screaming for Jackson. "Reggie . . . Reggie . . . Reggie." Reggie was escorted out to take a bow and wave his hat to the cheering populace. They still wouldn't leave, and he had to be escorted out again.

In the clubhouse, Reggie was thanking God, praising George Steinbrenner, and drawing dubious sociological conclusions. You can always tell when Reggie is becoming a sociologist because he takes the long, objective view of mankind's struggle, and refers to himself in the third person. "If Reggie plays well, if we win and if Billy and Reggie get along and George looks good, sociologically this city will be in better shape. I may be crazy, but that's what I believe."

Until that moment, nobody had been thinking of Reggie as a black man. As soon as anybody develops a personality—and the Lord and George Steinbrenner know that Reggie has done that—it becomes impossible to think of him as anything except a person. Unless he keeps reminding you. Reggie thought, apparently, that they were cheering a black man who had done something great. They were, in fact, cheering a ballplayer they knew to have been undergoing a very rough year, and they were showing that they recognized the drama of the moment, understood that they were part of it, and, in fact, were demanding their fair share in it. Hadn't Reggie written that into the scenario from the beginning? "What can I do to turn that city on?" Could anything be enough?

The Red Sox had come to town, conceding that they

had to win two out of the three games to remain in contention. They now had to win the third game to keep the last, flickering hope alive. It had come down to Torrez vs. Tiant. For five years, Luis had been the man the Sox had gone to in the crunch. This year, Luis was coming to the last few games with only ten victories. He lasted long enough to win his 11th.

Mike Torrez couldn't get his shoulder loosened. The Red Sox didn't hit him much, but after four innings, with the score tied at 1-1, he asked to be taken out. Since Tidrow was going to start in two days, Martin took an all-out gamble and sent Sparky Lyle out in the fifth, the earliest he had been in all season. Also the earliest out. The Red Sox scored six runs off him in the sixth. Carlton Fisk, who had nothing to show for five 400-foot drives in the two previous games, knocked in the tie-breaking run with a ground ball that sneaked over second base. That's the way the whole inning went. Four singles, only one of which was hit hard, a walk, and then Denny Doyle, the number-nine hitter, slashed a ground ball over first base and into the corner for a base-clearing triple. The Red Sox had found the way to win a ball game at Yankee Stadium. Don't hit the ball too far.

The Yankees never did quite forgive Mike Torrez. "Did you ever see such a choke up?" one player growled to a reporter. "Here we have a chance to finish them off, and that sonofabitch gave them a life." There is always, as all players understand, a psychological lift in getting the starting pitcher out in the middle innings.

Billy Martin didn't want to come right out and say how he felt about it. All he would do was look meaningfully at the inquiring reporters, and say, "Oh, you learned something, did you?"

There are two conflicting truisms that come into play here. A pitcher isn't supposed to stay in there if he can't do the job, that's obvious. On the other hand, he is supposed to be enough of a competitor to push himself to the limit. Mike's arm wasn't hurting, he simply hadn't been able to work his shoulder loose. He was getting by. A good pitcher like Torrez can win without his good stuff; he's supposed to stay in there and battle it through.

But the age of the free agent was creating its own truisms. Torrez wasn't signed. The Yankees had indicated that they weren't interested in coming close to what he was asking. At the end of the year, he was going to be putting himself on the market. If he was thinking, "Why should I take a chance of blowing a million dollars?" who could blame him?

George Steinbrenner, for one. Steinbrenner could never quite forget that in one of the most crucial games of the year, Torrez had asked out. Even after Mike had come into *the* most critical game of the year, the fifth game of the play-offs, to shut the door on the Kansas City Royals, Steinbrenner was still asking sportswriters whether they thought this guy Torrez had any guts.

By the sheerest of coincidences, another member of the Celebrated Unsigned had made his appearance in the Yankee clubhouse just before the game. As incomprehensible as it seemed at first glance, the Yankees had signed Dave Kingman, who had become the traveling minstrel of the free agent era, lugging his asking price, $2.5 million for five years, behind him. The New York Mets had, to all intents and purposes, given him to San Diego at the trading deadline; San Diego, unable to reach a meeting of the minds, had put him on waivers; California had claimed him nine days earlier and, having presumably discovered that they were a million or so apart, put him right back on the waiver list.

Clearly, Kingman was exactly what the Yankees needed, a discontented ballplayer. Everybody's first reaction was, "You're kidding!" Was nothing ever going to be enough for George Steinbrenner? Between Piniella, the unexpected bonus, and Cliff Johnson, the quiet acquisition, the Yankees no longer had a DH problem. What did they want with a guy who could do only one thing, hit the ball out of sight once in a while?

But it wasn't Steinbrenner, it was Gabe Paul. Kingman's salary demands had looked so ridiculous that everybody had focused on what he couldn't do. Which was everything except hit home runs. Gabe Paul had focused on what he could do. He could hit the ball farther than anybody playing baseball. With all his bouncing around, he had still managed to hit 22 home runs, and knock in 71 runs, in only 210 times at bat.

The Yankee lead was only two and a half games, and the next six were in Detroit and Boston, where anything Kingman got up into the air had a chance of going out of the park. Just sitting on the bench, Kingman would give the opposing manager something to think about when he was considering a pitching change. Gabe wasn't thinking just in terms of the remaining few games of the season, he was hoping to sign Kingman for the coming years.

There was also his effect, whether Gabe considered it or not, upon the Living Presence and the MVP. The first time Kingman started in Detroit, there were home runs flying everywhere. Kingman struck out on three pitches his first time at bat, and hit the ball into the upper deck for two runs the next. Munson had already hit a two-run home run in the first inning. Jackson, not to be outdone, hit two home runs. Nettles, who had gone into a terrible slump, hit a two-run home run to give him 97 RBI's, an all-time record for a Yankee third baseman.

The next day, Kingman hit another two-run home run into the upper deck in the second inning. Reggie hit a three-run homer in the third, to bring his RBI total to one hundred.

While the Yankees were sweeping Detroit, the Red Sox were losing two out of three to Baltimore. Just as Martin had predicted. The Yankees were coming to Fenway Park with a four-and-a-half-game lead, and only twelve games left to play. If the Red Sox didn't win both games, they were dead. If they won them both, they weren't necessarily alive.

It was Cleveland vs. Figueroa again, a replay of the dramatic 2-0 game in New York. Everybody had anticipated that Martin would be starting Kingman, on the assumption that anything he hit in the air would damage the left-field wall. Against a right-handed pitcher, Martin started his normal line-up, Roy White in left field and Piniella as DH.

It was Reggie Cleveland's revenge. And Carlton Fisk's. And Fenway Park's. Fisk got things going with a three-run home run into the net. He also had a triple that led to another run. The score was 4-2 when Kingman was sent up to pinch hit for Dent, leading off the eighth. Munson, in his drive for his third straight year in the .300-100 Club, had driven in both Yankee runs with a home run and a double.

Kingman, the joke, had become Kingman, the Superman. Off in the night, well beyond Fenway Park, there is a billboard which is traditionally occupied by the more intrepid sons of Boston when there is a sellout crowd. Either in tribute to Kingman's awesome power, or in memory of the midnight ride of Paul Revere, they had come equipped with flares to point the way. And damned if Kingman didn't send one out to them. He just seemed to reach over for a high outside pitch, and the ball shot out there as if it had been detonated. Who knows where it would have landed if it hadn't ricocheted off the top of one of the light stanchions. Bunker Hill, maybe.

You have to sympathize with Billy Martin, you really do. Yaz, the 38-year-old marvel, had gotten the run right back with a home run of his own, but Martin had to explain to the second-guessers why he hadn't started Kingman (they had signed him to play in Fenway Park, hadn't they?), and why he hadn't sent him in to pinch hit for Dent in the fifth inning, when there had been two runners on base. Dent, after all, had hit into a double play. Sure. A wicked line drive that had gone to the shortstop on one hop.

OK. Why hadn't he used him as DH? "Take out Piniella?" Piniella was hitting .332. Piniella had gone two-for-two on the day. "You see a guy hit a home run, and ask why I didn't use him. But if he had struck out, you wouldn't be asking."

He gave the best arguments against second-guessing ever heard, but it did no good. The moving finger had writ.

And then it was two and a half. The final game, played on a cold, damp night after a delay of a day, was a rematch between Tiant and Torrez. Mike started, Mike finished. The only thing he didn't do, was win. It wasn't his fault.

The day's postponement had not been unwelcome to

Don Zimmer. Bill Campbell, having "hyperextended" his pitching arm in the Baltimore series, had been given a shot of cortisone just before the first game, and although Zimmer had sent him out to the bull pen as a kind of decoy, he had known that Campbell was out of action for at least two days.

On the Yankee side, Mickey Rivers had been out of action, for the fourth straight game, with a twisted ankle. Mickey is a slow healer. So slow that Munson sat him down on the day of the delay, and explained that his teammates sure would appreciate it if he could figure out a way to heal faster.

Before the game, Yastrzemski was telling the New York writers what a great player he thought Rivers was. "Everybody talks about Munson, about Jackson, about Nettles, but the guy who's MVP to me, at least when they play the Red Sox, is the guy in centerfield. He makes catches against us that are unbelievable."

So what happens? After George Scott had walked, with two out in the second, Fred Lynn hit a long fly to the fence in left center. Rivers went after it. Mickey, the ball and the fence all seemed to come together at the crease, and the ball either ticked the wall just above his glove and ricocheted down to bloody his nose or— what looked more likely on the replay—the ball came down between his glove and the fence, and hit his face on the fly. Very embarrassing. Mickey had a bloody nose and a rapidly swelling cheekbone. The Red Sox had a run.

Between them, George Scott and Lou Piniella were involved in everything that happened all day. Not only the runs that scored, but also the runs that didn't. In the fourth inning, with Fisk on first base, Scott hit a line drive to right field. Reggie had been playing that kind of ball very tentatively all year, and on the wet field he was downright timorous. A couple of steps in, and he could have made a catch. Instead, the ball bounced in front of him, went off his glove, and while he was chasing it, Fisk was scoring all the way from first. After the Yankees had tied it, 2-2, Scott stepped up again in the sixth, and drove the ball into the bull pen in right center to make the score 3-2.

Both Yankee runs had been driven in by Lou Piniella. A home run in the fifth, and a line single off the fence in the sixth.

Once the Red Sox were in the lead, Campbell sent word to Zimmer that he was able to pitch. The rain had given him the extra day he needed. He wasn't great, but he was good enough. George Scott saved him twice, and Campbell saved himself the other time. The first batter he faced was Kingman, pinch hitting again for Dent. Kingman hit a little dribbler toward third, and Hobson booted it. Rivers, always tough in the late innings of a close game, lashed a line drive toward right field. Scott, holding the man on, dove into the hole, caught the ball flat on his face, and scrambled back to first to double up Kingman.

With one out in the eighth, Jackson got his second single, and Chambliss followed with a double into the left-field corner. Zimmer went out to talk to Campbell, and to everybody's surprise, Campbell preferred to stick to the righty-lefty percentage and walk Nettles, who wasn't hitting, to pitch to Piniella, who was. Piniella was hitting .336. He was 14 in his last 30 times at bat, and 4 for 5 in the series.

Campbell comes out of a windmill of arms, and kind of falls into the pitch. When he's right, he has a wicked curve that breaks out and down. He got it breaking sharply on the outside corner for a strike. Then a ball. Then another breaking ball down on the outside corner, which Piniella, with his stiff-kneed swing, fouled back. Another ball, low and outside. And then Fisk called for a screwball, which is a pitch Campbell would normally throw only to a left-handed batter. A great call. Everything had been breaking sharply down and out; this one broke sharply in and down, catching the inside corner and leaving Piniella standing dumbfounded, and, it seemed, nodding to Campbell in appreciation as he walked away. No alibiing for Sweet Lou.

In the ninth inning, with one out, Mickey Rivers slapped a ball into the hole between short and third. The man who ignites the Yankees was on first base, and Roy White, the man who had broken the Red Sox' heart in New York, was coming to the plate. White lined the ball toward first, and in an almost exact dupli-

245

cate of the play he had made off Rivers, Scott dove for the ball, caught it flat on the ground, and scrambled back to first to double up Rivers and end the game.

Boston had taken the season series, 8-7. The Yankees were still two and a half games ahead, and there were only ten games left to play.

"Don't tell me about Boston and Baltimore," Nettles had been saying. "We've still got three games to play against Toronto." He was dead on. If the Yankees kept winning, it didn't matter what anybody else did, and in their twelve previous games against the dreaded Blue Jays, they had only been able to get an even split.

They won six in a row, and clinched a tie. With all the criticism that was directed against Billy Martin for the handling of his pitching staff, a stormy case could be made that it was his patient maneuvering of that vastly overrated staff that won the pennant. When it had begun to fall apart in the last week of August (Lyle had four victories in relief in that one week, and Clay another), he slapped a curfew on the team for the only time all season, just to make sure that his starting pitchers were rested, and junked the four-day rotation. The team that wins a tight pennant race is the team that has the pitching down the stretch, and the Yankee pitching down the stretch was the best it had been all year.

They clinched the tie by beating Cleveland, 10-0, with Don Gullett pitching the shutout, and Reggie Jackson hitting a grand-slam home run. The victory brought Gullett's season record to 14-4. The home run gave Reggie 109 runs batted in, more than any New York player had achieved since Mantle's 111 in 1964. It was also Reggie's twentieth game-winning hit. Chris Chambliss was next in line with twelve.

At the end, it was the Red Sox and the Orioles who knocked each other off. Two days before the end of the season, the Red Sox eliminated the Orioles while the Yankees were losing. On the day before the season ended, the Yankees were in the clubhouse, on a two-hour rain delay, while the Orioles were eliminating the Red Sox on two home runs by Eddie Murray. It seemed the least he could do.

Nothing remained except for Thurman Munson to

go back out after the rain stopped, in pursuit of his goal of .300 and 100 RBI's.

At the time of the Hendricks flap, Martin had said, "It's going to show, later on. When he doesn't hit, they're going to wonder why."

There was not a thing for them to wonder about. In the tie-clinching game, Thurman had raised his average to .304 with a single, double and home run. He still needed two more RBI's. He had doubled a run home before the rains came. If the game had been washed out, his ninety-ninth RBI would have gone with it. The game resumed, he got two more hits, knocked in another run, and left with a batting average of .307 and 100 RBI's.

Reggie Jackson would cap his season in grace and splendor, with a grand-slam home run. For Thurman Munson, it was out in the cold, wet stadium with the second-liners, while the other regulars basked in the warmth of the victory champagne.

For Thurman Munson, it always has to be the hard way.

14

REGGIE . . . REGGIE . . . REGGIE

"It was like in a fairy tale and like in a horror movie where Frankenstein comes out talking, but in the end the wicked witch turned good."

—Bucky Dent

Once the Yankees began their drive in August, there was an almost palpable effort to do nothing that would rock the boat. Munson and Jackson would go out to dinner together on the road, usually accompanied by Fran Healy. When Martin was going to bench Jackson against a particular left-hander, he would call him into his office ahead of time. "I got a great idea, Big Guy. We'll DH you today and sit you down tomorrow. We've got a big series coming up and you'll be strong and ready to go." And Reggie, who had to know exactly what was happening, would say, "Yeah, that's a good idea, Skip. I like that."

The odd thing about the relationship between Martin and Jackson is that they were never unpleasant to each other face to face. Jackson probably dropped into the manager's office more than any other player on the team. Jackson has a need to be accepted by the owner and the manager, even when it's an owner like Finley,

248

whom he despised, and a manager like Martin, whom he disliked. Reggie respects authority. More, in all probability, than he'd like to. Jackson would come into the office and moan a little about his sore elbow or banged-up knee, and Martin would go to more pains than anybody imagined to pump him up. "We need you, Big Guy," he'd tell him, gagging a little on the "Big Guy." "Big Guy" has a connotation in baseball. It means exactly that—the man who'll do what has to be done to win the games that have to be won.

"How do you feel today, Big Guy," he'd call out as he passed Reggie's locker, and, whether Reggie groaned or brightened, the purpose was accomplished.

It was all a façade. One writer, rejoining the team late in the year, was so taken aback at the good will radiating around the clubhouse that, just for his own background information, he asked Munson whether it was possible he and Jackson had really become friends.

"Don't believe everything you see," Thurman advised him. "How could I ever like that motherfucking sonofabitch after what he said about me? I could never like him. A lot will come out later."

Toward the end of the year, Billy Martin was asked how he really felt about Jackson. "Off the record? He's a piece of shit."

Jackson didn't only drop into the manager's office, he also spent a lot of time with the owner. It was a practice that offended Billy's basic sense of discipline, not to mention its effect on his sense of security. "Who ever heard of such a thing?" Billy would say, bitterly. "A player and an owner going out together."

Munson wouldn't go up to Steinbrenner's office without letting Billy know. "Any words for your pal up there, the shithead?" he'd say. "Anything I should tell him?"

Munson had one overriding interest, as we know. To get the money he felt he had been cheated out of. And if the talk got around to the shambles the clubhouse was in . . . well, it was true, wasn't it?

While George was telling everybody within earshot—off the record—about how the players wanted to get rid of Martin, he was also telling them, "Thurman's a great ballplayer, but he thinks he's smart and he isn't.

I know what he's doing. But he wants his share of the attention, too."

That was one of the problems. Everybody understood what everybody else was doing. If there were rumors going around that Billy was through at the end of the year, win or lose, it could have been because stories were leaking out of the front office that "Reggie's lawyer" wanted to renegotiate the contract on the basis that Martin would be gone. "My guy can't live this way any more," he was supposed to be saying. "And you claim you're with my guy. We're being destroyed here, it can't go on."

Billy Martin never felt threatened by Reggie Jackson himself. The threat was entirely in what he represented, the power he held by virtue of the $3,000,000 contract. "He's not a hater," Billy could still say at the very end of the season, "he doesn't know how to hate. Raschi and Reynolds knew how to hate. *I know how to hate.*" When you hate you want to hurt. Reggie never sang a song of hatred; his plaint was always that everybody on the team hated him.

And that's the way it went as the Yankees charged on to the pennant. After the second game of the World Series, Thurman came into a steakhouse where Gabe Paul was sitting with his party, and Gabe invited him over for a drink. Munson came over—and, within full hearing of the people at the adjoining tables, said, "I don't want to drink with you, Gabe. I love you, but I won't play another year for Steinbrenner. He lied to me and I won't play for him. And I won't play another year with that prick, Jackson."

With postseason play about to get underway, Billy Martin did what Jackson had done at the beginning of the season. He put the spotlight squarely on himself. "I felt like Caryl Chessman," he said in describing how many times he had expected to be fired.

He had been fired four times, he said, and had been saved only because the newspapermen had written about it. And if the implication of that was that George had been afraid to face the terrible wrath of the people, that's precisely what Billy had taken to calling himself during his times of trouble, "the people's manager." He still had a warning for George. "If I get fired I'll beat him. If he buys $50 million worth of players, I'll beat him with another club and he knows it . . . If I come back, I'll make him cry."

It had started on the evening of the victory party. George had remained up in his office until Lou Piniella snuck out into the corridor and phoned him. "You're making a mistake, boss," Lou told him. "You ought to be here." Even at that, George had made little more than a ceremonial visit, and it had been left to Gabe Paul and Billy Martin to exchange the toasts.

"Salute," said Paul, giving the Italian toast. *"L'chaim,"* said Billy Martin in Hebrew. "Stick with us Dagoes," he said, "and we'll make all of you Jews Dagoes."

Claim credit? He had done it, to listen to him, not alone by holding a team of contentious players together, but also by overcoming the interference and petty shit from the front office. "If he ever gets to working with me," he said about Steinbrenner, "it could be a lot easier." He felt so strongly about it because it proved a point. "No matter who you signed, it takes a melting pot to win. The melting pot came to be and that's what it took. They came together."

They couldn't have won without him was what he was clearly saying, and he very well might have been right. On the other hand, it could be argued that another kind of manager, a manager who didn't put himself into an adversary position with his star, might have been able to lower the melting point considerably.

Reggie Jax, who had tried to lower the melting point in those final weeks—when he could think of it— came into the manager's office, after Martin had settled down, to offer him a drink from his bottle of champagne.

"I'll drink if you will," said Martin. And, after they had drunk their victory toast: "You had a hell of a year, Big Guy. I love you."

The day before the play-offs were to begin, Martin said, "If we win everything, I think it's a must for George to come with another contract. If he didn't, I'd have to seriously think about asking permission to talk with other clubs."

Having satisfied the First of the seven commandments

by winning, wasn't he breaking the seventh commandment ("Is he honorable?") by making that kind of threat? "Only One Person can give you commandments," Billy said. "How the hell do I know if he'll fire me. If I was him I'd give Billy Martin a five-year contract. What's money to George? If I'm fired it will be his loss. He'll find out these guys aren't that easy to manage . . ."

Steinbrenner, incapable of not answering back, reacted predictably by saying that Billy was reacting predictably. "He's crazy if he tried to take credit for our success." Not that he hadn't expected it to happen. "I would just tell him that he's not indispensable. That this is just another example of his immaturity." Would Billy have taken the blame if the Red Sox or Orioles had won, Steinbrenner wanted to know. "If he's playing this thing out in the papers—and this is a form of coercion, in a way—then he's crazy. Because he's taking away the credit from the player. If you look at his record closely, you'll see that he's done this in every place he's been. If he's successful, he'll come back to you and want more. We were warned about this when we hired him. So it had to come, sooner or later."

Like everything else, he was leaving the matter in the capable hands of Gabe Paul.

"My policy," said Paul, "is not to negotiate contracts in the newspapers."

Billy's policy was to do exactly that. By forcing the issue, he was writing the sub-story to the play-offs and World Series. "Is Billy Martin going to be fired? Win or lose?"

When the question was put to Steinbrenner directly, all he would say was, "We'll have to wait and see."

There are three seasons. There are the 162 games for the divisional championship. There is the divisional playoff for the American League championship, which the Yankees had won the previous year without Reggie Jackson, as Martin had pointed out endlessly. And there is the World Series, which the Yankees had not been able to win—as Jackson was not reluctant to remind you—without him. The divisional playoff is a kind of instant ordeal in which the prize you have struggled and bled for in over 162 games can be taken away in three games.

Kansas City was favored to beat the Yankees, you know. The Yankees had won 100 games? The Royals had won 102. The Yankees had won 40 out of 50 down the stretch? The Royals had won 43 out of 53. The season series had been split exactly; each had beaten the other 4 out of 5 on its own home grounds. Three of the five games were going to be played in Kansas City and you couldn't beat Kansas City on their Astroturf, said the conventional wisdom.

The counterwisdom, which might be called the "wisdom of the Pinstripe," said that the Kansas City Royals did not know how to beat the New York Yankees in this kind of a series.

Pinstripe wisdom went to the back of the class when the Yankees were able to win only one of the two games at Yankee Stadium. When they lost the first game in Kansas City they were one game away from extinction. They were going to have to beat the Royals twice, in Kansas City, on Astroturf, and they were going to have to do it with a pitching staff that had begun to unravel. Ed Figueroa had pulled a muscle in his side on his last start during the regular season and hadn't pitched in nine days. Don Gullett's shoulder had tightened up in the opening game of the series, the same kind of injury that had put him out for thirty-five days. Catfish Hunter hadn't pitched in twenty-eight days. Dick Tidrow had pitched 6⅔ innings in relief of Gullett. Guidry had pitched a brilliant 3-hitter to win the second game, and Torrez had lost ("I was chopped to death") the first game in Kansas City.

The other problem was that there had been no hitting from the left-handed batters, where all that power was supposed to be. Reggie Jackson had one single in eleven times at bat, Nettles had one infield single in eleven times at bat and Chambliss had one infield single in nine times at bat.

Teetering on the brink, Martin named the semi-injured Ed Figueroa for the fourth game and, to even it up a little, began to practice a little voodoo on the Royals' pitcher, Larry Gura.

Gura had pitched for Martin very briefly in Texas

and New York, and was numbered among the growing cadre of Martin haters. Whitey Herzog seemed to believe that Gura's hatred of Martin gave him an extra incentive. Which was fine with Billy. Herzog had started Gura twice in the previous year's playoffs, and the Yankees had beaten him twice.

With Gura pitching for the Royals, Martin was willing to guarantee that there would be a fifth game. "If I had my way," he said, in a voice that had been reduced to a whisper, "I'd put a bodyguard around his house today and get him a chauffeur so he doesn't get in an accident on the way to the ball park."

He was, of course, talking for Gura's benefit. Gura is a left-handed control pitcher. "The more he wants to beat us, the more fine he'll try to make his pitches. And when he gets too fine, that's when he can't get anything over."

Gura departed after the second inning, with the Yankees leading, 4-0. "He was throwing nothing but fast balls and sliders," Herzog complained. "And he can't pitch that way. I don't know what he was thinking about."

The injured Figueroa left soon after, with the Yankees leading, 5-4, and Sparky Lyle came in to hold the fort the rest of the way. It had come to the fifth game again. Billy Martin announced that he was going to pitch Ron Guidry with two days' rest. Guidry, who preferred five days, didn't sound all that thrilled. "Usually I feel stiff for two days," he said, "On the third day, I begin to loosen up."

None of the left-handers was hitting except Mickey Rivers. Mickey had rapped out four hits giving him 8-for-18 for the series. Naturally, he asked to be traded. "I don't want to hurt the cause," he said. "But I want to leave."

Steinbrenner had been attending a Parents' Day ceremony at the University of North Carolina. When he got back for the fifth game, Billy had something to tell him. He was benching Reggie Jackson. Reggie had one single in 14 times at bat, he was having all kinds of trouble fielding balls on the Astroturf, and Paul Splittorff was exactly the kind of left-hander that Martin liked to sit him down against. On the season, he had

254

two hits against him in 15 times at bat. A home run and a double.

Look, you could make a case on the statistical data if you wanted to. But there are statistics and there are statistics. We are talking about Reggie Jackson in the fifth game of the playoffs. We are talking about the walkdown at high noon, the moment of truth, that rarified atmosphere in which Reggie Jackson—off his record over ten years—pumps a richer, finer adrenalin. Billy Martin didn't make his reputation by becoming a slave to statistics, *deedeedahdit*. "My secret of managing," he had said when he was under fire, "is in getting to the heart of a player."

It's difficult to believe that Billy didn't know what he was doing. If the Yankees lost, Billy was gone. And he would not be going down alone. The fear that Jackson had expressed from the very first week of spring training would become a reality. Having won a pennant without Jackson, they would have lost with him. "Everybody will say it's my fault," Jackson had said, "and Steinbrenner will look like a fool." The one thing Reggie could not possibly have imagined was that he would suffer the ultimate humiliation of being benched, in the climactic game, for a conspicuous failure to perform.

And Billy had put himself right back in the spotlight again, hadn't he? Billy Martin, the embattled manager, doing it his own way.

It wasn't Reggie Jackson's scenario being played out now; it was a new script, written by Billy Martin, directed by Billy Martin, and starring Billy the Kid. Fran Healy was sent to break the news to Reggie. The only word we have is that Reggie took it well. There being nothing he could do about it, he'd have to accept it. He remained in the clubhouse until the very end of the batting practice and, when he finally emerged, he said all the right things. Sure, he had been surprised. "You've got to be down, your pride has got to be hurt. But if a man tells me I'm not playing, I don't play. I sit down and pull for the club. I'm not the boss, I'm the right fielder. Sometimes."

He not only rooted hard from the bench, he led the cheering. When the Yankees were out on the field, he kept up a pleasant enough conversation with Billy. Although there was going to be another flare-up before long, the personal relationship between the two men improved in a very real way that day.

Oh yeah, the ball game. The game that had to be won. The previous year, they had gone to the ninth inning of the fifth game before they won. This year, they went into the ninth inning trailing. Pitching with two days' rest, Guidry had nothing. After three innings, the Yankees were behind, 3-1. Mike Torrez had offered to go down to the bullpen. Pitching with one day's rest, Torrez stopped the Royals cold into the eighth. The Yankees had scored their run on a single by Rivers, a stolen base, and a single by Munson. After that, they could do nothing with Paul Splittorff. Willie Randolph's single to lead off the eighth was a turning point of the game because it got Splittorff out of there. All year, Whitey Herzog had gone to the lefty-righty percentage in the late innings. With Munson coming up, he went to his ace right-handed reliever, Doug Bird. Bird struck out Munson, but Piniella singled Randolph to third and, with a right-handed pitcher on the mound, Reggie Jackson was sent up to bat in the DH position in place of Cliff Johnson. ("I wanted to succeed more than any time in my life.") Reggie didn't do anything so dramatic. Behind in the count, 1-2, he got a slow curve and hit a lazy single into center field to score Randolph. But that's Reggie. It might not have been much of a hit, but it was a hit. And it was a 3-2 game.

In the ninth inning, Herzog sent out his 20-game winner, Dennis Leonard, to get the last three outs. Paul Blair, the man who had started instead of Reggie, wanted a base hit more than at any time in his life, too. But for an entirely different reason. Blair was in his thirteenth season. His fellow ballplayers had always considered him to be the best center fielder in the game. Ever since he was hit in the face by a pitch in 1970, he had pulled away from the ball at the plate, and the Yankees had made the trade for him after Earl Weaver made it abundantly clear that Blair's hitting had fallen off to the point (.197) where he had just about lost his usefulness. Thurman Munson, the student of hitting, had worked with him on holding the bat in a way that would allow him to protect the outside of the plate. Instead of sending up a pinch hitter for him in the late innings, as Weaver had done, Martin had let him hit for himself, and Blair had come through with six game-winning hits. Blair was grateful to Billy Martin. Billy Martin had given him a whole new career. And now, in the most critical inning of Billy Martin's career, Paul Blair was leading off and, as he had been doing all year, Billy was letting him hit for himself. Yeah, he wanted a hit, all right.

Leonard got two strikes on him and then threw two perfect sliders, low and away. Blair was able to get his bat there in time to foul them off. Leonard came back with a fast ball, tight, almost jamming him, but Blair fought it off and blooped a hit into center field. "You just won it for us right here," first-base coach Bobby Cox told him. They knew it in the dugout and they knew it in the bullpen. Blair was so excited that he was trembling. He knew it, too.

Roy White, batting for Dent, ran the count down to 3-2, fouled off a couple of very good pitches and walked. That was all for Leonard. Anticipating that Rivers would bunt, Herzog brought in Larry Gura, his best fielding pitcher, for a play at third. All that bunting practice Rivers didn't take paid off. Having failed to bunt, Mickey whistled a line drive over second base to tie the score.

Into the game came Mark Littell, the same pitcher who had thrown the home-run ball to Chambliss in the ninth inning of the fifth game a year before. Willie Randolph, who had started the whole thing an inning earlier, hit a long fly to center field to score White. In the first inning of the first game at Yankee Stadium, the Royals had scored two runs. Here, in the ninth inning of the fifth game, the Yankees were going ahead for the first time in the entire series.

After the game, Blair made sure everybody knew that it had been Munson's instructions that allowed him to stay alive. "Yeah," Munson said. "The beachball [Munson] can't stir the bleeping drink but he can show you how to hit."

Everybody else was right in character too:

George Steinbrenner found lessons in Reggie's ordeal that in earlier times would have been preserved by monks in illuminated script. Reggie had become a man in George's eyes. "When he came in, he delivered a hit instead of sulking. That shows everyone in New York he's a team man."

Billy Martin was giving them nothing. Why had he sent Howard and Healy to break the news to Jackson instead of doing it himself? "How do you tell a guy he's been butchering the outfield and not hitting worth a damn? How do you do that diplomatically."

And Reggie . . . uh, Reggie was being the quintessential Reggie. At his own locker the old drink-stirrer was putting another touch on the Autobiography. "All season," he said, clutching his throbbing heart, "I had to eat it in here. Thank God. I can't explain it because I don't understand the magnitude of Reggie Jackson and the magnitude of the event. I am the situation."

Reggie was taking his scenario back. Right now, if you stopped ten baseball fans and asked them what Reggie Jackson did in the fifth game of the playoffs, nine of them would probably say that he came up in the ninth inning as a pinch hitter and drove in either the tying or the winning run.

During the victory celebration, Martin pounced upon Steinbrenner and doused him with champagne. "That's for trying to fire me," he yelled.

"What do you mean 'try,' " Steinbrenner said. "If I want to, I'll fire you."

The playoffs are only a preliminary to the main event. If Reggie didn't understand the magnitude of himself after a lousy little humpbacked single, it was going to take a lifetime of scholarship and dedication to plumb the depths of himself after his performance in the World Series.

Having won the pennant, Billy Martin was in better spirits. "I got him now," he was telling friends. "He can't touch me now." He didn't seem to be saying that Steinbrenner could no longer fire him. He seemed to be saying that Steinbrenner could no longer humiliate him. At the very least, he would never again have to hear George Steinbrenner boast that he was going to do what nobody else had ever been able to do—drag Billy

Martin to a second straight pennant and make a man out of him.

I wonder if there has ever been a World Series played before where the manager of one of the teams was fighting—or at least thought he was fighting—for his job. Or could say about his owner that win or lose, "He can't hurt me any more."

The matchup with the Los Angeles Dodgers was perfect. The orchestration was inspired. Yankee dissonance versus Dodger harmony. Dodger manager Tom Lasorda, who liked to talk about bleeding 'Dodger blue' had a routine worked up with several of his players. On instruction from Lasorda, the player kneels.

"What do you say?" chants Lasorda.

"I believe," answers the player.

"Who do you love?"

"The Dodgers."

"Where do you get your mail?"

"Dodger Stadium."

"What would you give for the Dodgers?"

"My life."

"What do you say?"

"I love the Dodgers."

"And the Dodgers love you."

Tom Lasorda and Billy Martin were close friends. When it came to loyalty to a ball team, Billy Martin's feeling about the Yankees is almost mystic. "If Lasorda bleeds Dodger blue," Billy said during one of those tearful sessions when he was sure he was going to be fired, "then my stool has pin stripes."

The World Series is supposed to be fun. You're a winner even if you lose. Only the Yankees of 1977 could have turned such a lovely occasion into a series of controversies. Why should ten days in October be any different?

GAME ONE

There is a mixup on tickets for Joe DiMaggio, who was supposed to throw out the first ball. Joe goes storming out, vowing never to set foot in Yankee Stadium again. George Steinbrenner puts the blame on assistant ticket manager, Jerry Waring, if you can believe that mounds of prime World Series tickets are entrusted to an assistant ticket manager. Steinbrenner tries to explain over the phone. DiMag hangs up.

Whitey Ford throws out the first ball instead. Fifty thousand New Yorkers say, as one: "I'll bet it's a wet one."

What had actually happened was that Steinbrenner had invited Governor Hugh Carey, a fellow Democrat, to replace DiMaggio and had been informed by Commissioner Kuhn that there is a rule that no elected official except the President or Vice President can throw out the first ball in a World Series game. Honest to God. I wonder what would have happened if they had let the Governor throw out the ball and hadn't told anybody about the rule?

Reggie Jackson, having had some time to brood over it, wasn't being such a great sport about being benched in Kansas City any more. "I just play here" is his growling answer to all inquiries.

Thurman Munson is dropping hints again about how lovely life could be in Cleveland. "Nothing means much to me with all the controversy that went around here all year. I love the Yankees and the tradition. I'm not talking as if this is my last five or six games as a Yankee, but tradition is the only thing that makes it hard to walk away from this. Where else is there to play baseball but New York. . . . But I've got my own tradition."

He could also go to Philadelphia and become a lawyer.

The Game: Yankees win, 4-3, in 12 innings. Already they've done better than last year. Don Gullett, of all people, is back to pitch the opening game. Lyle relieves in the ninth and is the winning pitcher.

The key play came in the sixth inning, when Steve Garvey tried to score all the way around from first base on a hit-and-run single to right center. Jackson had moved on the ball so tentatively that Rivers had finally cut in front of him to make the play. ("I looked at him, and he looked at me. Well, somebody better get that, we're playing to win. If I see somebody laying back, I'm going to run, too.") A typical Rivers throw, with the ball kind of dying as it bounced. Munson had to move up the line and dive back to make the tag. The umpire called Garvey out. To everybody else, including the instant replay, he was safe.

In the twelfth inning, speaking of instant replays, the heroes of the final game in Kansas City became the heroes again. Willie Randolph doubled and Paul Blair singled him home. Blair had been sent out to right field in the ninth inning to take Reggie's place after the Yankees took a brief lead.

Post-game: If you think Gullett was a surprise in the first game, wait until you hear who Billy Martin has for the second. Catfish Hunter. The Cat hasn't pitched since September 10, when he was the starting pitcher in that 19-3 slaughter by the Blue Jays. All the while that Reggie was suffering in public, Catfish Hunter was suffering in private and putting the best possible face on it in public. At the beginning of the season, he had told *Newsday's* Joe Donnelly, "If I can still throw where I want to and get hitters out, if it hurts and I can still do it, that's not pitching with pain. That's pleasure. If you throw down the middle, if you are hanging a curve ball all the time, that's pain."

At the end of the year he had confided to Donnelly that far from telling him that everything was all right as the Yankees had reported, Dr. Jobe had informed him that the rotator cuff on his shoulder and the bone that forms the shelf on top of the shoulder were rubbing against each other when he threw. Which explained why he couldn't come overhand. In addition to the arm trouble, he had begun to suffer pain in the groin. The Yankee doctor had met him in Syracuse at the time of that exhibition game and had diagnosed it as a hernia. Hunter had just learned that it wasn't a hernia, it was seminal vesiculitis, which is an inflammation of the bladder glands and can be treated by injections.

Never mind what's going to happen, it's a good move by Martin. He has nobody else to pitch except Tidrow, and he's beginning to think he's going to need Tidrow in relief. He has a game in hand, there will be a day off tomorrow for travel, and by pitching Hunter he is getting his entire pitching staff lined up. His entire

261

pitching staff at the moment consists of Guidry and Torrez (for the third and fourth games), and then Gullett (if he's okay), Figueroa (if he's okay; it doesn't seem to be the pulled muscle that forced him out of the Kansas City game, but tendonitis of his index finger), Hunter again (if he's pitched well) or Tidrow (if there's nobody else) and, if there's a seventh game, Guidry.

Catfish has been there before. He's the kind of pitcher who could rise to the occasion. If he does, Billy Martin will be hailed as a hero and carried through the streets in triumph. If Catfish is hit like Catfish has been hit all year, Billy is going to be skinned, filleted and fried in oil. The Yankee players are in agreement that if anybody can come back from such a long period of inactivity, it's Hunter. Except for Reggie Jackson. "They probably should have pitched him somewhere along the line, don't you think?" he asks, acidly. It has hurt Reggie to see Hunter humiliated during the year. He does not want to see him humiliated in front of a national audience.

GAME TWO

Steinbrenner picks up a small boy in the street to throw out the first ball. The boy is black. Steinbrenner is still in there pitching. It is a message to the Commissioner. It's okay to pick somebody off the street to throw out the first ball, but you can't have a Governor do it. It is also a wasted gesture, since nobody knows the Governor Carey story yet.

Question: What would happen if nobody threw out the first ball?

Billy Martin says that his battles with Steinbrenner have been exaggerated. "Our relationship is a lot better than most people think. Actually we are the same in many ways. The only difference is he's rich and I'm poor."

The Game: Los Angeles wins, 6-1, as Cat is bombed. A 400-foot double by Reggie Smith off the center-field fence followed by a 400-foot home run by Ron Cey into the left-field bleachers. A home run by Steve

Yeager, 400 feet into the left-field bleachers. A home run by Reggie Smith, 425 feet into the right-field bleachers.

Firecrackers, smoke bombs, beer cans, ice cubes and garbage descend upon the Dodgers during the game. Reggie Smith is hit on the top of the head with a hard-rubber ball after the final out and suffers neck and back spasms. Kids run out on the field all through the game. Steinbrenner does not congratulate the fans on behalf of management.

Post-game: Reggie, who has one single in six times at bat, is afraid he's going to be benched in the third game against left-hander Tommy John. "All I hear is how I'm making too much money and not hitting enough." Just like old times.

When Martin is asked about it, he says Jackson won't be benched. But he can't resist adding, "Splittorff isn't pitching, is he?"

"I don't care what he said," Reggie says when the Splittorff crack is repeated to him. "I don't have to take that from nobody. Especially him. I know what I can do, and if he knew that, he might be a lot better off."

He also has a few words to say about Martin's decision to pitch Catfish instead of Tidrow. "He hasn't pitched for a month, how could he do anything? In a World Series, how do you make a decision like that on a guy like Hunter? Cat did his best, but he hasn't pitched in so long . . . Ah, the hell with it."

Reggie is sinking into one of his delayed depressions. When he accidentally spills some beer on a reporter's pants, he says, "When I drink beer, maybe I should have Blair hold it for me."

Art Fowler, who had been given the locker alongside Jackson when he came in August, is getting an earful. Usually, Art is back in the manager's office. "I often wonder how you guys can listen to this crap," he observes helpfully.

OFF DAY

Most of the Yankee controversies took place on the

road, probably because the players were forced into proximity with each other over longer periods of time. On the plane to Los Angeles, Thurman Munson bellied up to ticket manager Jerry Murphy and demanded to know why the players were getting only one box seat each, with the rest of their allotment in the reserved sections.

The Dodgers hadn't given them many box seats, that was why. "The reserved seats we gave you are better than the other boxes we have."

"How many box seats does George have?" Thurman demanded.

Thurman was keeping tabs. "In New York he had over three thousand, and all we got was four box seats each, and the rest reserves. Now, we get one box seat and you try to tell us the reserves are better? What are we, dumb?" Thurman was getting himself worked up. "I'll tell you this, unless we get more boxes, I'm not playing in the rest of the World Series. No way!"

From the surrounding seats, there came a low, growling ground swell of support for Captain Munson. And then a scream for Reggie Jackson. Thurman and Reggie had finally found a common cause. Reggie doesn't bring his complaints to ticket managers, though; he goes screaming to Gabe Paul. "Do you know where these tickets are? They're in the fifth deck! Do you expect my friends to sit up there?"

Paul's explanation that the Dodgers had a huge season-ticket list doesn't impress Reggie a bleep. "These bleeperblupper tickets are a disgrace." Others might *say* they wouldn't play but Reggie wanted Gabe to know he meant it. "I won't put on my uniform until I get better seats." He would sit in the clubhouse until Bowie Kuhn brought them.

Billy Martin wasn't going to let that go by: "Right after Reggie said it, two of my top pitchers went up to Gabe Paul and told him if he really wanted to help the Yankees he shouldn't give Reggie any tickets."

Thurman Munson wasn't going to sit around waiting for Kuhn. "I'm thinking of hiring a helicopter and hovering over the infield. It would be closer than my tickets."

Informed of Reggie's comments about Hunter during a workout at Dodger Stadium, Billy said, "He can kiss my Dago ass." To which Reggie, standing by the batting gate, responded softly, "If I had an ethnic origin, I'd tell him what he could kiss."

As the session progressed, and succeeding reporters approached Martin about Reggie's comments on both Hunter and Splittorff crack, Billy had a few other things to say. Knowing a soft underbelly when he sees one, he observed that he might have to alter his plans about his right fielder. "He was told in Kansas City the day of the last playoff game that he would be playing in every game in the World Series, but if he's going to say things to hurt the ball club, and if he doesn't hit Tommy John, I may have to think about making a change. He has a little growing up to do."

He said: "Where's his memory, what happened to that one sixty I.Q. he says he has? Why do we have to have all this kind of talk now? Do your job and if you can't do your job, then shut up. He has enough trouble in right field."

He said: "A true Yankee doesn't criticize another Yankee player or the manager. We're all supposed to be working together to win. The way to do that isn't with the mouth, but with the bat and glove."

Billy says that a lot, "A true Yankee . . ."

After the workout, another group of helpful reporters wanted to know whether he had discussed the matter with Reggie. "I've got nothing to talk to Reggie about. He has his job to do in right field and he's getting paid a lot of money to do it. My job is to manage, and I'm not being paid a lot of money to do it . . . Why should I pay any attention to him? His teammates don't."

He said: "Did I criticize him the other day when he didn't run after a ball? Mickey Rivers had to come over from center field to get it. If I'm gonna back that prick, why doesn't he back me? What is this, a one-way street?"

He said: "He's a man of moods. In Oakland, the players criticized the manager. The manager runs the club here, and he should have learned that last summer."

He said: "He's putting a lot of pressure on himself. Now he'd better get a couple of hits."

Thurman Munson had a few words to say, too. Like: "Billy probably just doesn't realize Reggie is Mr. October." (Earl Weaver had said that Reggie was the best October player he had ever seen, meaning that he was a terror down the stretch. Mr. October had sounded to Reggie like a good way of putting it.) Munson was off on his own thing. "I've been in the middle of controversy all year that I didn't cause. There was the magazine article where Reggie put me down. Then I'm told by Steinbrenner if I don't get along with Reggie, then they're going to fire the manager . . . You'll never read an article that I haven't stuck up for Billy. I've got five more games at the most to put up with this crap. All year I've been trying to live down the image I was jealous of somebody making more money. Somebody asked me, Did you bury your pride? No, I postponed it."

He said: "We have a chance to win a Series ring, and a guy is second-guessing the manager. If I was hitting .111 I wouldn't be second-guessing the goddamn manager. And I'm going to stop talking, because the more I talk the madder I get."

Sparky Lyle, with his talent for pith, summed it up in a nutshell. "So what else is new?"

The call came that the bus was leaving in ten minutes. "Leave without me," Reggie shouted. There was a silence in the circle of writers around him. Eyes poised, pens at the ready. Reggie moved his lips into the grimace of a smile. "Change of mood," he informed them, getting ready to leave.

GAME THREE

Gabe Paul held an afternoon press conference. "This is another chapter," he said, "in the tumultuous life of the 1977 Yankees. Controversial ballplayers are many times better ballplayers because they are not afraid of the consequences . . . What I do mind is a miser who's going to worry about what's going to happen. We have fellows who don't worry about what happens."

That's known as putting the best possible face on it.

On Jackson's criticisms about the use of Hunter, he said, "I have looked through the contracts, and I don't see where players have a right to determine policy." Asked whether he agreed with what Martin had said about Jackson, he said, "I don't think there will be any lack of backing for Martin in this thing."

And while he refused to say a decision had been made on Martin's future, he did say, "I don't know if we'll have to. The only time you sit down and make a judgment is when you think something is wrong." If there was nothing to act on, you didn't act. He as much as said that Martin had two more years left on his contract, and so what was there to talk about. Gabe had already made the decision to keep him. He still didn't think Billy was a great technical manager, but he had been impressed with the way he had held the team together, refused to be discouraged, and had somehow managed, through the force of his own personality, to keep the ball club stimulated.

The man who had never wanted him had become an admirer.

Gabe had seen unhappy teams before. "Some of the unhappiest players have played the best ball. We judge players by what they do on the field. If we want all nice boys, we'll go on the church steps and collect them."

Yes, he had talked to Steinbrenner, and George was unhappy about the latest mess. "I was so excited about it myself that I woke up this morning and went down and bought a new pair of shoes."

As to the great ticket controversy: "We gave the Dodgers locations better than we got." But he didn't think ballplayers gave a thought to ticket locations when they were up at the plate.

Catfish Hunter, out on the field early, was asked where Thurman and Reggie were. "I think they're inside waiting for Bowie Kuhn to bring them some tickets," he said. A few moments later Munson came out into the dugout. "There he is!" Cat shouted. "Go get him!"

When Reggie came out, he stood near first base and

delivered himself of a statement that could have been written by a public relations man. "In the emotion of wanting to win the World Series maybe I said something I shouldn't have said that was taken the wrong way. I have no desire to comment on anything Billy Martin does in handling the ball club because he has won the pennant two years in a row, and I'm pleased to be a member of this club. I've had a good year because of the way he handled me."

Maybe somebody reminded him that it was going to be very difficult to fire Billy as long as his firing could be attributed to his inability to get along with Reggie Jackson.

Billy Martin was eating a popsicle in the dugout under the watchful eyes of an appreciative audience. There wouldn't be any more misunderstandings, he told them drily, "because the next time I'll talk to Reggie first and ask him what he meant."

One player summed up his view of all the Martin-Jackson controversies thusly: "I don't know which one I dislike more."

"Why can't we have a peaceful World Series?" another Yankee asked. After debating the problems back and forth for several minutes he came to the astonishing conclusion that "Reggie is disruptive."

Since both Billy Martin and Tom Lasorda are friends of Frank Sinatra, Billy had ordered a cap made up for Sinatra with two peaks, N.Y. on one side and L.A. on the other, so that he could reverse the cap according to which team was at bat, who he was rooting for, or which way the sun was shining.

In other words, he could do it his way.

George Steinbrenner and Gabe Paul sat with the players' wives in the seats the players had objected to so violently. They were in the loge section, one tier up, behind home plate. After all the turmoil, the wives thought the seats were great. Behind them were some Los Angeles people George had invited as his guests. Since no good deed ever goes completely unpunished, one of George's guests became so excited when Dusty Baker tied the game with a three-run home run in the third inning that he leaped up and spilled his beer all over George.

The Game: Torrez beat John, 5-3. The Yankees' three runs had come in the first inning. Mickey Rivers plopped a blooper over first base, the ball fell dead, and Mickey was on second base. Randolph hit a professional ground ball to the right side of the infield, moving Rivers to third; Munson, also going the other way, doubled past first base; Reggie Jackson, back in the eye of the storm, blooped a wrong-way single to left and went to second when Dusty Baker overran the ball. Lou Piniella slapped a single through the box.

They came right back after Baker's homer and scored the winning run in the fourth on infield singles by Nettles and Dent, a sacrifice bunt by Torrez (there was no DH in this World Series), and a ground ball by Rivers. The final run came in an inning later on a walk to Jackson, a single by Piniella and a line single to right field by Chris Chambliss, only his second hit in the Series.

Steinbrenner's shipping company lost an $800,000 jury verdict to a seaman who had fallen down an open hatch and broken both legs.

You win one, you lose one.

Post-game: An L.A. sportscaster, who had apparently teethed on old Howard Cosell transcripts, stuck a mike in Reggie's face and intoned, "Reggie Jackson, once again you find yourself in the center of controversy, and you must admit that you enjoy it, don't you?"

"Mister," Reggie said, "on a day like yesterday, I'd like you to put on a pair of glasses and number 44 on your back and walk around and see what it feels like. I shouldn't be the most well-known player in the game but I'm known more for crap than for playing. It's not fair to a guy like George Foster."

Munson couldn't understand why everybody was asking him whether he wanted to be traded to Cleveland. "Did I ever say I wanted to be traded to Cleveland?" Well, no. He had been saying he wanted to go home to Canton, which is fifty miles from Cleveland.

The Dodgers had read about the battling Yankees, and couldn't quite believe it was real. "So the soap opera goes on," said Tommy John. "Will Billy Martin find success and happiness in a continuing shower of champagne?"

"The circus is back in town," Lou Piniella groaned.

GAME FOUR

The Dodgers were starting Doug Rau, who had pitched only one inning in seventeen days, and none of the Dodgers objected. The Yankees didn't object either, they had him out of there before a man was out in the second inning. Once again, they did it with a combination of the "other way" hits and infield hits. Reggie started it with a ground ball double down the third-base line, Piniella brought him home with a single to right, and Chambliss lined a double to left. Nettles brought in one run with a routine ground ball and, with the infield pulled in, Dent snuck a single through the right-hand side.

With Guidry pitching a 4-hitter, the Yankees won, 4-2. The fourth run came on Reggie's home run in the sixth. Martin didn't send Paul Blair out into right field until the ninth inning, and when the game was over, Jackson embraced Martin and thanked him for giving him the extra time at bat.

Post-game: Reggie nominated Billy Martin for the Nobel peace prize for managing, and was perfectly willing to settle for a Survivor's Medal himself.

"I accept," said Billy Martin through the ever-ready auspices of the New York press, "With deep humility, I accept. Thank you very much." Since one good nomination deserves another, it was suggested that Billy might find some honor worthy of being bestowed upon Reggie Jax. "How about the Good Guy Award?" Billy said.

The Dodgers were either congratulating the Yankees on their ability to take the outside pitch to the opposite field, or griping about all those bloopers and chippies. "We're taking advantage of what they're giving us,"

Piniella agreed. "But the key to beating the Dodgers is to keep them from hugging each other too much."

Speaking of hugging, it was getting difficult to tell the Dodgers from the Yankees. When he was asked about the eerie twenty-four hours of peace that had settled upon his clubhouse, Billy Martin urged a little patience and understanding upon his friends in the press. "I'm trying to think of something for you for Monday when you need it," he told them. "Don't worry, we'll come up with something. We always do."

GAME FIVE

Unless the Dodgers were able to win a game in Dodger Stadium, there wasn't going to be any off day for the return to New York. Just as in the opener, it was Don Gullett against Don Sutton. Gullett was still insisting that his arm was okay when he left in the fourth inning, trailing 5-0. After six innings, it was 10-0. Tidrow, who a lot of the players felt should have started, didn't get in until the score was 8-0, and immediately gave up a single and another home run by the Dodgers' Reggie, Reggie Smith.

The Yankees' Reggie scored the first New York run after he had led off the seventh with a single. With two out in the eighth inning, Munson and Reggie had consecutive home runs. For Reggie Jackson, it was also his second home run on consecutive days. Sutton, who is a friend and fan of Munson's, could be seen to be jawing at him as he ran around the bases. "I asked him couldn't he hit it any better than that. He just ducked his head and smirked. But I didn't like it when Jackson followed with his home run. I object to guys who trot the bases like they had saved the world from utter chaos."

Stick around! Reggie could have told him. If it was strutting he objected to, Reggie was going to give him a case he could take to the Supreme Court.

Post-game: Martin announced that Ed Figueroa would start Game Six in New York. An hour later, he announced that Figueroa was not 100 percent. Torrez was going to start.

The *Time* Magazine World Series issue was out, containing Bob Ajemian's story about the Steinbrenner meeting in the Milwaukee hotel room. Actually, the advance release had been delivered to the press in Los Angeles, and the shit had already hit the fan. If Munson and Piniella were outraged by the revelation of a meeting that was supposed to be kept secret, Jackson had every reason to be unhappy, too. There was a line in there that Jackson had already told Steinbrenner he would refuse to play another season for Billy Martin. Although Jackson said for the record that it wasn't true, he also said that the source must have been "someone who never betrayed me before." Reggie uses the language with some precision. The best interpretation of what he was saying seemed to be: Talking about it and meaning it are two different things.

Martin had huddled with Steinbrenner and Paul on the plane, and an agreement was reached. Billy wouldn't get a new contract, but he would get a good bonus and an announcement that the Yankees appreciated him, stood behind him and wanted him to fulfill the remainder of his contract. George agreed that he would not interfere the following year, and Billy agreed that he would not attack George in the press. It's possible that they believed one another.

Ed Figueroa was near tears when he left the plane, and demanding to be traded. Martin had told him before the first game in L.A. that he was going to pitch the sixth game if they had to go back to New York. "Billy has been lying to me for two years," he said. By Tuesday morning, he had informed the club he was going home to Puerto Rico. By Tuesday afternoon he had changed his mind. "I thought about it and decided it wouldn't look good, even though I don't want to play for the Yankees next year, I want to be a part of the club until the Series is over."

It's the kind of mixup that's inevitable in Martin's system. The pitching coach reports to Martin, the trainer reports to Martin. Boyer had told him he was okay, Monahan apparently told him that he was okay;

but to the question of whether Figueroa had said he was 100 percent, the answer seemed to be that he hadn't. Mostly, it appears, because he wasn't asked. The logical thing would be for Martin to ask him. But Martin doesn't operate that way. Possibly because players tend to lie to managers about such things, and possibly because it gives Martin a wide latitude to use this kind of "misunderstanding" when he wants to change his plans.

Billy didn't even go over to tell Figueroa he wasn't pitching. He had told Torrez he was it and then sent him over to break the news to Figueroa.

For Mike Torrez, it had been a bittersweet season. His fourth successful one for four different teams. With the Yankees showing no inclination to meet his salary demands, it was beginning to look as if it were going to be five out of five. He had anchored the staff through the August streak that put the pennant race away. He had kept the Yankees in the fifth playoff game, with five innings of gutty pitching on one day's rest. When he was finally removed from that game with two out in the eighth, Thurman Munson handed him the ultimate accolade: "You are an OUTSTANDING fucking Mexican."

Exactly. When Mike Torrez went in to win Game Three, he became the first Mexican-American to ever win a World Series Game. (No, Mike Garcia didn't. The Giants beat Cleveland four straight, remember?) He was going to become the first Mexican-American to win two World Series games. He was about to go the distance for a second time; he was going to win the clinching game. And, once again, nobody except him was going to know or care. Mike Torrez doesn't know how to promote himself, and, let's face it, Mexicans aren't a fashionable minority.

GAME SIX

Billy Martin was called by Gabe Paul late in the morning and asked to come to the Yankee office. Since they had settled the thing on the plane, it had occurred to Paul that it would be better to make the announcement; if they waited until after the Series was over, they would never be able to convince anybody that Billy wouldn't have been fired if the Yankees hadn't won.

Besides, the *Time* story carried the implication that Steinbrenner was greasing the skids for him. With one game left, it seemed like a very good idea to let the players know that Martin was going to be back.

At a hastily called press conference, Gabe Paul read a brief statement:

We are pleased to announce that Billy Martin will continue as Yankee manager and has been rewarded with a substantial bonus in recognition of the fine job he has done. We hope this will put to rest the unfounded rumors that a change was about to be made. Billy's contract runs through the 1979 season.

He was getting a bonus of $50,000, which included a Golden Jubilee Lincoln Mark V, worth about $13,000, and the club was going to pay the $400-a-month rent on his apartment. As Phil Pepe wrote: "What the Yankees did was announce that Billy Martin, who has a two-year contract, has a two-year contract."

Martin's scenario had come to an end on the morning of the sixth game. If Billy didn't get everything he had set out to get, he did get a great deal, including, most of all, the public acknowledgment that he had done the job and remained his own man to the end.

On the night of Game Six, Reggie Jackson's scenario was going to explode to its own triumphant end.

The Game: The Dodgers scored two unearned runs off Torrez in the first inning on an error, a walk and a triple. Reggie walked on four straight pitches to open the second, and Chambliss hit a home run deep into the right-field seats to tie it. The next time Reggie came up, the Dodgers had gone back into the lead on a home run by Reggie Smith. Munson had singled on the first pitch of the inning and Jackson hit Burt Hooton's next pitch on a line into the lower right-field stands to put the Yankees ahead.

In the fifth inning, he hit a line drive off Elias Sosa into the same spot, a shot—a ball hit so hard that it went into the stand with something approaching the speed of light.

After something has happened, it seems to have been inevitable. Reggie did write the scenario the first day of spring training, after all. But, you know, after Reggie's first home run he really shouldn't have been given anything to hit on the first pitch. After he'd hit two, you could see that he was floating. When he came back to bat again, he was so charged up that you could almost see the smoke chugging out of his ears. Charley Hough is a knuckle-ball pitcher, and knuckle-ball pitchers don't necessarily knock batters down; but, at the very least, you'd have expected that he'd stall around for a while, give Reggie a chance to chase a couple of bad pitches, run the count down.

The first pitch was a knuckle ball that didn't do much knuckling. Instead of darting downward, it just kind of rolled over the plate about knee-high. Right into Reggie's power wheel. He had never been so pumped up in his life, and he had never got a pitch hung there for him more perfectly. Put them together and it's a 475-foot drive into the center-field bleachers, the only ball ever hit up there except for Jim Wynn's shot on opening day.

Stick around, Reggie had said. Remember?

Tote it up, and the records fall like Big Timber. Only Babe Ruth—for whom a candy bar had not been named—had ever hit three home runs in a single World Series game before. The Babe had done it twice, in 1926 and 1928. But not even Babe Ruth had ever done it on three successive times at bat, let alone on three successive swings. Add the home run Reggie had hit on his last time at bat against Don Sutton, and it was four home runs on four consecutive swings. That will never be equaled. Never, never, never, never. Four consecutive nevers.

Add the home run he had hit off Ray Rhoden in Game Four, and it was five home runs in three consecutive games, off five different pitchers.

Nobody had ever hit five home runs in a World Series before.

Tote it up and he had nine hits in 20 times at bat

(.450) for 25 total bases. He had scored ten runs and driven in eight.

After the first home run, the mobile camera moved in on him in the dugout, and he held up one finger and mouthed the words, "Hi, Mom." Well, you see a camera coming in on you and you feel the need to do something. After the second home run, the camera came in and he held up two fingers. He had settled down beside Ray Negrone. Elbowing him, he whispered, "Two . . ."

"How about three?" Negrone said.

"Whew. I don't know about that."

The fans were yelling for him. "Why don't you go out and take a bow?" Negrone said.

Reggie didn't feel it would be right to do it in the middle of the game, even though players had been doing it all year. Even though the Dodger home-run hitters had been doing it in Los Angeles. There's a conservative streak in Reggie; that division in his personality again. "All I want to do right now is win this thing," he said.

After the third home run, he comes back and, if you have seen the films of it, he seems to be looking for somebody as he walks down the dugout. Negrone had been sent to the locker room, and had come back just in time to see Reggie crossing the plate. Reggie has to turn back to see a grinning Negrone coming down behind him; after they have hugged, Reggie turns, and his eyes catch Willie Randolph's. There is a moment of hesitation while Reggie and Willie, who have sat in that corner of the clubhouse all year, close together and yet far apart, think about it. And then Willie Randolph breaks into a big smile and they almost rush into an embrace.

The cheering is rocking the place. Reggie holds up three fingers for the mobile camera. "Three."

"You ought to go out," Negrone tells him. "You owe them that much."

So Reggie Jax, to whom the applause of the crowd is mother's milk, has to be persuaded by the former bat boy to do something that goes a little against his grain, interrupt the ball game to take a bow.

The same division in him is shown when he is called to the TV camera in the dressing room immediately after the game. "I'm not a superstar," he said, "but I can always say that on this one night I was. Tonight I was a superstar." He means that. When Reggie wrote a book in 1975, the publishers wanted to call it that. *Superstar!* Reggie balked. He wasn't a superstar, he protested. The superstars were the guys whose pictures he had collected on bubble-gum cards. The guys in the Hall of Fame.

Joe DiMaggio, in a reconciliation with the Yankees, had thrown out the first ball that night. Before the game, Joe had come back to the clubhouse and talked to Reggie, and it was after Joe had left that Reggie began to walk on clouds.

He is a myriad of personalities. He is a constant astonishment. He is an enigma. Never more than in the dressing room after the game. After an hour and a half or so of interviews and champagne, he was still riding high. When he was told the record he had broken for most total bases in a Series had been held by Billy Martin, he threw back his head in delight. "Reggie and Billy," he chuckled. "Billy and Reggie."

The Reggie and Billy Show was about to begin.

Reggie went into Billy's office and they began to talk about the coming year. "Billy Martin," he said. "I love the man. I love Billy Martin. The man did a helluva job this year. There's nobody else I'd rather play for. Next year, we're going to be tougher, aren't we, Skip?"

Martin nodded. "You bet we are. We'll win again next year."

"Next year is going to be different. We'll win because we have a manager who's a tough bastard and I'm a tough bastard. If you fuck with Billy Martin you're in trouble and if you fuck with Reggie Jackson you're in trouble."

Yeah, he was asked, but what if they clashed with each other?

"Then *look out!*" Jackson bellowed, and threw back his head and roared.

Reggie had won the car awarded by *Sport Magazine* to the MVP of the Series. *Sport Magazine.* Another circle was coming to a close. "They're giving me the car Thursday, Skip," Reggie said, as he made ready to leave. "I'd appreciate it if you'd be there."

"I'll be there," Martin said.

"No, that's all right. It's too early in the morning."

"Don't worry about it, Big Guy. I'll be there."

"Aw, no, you don't have to come. It's ten o'clock in the morning."

"I don't care. I'll be there."

"Oh, no. No."

"I'll be there. I want to be there."

"No, no. I can't ask that."

"I'll be there. You can bet on it."

He wasn't there.

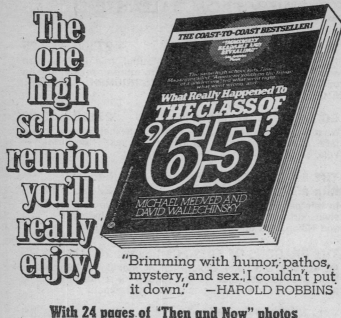

NEW FROM BALLANTINE!

FALCONER, John Cheever   27300 $2.25
The unforgettable story of a substantial, middle-class man and the passions that propel him into murder, prison, and an undreamed-of liberation. "CHEEVER'S TRIUMPH . . . A GREAT AMERICAN NOVEL."—*Newsweek*

GOODBYE, W. H. Manville   27118 $2.25
What happens when a woman turns a sexual fantasy into a fatal reality? The erotic thriller of the year! "Powerful."— *Village Voice.* "Hypnotic."—*Cosmopolitan.*

**THE CAMERA NEVER BLINKS, Dan Rather
with Mickey Herskowitz**   27423 $2.25
In this candid book, the co-editor of "60 Minutes" sketches vivid portraits of numerous personalities including JFK, LBJ and Nixon, and discusses his famous colleagues.

THE DRAGONS OF EDEN, Carl Sagan 26031 $2.25
An exciting and witty exploration of mankind's intelligence from pre-recorded time to the fantasy of a future race, by America's most appealing scientific spokesman.

VALENTINA, Fern Michaels   26011 $1.95
Sold into slavery in the Third Crusade, Valentina becomes a queen, only to find herself a slave to love.

**THE BLACK DEATH, Gwyneth Cravens
and John S. Marr**   27155 $2.50
A totally plausible novel of the panic that strikes when the bubonic plague devastates New York.

**THE FLOWER OF THE STORM,
Beatrice Coogan**   27368 $2.50
Love, pride and high drama set against the turbulent background of 19th century Ireland as a beautiful young woman fights for her inheritance and the man she loves.

**THE JUDGMENT OF DEKE HUNTER,
George V. Higgins**   25862 $1.95
Tough, dirty, shrewd, telling! "The best novel Higgins has written. Deke Hunter should have as many friends as Eddie Coyle."—*Kirkus Reviews*